W9-AQL-394

*To his comrades, the officers, crew, and marines of the U. S. S. George Washington, with the warmest good wishes of*

*Woodrow Wilson*

G. A. Lazenby.

1924.

DR. G. A. LAZENBY, JR.

# THE LIFE
# OF
# WOODROW WILSON

# THE LIFE OF WOODROW WILSON

## 1856 — 1924

BY

JOSEPHUS DANIELS

Secretary of the Navy, 1913-1921

*Illustrated*

To My Wife

ADDIE WORTH BAGLEY DANIELS

"THE TRUEST AND TENDEREST AND PUREST WIFE EVER MAN WAS BLESSED WITH. TO HAVE SUCH A LOVE IS THE ONE BLESSING, IN COMPARISON OF WHICH ALL EARTHLY JOY IS OF NO VALUE; AND TO THINK OF HER IS TO PRAISE GOD."

## PREFACE

Upon the death of President Wilson on February 3, 1924, there was an immediate and widespread demand both in this country and abroad for an understanding "Life of Woodrow Wilson" which might be within the reach of the people while the grief at his passing was still poignant.

The perspective of time, with the full opportunity for careful examination of original papers and letters, must precede full portrayal and lasting appraisement of the life of the twenty-eighth President. In response to a desire for an early story of his life, with appreciation of his outstanding contribution to his country and the world, this volume has been undertaken as a labor of love. If it will help his countrymen to visualize the devotion of Woodrow Wilson to their weal and his consecration to human freedom, the writer will feel his purpose has not failed. It is hoped and believed that a reading of this Life will stimulate devotion to the principles and ideals for which he gave his life.

The author acknowledges obligations to friends and co-workers of the late President, and to those writers whose tributes and studies of Wilson have been freely drawn upon and found invaluable.

Josephus Daniels

CONTENTS

PAGE

INTRODUCTION . . . . . . . . . . . . . . . . . . . . . . . . . . . . 13

CHAPTER I. THE EPIC FIGURE OF HIS ERA

In Selecting Its Leaders "Nature Does Not Run After Titles or Seek by Preference the High Circles of Society"—Wilson Won in "Race Between Wilson and Hindenburg"—He Brought Home the Covenant Which to Him Was the Hope of the World—Won the Gratitude of Mankind . . . . . . . . 19

CHAPTER II. INHERITED TRAITS

His Scotch-Irish Ancestry—The Emigrant from County Down—The New Home in Philadelphia—Literary and Religious Character of the Early Wilsons—Moved to Ohio—The Call of the South—His Father's Dominating Influence on His Life—Tribute to His Mother in Her Girlhood Home . . . 27

CHAPTER III. BOYHOOD DAYS OF TOMMY WILSON

A Virginian by Birth—At School in Augusta, Georgia; Columbia, South Carolina; and Davidson College, North Carolina—Civil War Days—Life in the Carolinas—"Prep" School Days—Ball Player—The Boy Was Father to the Man . . . . . . . . . . . . . . . . . . . . . . . . . . 36

CHAPTER IV. AT OLD NASSAU

Received Stimulus in Study of Politics and Government—Excelled in Debate—Editor Princetonian—"Knew Exactly What He Wanted"—Estimate of Teacher and Classmate—"A Fund of Humor Inside"—Wouldn't Speak in Favor of Protective Tariff—A Product of Old Nassau Training— "No One Ever Disliked Him" . . . . . . . . . . . . . . . . . . . . . . . . . 46

CHAPTER V. FINDING HIMSELF

Studying Law at the University of Virginia—Incidents and Reminiscences—Started Law as Step to Political Career—There Was Incompatibility of Temperament—Took His Degree at Johns Hopkins—Married to Miss Ellen Axson—Beautiful Home Life—Death of Mrs. Wilson . . . . . . . . . . 54

CHAPTER VI. EDUCATOR AND LECTURER

Began Teaching Politics in Bryn Mawr, a College for Women—His Heart's Desire Disclosed—Two Years at Wesleyan—Returns to Princeton as Professor and Is Chosen President—Popular on the Platform. . . . . . . . . . 65

PAGE

CHAPTER VII. HIS FIGHT FOR DEMOCRACY IN EDUCATION

"America Will Tolerate Nothing Except Unpatronized Endeavor"—Raising the Standards of Education—Broadening the Curriculum—The Preceptorial System—The Controversy Over Student Clubs—Colleges Must Be Reconstructed from Top to Bottom—The "Battle of Princeton" . . . . . . . . 76

CHAPTER VIII. WRITER AS WELL AS MAKER OF HISTORY

Man of Letters to His Finger Tips—Made History Fascinating and Political Science Interesting—His Father Taught Him to Think in Definitions—That Training and Wide Reading Responsible for His Elegant Style—Made History as President as He Had Written It as Citizen . . . . . . . . . . 84

CHAPTER IX. GOVERNOR OF NEW JERSEY

Victory Over the Bosses—The Schoolmaster in Politics—Giving the Politicians a New View of the Administration of the People's Affairs—No Foe of the Organization When it Named Best Man—Cut Down the Jungles . . . 95

CHAPTER X. THE BALTIMORE CONVENTION

Wilson Owed His Nomination to His Progressive Principles and to Approval of the Fight to Organize the Convention by Progressives—Bryan's Magnificent Leadership Routed the Reactionary Forces and the Bosses—Wilson Would Make no Promises . . . . . . . . . . . . . . . . . . . . . . . . 105

CHAPTER XI. THE CAMPAIGN OF 1912

Wilson's Directing Hand at the Start—Made Few Promises—Wilson and Marshall Had Popular Records—No Democratic Division—Roosevelt's Vigorous and Effective Onslaught—"Thou Shalt Not Steal"—Part Taken by La Follette and Gompers—Wilson's Big Electoral Majority . . . . . . 115

CHAPTER XII. PRESIDENT AND THE PRESIDENCY

"Let the People in"—A Kindly Thought for the People Who Wanted to Hear the Inaugural Address—Looking Forward to a "Work of Restoration" —"Not a Day of Triumph, but a Day of Dedication"—His Conception of the Office of Chief Magistrate—Added Executive Initiative to Insistence That There Be No Infringement Upon the Rights of the Executive . . . . 127

CHAPTER XIII. CABINET MAKING AND BREAKING

Picking the Cabinet—"I Am Sweating Blood Over Choices," He Wrote—The Cabinet a Place of Common Counsel—Team Play Under Sound Leadership—Bryan's Resignation the First Break—Why Bryan and Garrison Resigned, and Why Lansing Was Asked to Retire . . . . . . . . . . . . 135

CHAPTER XIV. TARIFF REFORM, FIRST STEP PAGE

Tariff Legislation and Effect on Politics—Did Not Make Cleveland's Mistake—Drives Out Tariff Lobby—Abolishes "Every Semblance of Privilege" —Income Tax Introduced—Refuses to Sanction Gold Brick for Relief of Farmers . . . . . . . . . . . . . . . . . . . . . . . . . . . . . 155

CHAPTER XV. THE CURRENCY SYSTEM

The Federal Reserve Act—"Banks to Be Made the Instruments, Not the Masters of Business and of Individual Enterprise and Initiative"—The "Interests" in Opposition—Would Not See Money Kings Who Had Vainly Fought Him—Importance of the Federal Reserve System in the War—Rural Credits—How Wilson Converted Glass . . . . . . . . . . . . . . 165

CHAPTER XVI. THE WILSON POLICY IN MEXICO

"If I Am Strong, I Am Ashamed to Bully the Weak"—Taft Had "No Sympathy With Exploitation"—Wilson Refused to Approve Election by Assassination—No Recognition for Huerta—Vera Cruz Landing Followed by Huerta's Flight—Policy of "Watchful Waiting" Bore Fruit in Better Situation in Mexico . . . . . . . . . . . . . . . . . . . . . . . . . . 175

CHAPTER XVII. ISLAND TERRITORIES

Dewey's Theory of Capacity of Filipinos for Self-Government Put in Practice—Why Virgin Islands Were Acquired—Porto Rico and Hawaii Helped—Haiti and San Domingo Saved From European Control—Dollar Diplomacy Ended—Closer Relations With Latin America. . . . . . . . . . . . . . 189

CHAPTER XVIII. REDEEMING THE PLEDGES

Legislation Fulfilling Promises—Repeal of the Panama Canal Tolls an Early Test of Power—Clash Between Railroads and the Brotherhoods—Anti-trust Legislation—"Crime Is Personal"—"The Most Adequate Navy in the World" . . . . . . . . . . . . . . . . . . . . . . . . . . . . . 195

CHAPTER XIX. PATRONAGE AND MERIT SYSTEM

Began by Declining to See Any Applicant for Office—Always Asked: "Is He the Best Man for the Place?"—Firm in Support of Civil Service Reform —Would Have No Coalition Cabinet—Called Prominent Republicans to Important Service . . . . . . . . . . . . . . . . . . . . . . . . . 204

CHAPTER XX. WILSON AS A POLITICAL LEADER

Most Successful Politician of Generation—Regarded Himself as the Chosen Leader of the Party—Jackson Day Speech—Appeal for Democratic Congress —Had No Machine and Used No Patronage—Humor in Speeches . . . . . 209

CHAPTER XXI. A BREAKER OF PRECEDENTS PAGE

Appearing in Person to Read Messages to Congress—Harding and Coolidge Followed Wilson's Plan—First President to Go Overseas—No Secret at Cabinet Meetings—"A Gentleman at His Own Fireside" . . . . . . . . . 220

CHAPTER XXII. THE HUMAN SIDE OF WILSON

"He Is Respected, but He Walks Alone"—"My Constant Embarrassment Is to Restrain the Emotions Inside of Me"—Had a Passion for the Mass of Mankind—Thirteen Was His Lucky Number—When He Got Best of Pershing—Enjoyed Story at Own Expense . . . . . . . . . . . . . . . . . . . . . 228

CHAPTER XXIII. NEUTRALITY

Nearly All America Favored Neutrality Upon Outbreak of European War—Roosevelt at First Favored and Later Vigorously Opposed Policy—Diplomatic Correspondence—Armed Guard on Ships—Wilson Consistent in Demand—"Will Omit No Word or Act"—The McLemore Resolution—"Little Group of Wilful Men" . . . . . . . . . . . . . . . . . . . . . 243

CHAPTER XXIV. RE-ELECTED TO THE PRESIDENCY

Pauline Revere Rode Out of the West, Bringing Victory—The Hyphen Issue Loomed Large—Wilson Scorned Disloyal Vote—"He Kept Us Out of War"—Hughes Indulged in Petty Criticisms—Threatened Railroad Strike Averted . . . . . . . . . . . . . . . . . . . . . . . . . . . 266

CHAPTER XXV. ACCEPTING THE GAGE OF BATTLE

President Wilson, in Presence of Distinguished Gathering, Asks Congress to Declare War—Presented by Speaker Clark—A Fighter Without Hate—"The World Must Be Made Safe for Democracy"—"The Right More Precious Than Peace"—"God Helping Her, She Can Do No Other" . . . . . 277

CHAPTER XXVI. THE WORLD WAR

The Driving Power of the Commander-in-Chief of the Army and Navy—"Force to the Utmost"—"Do the Thing Most Audacious to the Utmost Point of Risk and Daring"—Real Comrade and Shipmate to Fighting Men—Winning the War—Victory Message to Congress. . . . . . . . . . . 281

CHAPTER XXVII. PEACEFUL PENETRATION

Moral Offensives Undertaken—The Fourteen Points Accepted—The Armistice Signed—Race Between Wilson and Hindenburg—German Opinion as to Wilson's Demand—It Meant Unconditional Surrender—Foch Said the Armistice Obtained the Remedy for Which the War Was Waged . . . . . 290

CHAPTER XXVIII. THE PRESIDENT IN EUROPE PAGE

Unparalleled Welcome Everywhere—People's Hopes Hung on Wilson—From First to Last His One Thought Was to Secure League of Nations—European Diplomats Delayed Conference—Accessible to Representatives of Small Nations—Well Supplied with Advice—The Battle Royal and Wilson's Victory on the Main Issues . . . . . . . . . . . . . . . . . . . . . . . . 298

CHAPTER XXIX. A VISION OF WORLD PEACE

When the League of Nations Was Born in the Mind of Wilson—Approved the Bryan "Talk-It-Over" Treaties with Thirty-one Nations—Sent House to Europe Before Serbian Killing to Sound Out Heads of Government—A Pledge to American Soldiers—"We Live in Our Vision" . . . . . . . . . 313

CHAPTER XXX. THE FIGHT FOR THE COVENANT

First Shot Fired at Boston, Heard Around the World—Treaty and Covenant One and Inseparable—The Round Robin—Senate Refused to Help Fix Amount of Reparations—The Propaganda of the Bitter-Enders—Lodge's Reservations Meant Nullification of the Covenant, Not Amending It . . . 318

CHAPTER XXXI. AN APPEAL TO CÆSAR

"The Only People I Owe Any Report to Are You and Other Citizens"—Goes Joyfully on Speaking Trip for the Covenant—It Takes Him to the Pacific Coast—Article Ten—Shantung—Entangling Alliances—Prophecy of Entry "Into Pastures of Quietness and Peace" . . . . . . . . . . . . 326

CHAPTER XXXII. BROKEN AT THE WHEEL

The Great Casualty of War Returns to Washington, Which He Was Never to Leave Again—Happy in the Affection and Comradeship of His Devoted Wife—His Marriage to Mrs. Edith Bolling Galt, of Virginia, Crowned His Life with Happiness—The Beautiful Friendship Between Wilson and Dr. Grayson—The Physician's Tribute. . . . . . . . . . . . . . . . . . . . . . . . . 335

CHAPTER XXXIII. THE INVALID PRESIDENT

An Intimate Picture of His Closing Days as Told by Old Schoolmate—"The Road Away from Revolution" His Last Article—Honoring the Unknown Soldier—At President Harding's Funeral—Message on Armistice Day Broadcasted—His Last Reception—The Better Way . . . . . . . . . . 344

CHAPTER XXXIV. THE END OF THE ROAD

"The Old Machine Has Broken Down"—"You've Done Your Best for Me"—"But It Is Better that I Should Die Than Live on, a Helpless Invalid"—"Tell Mrs. Wilson I Want Her"—"I Am Ready" . . . . . . . . . 356

CHAPTER XXXV. SPIRITUAL SATISFACTION PAGE

To the Christian Man "Old Age Brings Higher Hope and Serene Maturity" —The Quest of Life Is "Satisfaction"—Found in Spiritual Air—"Rather He Was Ruling Elder than President," Said His Father . . . . . . . . . 358

CHAPTER XXXVI. "THE WAY OF PEACE"

Impressive and Touching Simplicity Mark the Funeral Services at the Home and at the Cathedral—Comrades of the World War Bore His Body—The Vacant Chair Before the Fireplace—Prayer that the High Vision of a World at Peace Might Be Realized. . . . . . . . . . . . . . . . . . 362

INDEX . . . . . . . . . . . . . . . . . . . . . . . . . . 377

# ILLUSTRATIONS

Portrait of Woodrow Wilson................*Frontispiece*

PAGE

Birthplace of Woodrow Wilson.................... 12
Mr. and Mrs. James Wilson........................ 13
Wilson as President of Princeton................. 50
Wilson as Senior at Princeton.................... 50
Woodrow Wilson and His Family in Early Days... 51
President Wilson in 1884......................... 58
An Academic Procession at Princeton............. 59
Governor Wilson and His Family.................. 98
Governor Wilson at Sea Girt..................... 99
The Baltimore Convention in Session.............. 106
Incidents of the First Campaign.................. 107
The Nominees for the Presidency and Vice-Presidency 130
First Inaugural.................................. 131
Wilson's Three Cabinets.......................... 138
President Wilson and Secretary of the Navy Josephus Daniels.................................. 139
At Work in the White House...................... 194
Alumni Day at Princeton......................... 195
An Antidote for Diplomatic Worries.............. 202
President Wilson and His War Advisers........... 203
Columbus Day in New York........................ 274
The Big Four..................................... 275
Announcing the Terms of the Armistice Which Ended the World War................................. 282
The Corner-stone of the Amphitheatre at Arlington 283
President and Mrs. Wilson with the King and Queen of Belgium................................... 306

PAGE

At the St. Germain Conference.................... 307
The American Commission to Negotiate Peace..... 314
On the Bridge of the *George Washington*.......... 315
The Last Home of Woodrow Wilson.............. 322
Mr. and Mrs. Wilson in the Funeral Procession of the Unknown Soldier........................ 323
The Ex-President on His 65th Birthday............ 330
The Last Rites.............................. 331
Washington Cathedral.......................... 331

BIRTHPLACE OF WOODROW WILSON, STAUNTON, VIRGINIA
In the parsonage of the Presbyterian Church, "Tommy" Woodrow Wilson was born on December 28, 1856

**MR. AND MRS. JAMES WILSON**
The grandfather and grandmother of Woodrow Wilson

# INTRODUCTION

"I AM ready."

These were the last words of Woodrow Wilson. They are what might have been expected of the man whose inflexible purpose in life was readiness. His philosophy was preparedness. He spared himself no toil, no sacrifice of comfort, no affection, nothing that diverted him from the task which he set for himself. From early youth he always prescribed hurdles that called forth full absorption of all his powers. In his boyhood home, his scholarly and critical father, known for his precision in the employment of words, gave him the example of thoroughness and accuracy. Like one of his gifted predecessors, his youthful mind was bent on solving hard problems. "Give me a stent," said John Quincy Adams, the only American to come to the Presidency by inheritance, or by the peculiar training his father's high station privileged him to enjoy. Father and son of the Wilsons were alike in their zeal to find the right word as the vehicle for their thought. "Tommy" Wilson's style, which enabled him later to voice American idealism in such manner as to constitute him the spokesman of a new day in the world, was the finished product of the preparation in the home of his preacher-father. It was a sin to the Presbyterian preacher to be guilty of the loose use of words, as of lapses in manners and morals. The son was early required to avoid every useless word and to go to the dictionary for the real meaning of every term employed. The result? It is seen in his writings and his speeches, those of his maturer years being so perfect it might be said of his sentences that they are vascular and alive and would bleed if a word should be cut out of them.

Mr. Wilson's mind was richly stored and disciplined to almost perfect precision. He gave the mental machinery one single groove in which to move. The study of government was his passion as boy, as man, as College President, and as Chief Executive of the Republic. All other knowledge and learning were accounted as handmaidens to the—"this one thing I do." His "single track mind" was never deflected to long consideration of any question that did not head up in how government should be best administered and made to advance the common weal.

Perhaps his mind, already tending to a career that proved to be a preparation for the Presidency, received its commanding direction from a volume, "Men and Manner in Parliament," that fell into his hands at Princeton. It dealt with brilliant parliamentary leaders—Gladstone, Disraeli, Cobden, John Bright and Harcourt,—and the author clothed their careers with a charm which won the admiration and quickened the enthusiasm of the young student. "No single circumstance did more to shape my studies than this volume which came to me when decision for life work was in the making," Mr. Wilson once said. The story of the burgeoning of British Government, "broadening down from precedent to precedent," and flowering into its noblest leadership in John Bright and Richard Cobden, captured the imagination of young Wilson and he became an authority on English parliamentary practice.

"I am ready."

During the twenty-five years Wilson was a teacher his classes found he came to them with full preparation.

He had not only mastered the only subject he ever essayed to teach, Government, with its corollaries of history and economics, but he clothed upon them life and interest. He always imparted vivacity and reality to his lectures. The science of government in his hands was no abstract subject. It was not remote. It was like the "thou art the man" of the prophet. History was no siccant repetition of dates and rulers. He made it glow with the hopes and aspirations of peoples. Economics in his hands made pupils see the true relations of life. Every student felt a master was giving the result of study, but there was no smell of the lamp. Always his class-rooms were crowded and students stimulated.

"I am ready."

When Congress assembled in extraordinary session in the Spring of 1913 to revise and reduce the tariff, Wilson was prepared to outline the way a tariff bill should be drawn. Addressing the body he said: "We must abolish everything that bears even the semblance of privilege or of any kind of artificial advantage, and put our business men and producers under the stimulation of a constant necessity to be efficient, economical, and enterprising, masters of competitive supremacy, better workers, and merchants than any in the world" and he urged the necessity of lightening the burden of the people as soon as possible. He added: "Only new principles of action will save us from a final hard crystallization of monopoly and a complete loss of the influences that quicken enterprise and keep independent energy alive." He was not only ready with the plan for tariff revision. He was prepared to fight for it. When lobbies of miners and sappers poured into Washington, endeavoring to secure tariff schedules of favoritism, by

2

a dramatic move he sent the fear of God into the harpies infesting the capital. As a result they hurried out of Washington, not standing upon the order of their going. His readiness to propose other reforms and to go to the mat for them enabled him to secure the passage of every measure he proposed to Congress until he was stricken. That is a record without parallel.

"I am ready."

Hurrying nothing, Wilson was prepared with "force to the utmost" when he led America into the World War. His swing around the circle in 1916 made sentiment for preparation for war and secured legislative approval of the largest naval program ever authorized in one measure by any nation. He made plans for the selective draft which only his super-leadership carried through Congress. He composed a delicate situation in Mexico so his country should have its house in order to prosecute the World War. His war state papers were the inspiration of the country. He kept pace with army and navy preparations, preached "audacity," pressed unity of command abroad, and was the heart of American mobilization and American contribution to victory.

"I am ready."

The war ended, while others hoped and drifted, he promptly sailed for Paris with the concrete ideal which finally emerged triumphant—an ideal for which he gave his health, to which as an invalid he clung with undying faith, and for which he became the great casualty of the World War. It is the ideal of Bethlehem and the angels and the star in the East. The story of Paris is the story of the one man who never faltered in faith that mankind could be lifted from sodden war into honorable peace, who never compromised his principles, never lowered his lance, never believed that the vision he had seen of world peace would fade:

> Never doubted clouds would break,
> Never dreamed, though right were worsted, wrong would triumph,
> Held we fall to rise, are baffled to fight better,
> Sleep to wake.

"I am ready."

The "broken machine," the body wounded in battle, when it could no longer hold the unconquerable spirit, surrendered the immortal soul. Wilson never knew defeat, for defeat never comes to any man until he admits it. Not long before the close of his life Woodrow Wilson said to a friend: "Do not trouble about the things we have fought for. They are sure to prevail. They are only delayed." With the quaintness which gave charm to his sayings he added: "And I will make this concession to Providence—it may come in a better way than we proposed."

The Unknown Soldier lies in Arlington with the heroic dead of all wars in which America has taken part. Sharing with him the national gratitude is the Known Soldier, the President who called him to arms and gave his life as truly for the Cause as if he had fallen on the battlefield.

Chapter I

# THE EPIC FIGURE OF HIS ERA

IN SELECTING ITS LEADERS "NATURE DOES NOT STOP AFTER TITLES OR [illegible] CIRCLE OF SOCIETY" — WILSON WAS IN [illegible] WILSON AND [illegible] THE COVENANT WHICH TO HIM WAS THE HOPE OF THE WORLD [illegible]

[illegible]

AN EPIC period is always represented by an outstanding and commanding epic figure. Issues and ideas are made flesh and dwell among men. It is only when a noble ideal is incarnated in a great man that it can be truly interpreted. The period in which Woodrow Wilson was Chief Executive was marked by the breaking up of old systems and the ushering in of a new era. Old geographies became obsolete. Ancient boundaries were wiped out. New nations appeared. Change was the order of the day in America in the new century epoch—change by legislation, change by dynamic forces let loose, change by war, and change by the events following war. Old things passed away in the years when Wilson was America's commanding figure. He was a voice crying: "Make straight the path." This peaceful revolution was as apparent in the days preceding the war as in the grim months of struggle. It was felt also in the time of stress and uncertainty which made the after-the-war challenge almost as difficult to

## Chapter I

# THE EPIC FIGURE OF HIS ERA

IN SELECTING ITS LEADERS "NATURE DOES NOT RUN AFTER TITLES OR SEEK BY PREFERENCE THE HIGH CIRCLES OF SOCIETY"—WILSON WON IN "RACE BETWEEN WILSON AND HINDENBURG"—HE BROUGHT HOME THE COVENANT WHICH TO HIM WAS THE HOPE OF THE WORLD—WON THE GRATITUDE OF MANKIND

*"Hundreds of years hence Wilson's name will be one of the greatest in history."*—Jan Christian Smuts, Premier of the Union of South Africa

AN EPIC period is always represented by an outstanding and upstanding epic figure. Issues and ideas are made flesh and dwell among men. It is only when a noble ideal is incarnated in a great man that it can be truly interpreted. The period in which Woodrow Wilson was chief executive was marked by the breaking up of old systems and the ushering in of a new era. Old geographies became obsolete. Ancient boundaries were wiped out. New heroes appeared. Change was the order of the day in America's twentieth century epic—change by legislation, change by dynamic forces let loose, change by war, and change by the events following war. Old things passed away in the years when Wilson was America's commanding figure. He was a voice crying, "Make straight the path." This peaceful revolution was as apparent in the days preceding the war as in the grim months of struggle. It was felt also in the time of stress and uncertainty which made the after-the-war challenge almost as difficult to meet as when the fighting was on. Indeed it seemed more difficult because the consecration and unity that cemented and glorified in war were gone.

No static man could have fitted into the period of 1913–1921. It called for a man who had no worship of tradition, no slavish adherence to precedent, and who made no fetish of the God of Things as They Are. The times called for a man who had been making ready for such a time as this for over two score years and ten. No man could fitly typify the day who had not, long before the call to leadership, gone through the processes which turn out the great man for the great occasion. What are those processes? Never did the extremities of the race call for a man when God did not provide the Man. He has no patent process. The man may come out of favoring surroundings such as produced Washington, or the rude pioneer life of the West may furnish a Lincoln. He may be fashioned in the quiet home of a scholarly preacher, inspired by the men whose lives are Light Fountains. The resources of God in Nature are not greater than in His leadings which cause the man and the occasion to meet. Speaking of Lincoln, the epic man of his day, when the Lincoln cabin was presented to the Government as a shrine, Wilson said:

"Nature pays no tribute to aristocracy, subscribes to no creed or caste, renders fealty to no monarch or master of any name or kind. Genius is no snob. It does not run after titles or seek by preference the high circles of society. It affects humble company as well as great. It pays no special tribute to universities or learned societies or conventional standards of greatness, but serenely chooses its own comrades, its own haunts, its own cradle even, and its own life of adventure and of training. Here is proof of it. This little hut was the cradle of one of the great sons of men, a man of singular, delightful, vital genius who presently emerged upon the great stage of the nation's history, gaunt, shy, ungainly, but dominant and majestic, a natural ruler of men, himself inevitably the central figure of the great plot."

On the beautiful Fourth of March, 1913, when Woodrow Wilson took the oath of office, what seer could have envisioned the tragedies and conflicts awaiting the generation represented in the great gathering? He had come to the high office after the divisions in an old political party. He was the creature of no machine. He was free from all shackles. He was emancipated from all prejudices. To most people that cloudless day betokened nothing more than an auspicious harbinger. The sun shone on a new figure—was he an epic figure and were the days just ahead, mercifully shrouded, to be the epic period of world disruption and war of such magnitude as to dwarf all other conflicts at arms?

Others may have seen only the orderly passing from control by one party and the incoming of the agents of another party. Now we know its significance was deeper. Did the central figure of that day realize the road of thorns over which he was to lead the Republic? It may be that, master of the lessons of history as he was, Woodrow Wilson sensed the tread of horses afar and heard the thunder of the guns that were to reverberate. If he had no premonitions of the grave issues ahead, who can explain the closing sentences of his inaugural? Reading the solemn, pregnant words in the light of what followed, who can say that it was not given the epic man to envision the grim days near at hand? Else why did Wilson say "men's lives hang in the balance"? Was it not prophecy of the shell-shock of the trenches? Was not world dependence upon America to promote world stability, after the debacle following the Armistice, foreshadowed in "men's hopes call upon us to say what we will do"? When gravely, seriously and bravely, never hesitatingly, he led this peace-loving nation into war, all minds went back to his words of "dedication" as he took the oath and declared, "I summon all honest, all patriotic, all forward-looking men to my side," adding, "Here muster the forces of humanity."

The "watchful waiting" in Mexico, which produced such a storm of criticism, was always regarded by Wilson as calling for the same qualities of devotion to his ideals as his "force to the utmost" when he was the incarnation of military leadership. There was organized pressure for war with Mexico. Some of it was promoted by those who had or wanted oil and other concessions. Some of it was urged by the party of expansion voiced by the declaration of Henry Watterson that every foot of land to the Panama Canal ought to be annexed to the United States. The Huerta usurpation opened the way to send the Army to realize that dream. "No," said Wilson, and he added, "There will be no glory in such a war." He resolved to be true to the American ideal, which was being tested, "whether we be sincere lovers of popular liberty or not" and "can be trusted to respect national sovereignty among our weaker neighbors." He resolved, when the fury of popular wrath dismayed some close to him, to see to it that the attitude of the American government should be as just toward a weak neighbor as it would be toward a powerful empire. It was "weakness" said the critics, but when the World War came it proved that in devotion to the old-time

American ideal he had been wiser than his critics. Was he less an epic figure when he defied the war-lust and territory-hunger and concession-selfishness, bidding him to war on defenseless Mexico, than when he led the nation in the War against War or when he was acclaimed by the people in Paris and Rome as the bearer of the torch of a new and larger liberty?

When the fate of mankind hung in the balance, Lloyd George compressed the thought of the world in this sentence: "It is a race between Wilson and Hindenburg." The hope of war-weary Europe was in Wilson. The race was won by the man whose wisdom and zeal in the prosecution of the war enabled America to play its great and decisive part in bringing the war to a victorious close. America, united and indomitable, mobilized in manhood and womanhood and resource, followed with faith and enthusiasm where he led. Wilson stood forth as the militant leader of a fresh nation, girding itself for victory.

It remained, however, for the conclusion of the World War for Wilson to meet the supreme test. The shibboleth of battle and the universal pledges of a lasting peace had caused the armistice to be hailed, not merely as an end of fighting, but as ushering in a warless world. Could that dream be fulfilled? To him, as he set sail on the *George Washington* for the Peace Conference, the vision of a world at peace, rebuilding on foundations where war could be prevented, was as clear as the glory John saw on Patmos.

At Paris were gathered the titled and the great of earth. All the hopes and hates and ambitions and jealousies of two thousand years centered there. Statesmen and diplomats were looking for national advantage.

They were still pinning their faith to alliances and protection by guns. The vision of organizing for peace did not possess them. It was a language they did not speak. There were, however, great hearts there beating high in hope of the New Day. Glad were they to be comrades of America's President who, having seen the heavenly vision, never let it fade. Representatives of broken peoples and small nations, long enthralled by the powerful, plead for an opportunity to live their own lives unmolested. To them Wilson was the one hope. They had been heartened and cheered by what he had uttered in the great war. But far away from Paris and its Babel of tongues and confusion and intrigue, were the peoples of Europe—the people who had never known freedom and a fair chance. Living under conditions like those of the feudal system, oppressed by obstacles that impeded progress, hopeless and cheerless peoples confidently felt that the great American would bring their deliverance. They had heard echoes of his "self-determination" and "a fair chance for all," and his humane utterances. Somehow dumbly they felt his coming would open new doors of hope and opportunity to them. Those in high place fêted him, but it was the wistful yearning of the burden-bearers that lifted him to a new consecration as they cheered his entrance to Paris. In Rome the humble received him as if he were the earthly Prince of Peace. They would have touched the hem of his garments in thankfulness that in his heart he had come to Europe to help them and such as they. The forgotten men and women sensed his spirit. It strengthened him and humbled him that the unlearned and the toilers understood his zeal for liberty for all while many in his own country and in Europe had thoughts only for selfish advantage or personal advancement. It steeled his heart to carry high the Covenant which to him had become the hope of the world. And he never forgot those who had given of their flesh and blood in war and who were upheld by the hope the ones they mourned had not died in vain. For weeks, in collaboration with kindred spirits out of all nations, he was the leader. One day at Versailles, his Treaty of Peace, buttressed by the League of Nations, came forth. It was the promise of a new heaven and a new earth. Woodrow Wilson had not failed the men who had fallen in the belief that their sacrifice would flower in a warless world.

In 1910 Theodore Roosevelt, in accepting the Nobel Peace Prize at Christiania, made a carefully prepared speech, in which he said: "It would be a master-stroke if those great powers honestly bent on peace would form a League of Peace, not only to keep the peace among themselves, but to prevent, by force, if necessary, its being broken by others." He added this significant prophecy: "The ruler or statesman who should bring about such a combination would have earned his place in history for all time, and his title to the gratitude of all mankind."

That is exactly what Woodrow Wilson, awarded the Nobel prize in 1920, accomplished. It is because of that crowning achievement he will live as the epic figure of his period. It detracts no whit from his "place in history" or his "title to the gratitude of all mankind" that the Senate of the United States failed to ratify the treaty all other nations signed. The "League of Peace" which Wilson brought from Paris is only deferred. His faith will yet be justified.

If Elizabeth Barrett Browning had been writing of Wilson, his ideals, his dream of doing a great deed "to help a people's need," she could not have more accurately portrayed the inception, the creation, and the reception of the Covenant of Peace than she did long ago in these words:

A great man (who was crowned one day)
Imagined a great deed;
He shaped it out of cloud and clay,
He touched it finely till the seed
Possessed the flower: from heart and brain
He fed it with large thoughts humane,
To help a people's need.

He brought it out into the sun—
They blessed it to his face:
"O great pure deed, that hast undone
So many bad and base!
O generous deed, heroic deed,
Come forth, be perfected, succeed,
Deliver by God's grace!"

Then sovereigns, statesmen, north and south,
Rose up in wrath and fear,
And cried protesting by one mouth,
"What monster have we here?
A great deed at this hour of day?
A great just deed—and not for pay?
Absurd—or insincere." * * *

But he stood sad before the sun
(The peoples felt their fate).
"The world is many—I am one:
My great deed was too great.
God's fruit of justice ripens slow:
Men's souls are narrow; let them grow.
My brothers, we must wait."

## CHAPTER II

# INHERITED TRAITS

HIS SCOTCH-IRISH ANCESTRY—THE EMIGRANT FROM COUNTY DOWN—THE NEW HOME IN PHILADELPHIA—LITERARY AND RELIGIOUS CHARACTER OF THE EARLY WILSONS —MOVED TO OHIO—THE CALL OF THE SOUTH—HIS FATHER'S DOMINATING INFLUENCE ON HIS LIFE—TRIBUTE TO HIS MOTHER IN HER GIRLHOOD HOME

"*My best training came from my father.*"—WILSON

"MY Boss will not let me do this."

That was what Woodrow Wilson said one day to a member of his Cabinet who had suggested dropping work for a diversion he knew would appeal to President Wilson. He gave the answer quoted.

"Your Boss——?" began the friend, wondering who could be the Boss of the President of the United States.

"I have a Conscience that is my Boss," said the President. "It drives me to the task and will not let me accept the tempting invitation."

The dominant force in Wilson was the inherited spirit of the Scotch Covenanter, mellowed by the saving grace found in appreciation of the humorous, the absurd, the strange. In duty he was the Covenanter. Speaking at one time of his inherited traits, Wilson said: "So far as I can make out I was expected to be a perfectly bloodless, thinking machine—whereas I am perfectly aware that I have in me all the insurgent elements of the human race! I am sometimes, by reason of long Scottish tradition, able to keep these instincts in restraint. The stern Covenanter tradition that is behind me sends many an echo down the years." He "belonged to that small but superb nation, north of the Tweed, which is bred in disciplined poverty, nourishing the body on porridge and the soul on predestination. He had all the qualities, all the sensitive and angular impulses of a thoroughbred. He was high-spirited as a race horse. By a pedigree religious rather than royal he was an aristocrat and he knew it."

The Scotch and Irish strains in Woodrow Wilson help to interpret the twenty-eighth President of the United States. The traits of both show for mastery in him and made him the scholar, the reformer, the fighter, full of vigor and full of humor. The saving grace of humor which shocked some members of Lincoln's Cabinet was quite as apparent in Woodrow Wilson. He was fortunate in having a Cabinet who loved stories, and some of them were good story-tellers themselves. Relief from the strain that comes through turning aside to the lighter vein saved him as it saved Lincoln. If the world saw in him chiefly the Covenanter spirit, it was because he lived in days when the stress of serious affairs left little time for the spirit of play and jest which was revealed chiefly to his intimates.

James Wilson, his grandfather, was the first of the family to come to America. He set sail from County Down, Ireland, in 1807. On the ship that sailed to Philadelphia, came also Anne Adams, an Ulster young woman, bound also for the land of freedom and opportunity. A sea voyage is notable for intimate confidences.

That voyage brought the young people into the haven of love which was followed by marriage the next year in Philadelphia. Good Presbyterians, both, it was Rev. George C. Potts, pastor of the Fourth Presbyterian Church, who performed the ceremony. The wife had vivid recollections of her North of Ireland home and loved to old age to talk of it, saying from that home she could see the white linen flying on the line in Scotland.

Ten children, seven boys and three girls, were born to the Wilsons, and all were reared by the "blue stocking" Presbyterian mother in the knowledge of the Shorter Catechism and Calvinistic faith and practice. Of the children, Henry, Edwin, and Margretta were triplets. These two sons bore such strong resemblance, one was often taken for the other. They made their identity known to their intimates by the manner in which they wore their watch guards—Edwin wore a fob, while Henry wore a chain about his neck.

The grandfather of President Wilson, upon his arrival, turned his steps to 15 Franklin Court, a former home of Benjamin Franklin, trained printer. He found employment on the *Aurora*, edited by William Duane, whose ardent espousal of Jefferson's growing Republican party caused him to be haled before the authorities on the charge of having violated the Sedition Law. Young Wilson had come to America, expecting to see the real new freedom, only to find his new home applying old world suppression of a free press. It was not to last long. Press censorship cannot live in the free air of America. Woodrow Wilson saw to it that there was no censorship of the press in the United States during the World War.

As evidence that the young couple admired the gifted and courageous Duane, who "suffered persecution" for his support, as Jefferson said, of "the great principles of the Revolution," they named their first child "William Duane." When Duane in 1812 was made Adjutant General of the Eastern District of Pennsylvania, James Wilson succeeded to the management of the *Aurora.* The boldness and audacity of that paper in its war upon Federalism foreshadowed Woodrow Wilson's like war on Imperialism a century later. The lure of what was then called the West caused the editor to trek to Pittsburgh, then having the promise of its subsequent growth. He crossed into Ohio, and after a brief stay in Lisbon, established a newspaper at Steubenville. His paper was called the *Western Herald,* wielded large influence and gave its publisher ample income for his growing family. Every one of his seven sons served their apprenticeship in the *Herald* printing office and became expert compositors. In 1832, in conjunction with four of his sons and two apprentices, James Wilson founded the Pennsylvania *Advocate* at Pittsburgh, Pa., the first issues being printed on the Steubenville press. Soon, however, he installed the first Washington handpress west of the mountains and the whole of one side of the Pittsburgh paper was printed with one impression. That was as much enterprise in those days as a rotogravure press in this decade.

James Wilson divided his time between the papers at Pittsburgh and Steubenville, living in his Ohio home. He was an editor whose editorials expressed his convictions and had a punch. For example, he may be said to have originated the attempt to humiliate a political opponent by writing his last name with a lower case letter, as he did in referring to Samuel Medary, a candidate for office, as "Sammedary" in this offensive paragraph: "Sammedary's friends claim for him the merit of having been born in Ohio. So was my dog Towser." Such newspaper political amenities, however, did not create social estrangement, for later Henry Wilson, son of the editor, married the daughter of Governor Samuel Medary, and the editor-father favored the occasion with his presence and the bride with his blessing. He not only was an influential editor of the Jeffersonian school, but was given the title of "Judge" because he presided as Justice of the Peace. He also served in the Ohio Legislature. He died at Pittsburgh in 1837 during a cholera epidemic.

The father of President Wilson was the youngest son and was named Joseph Ruggles Wilson. He was born in Steubenville, February 28, 1822, and was taught the trade of printer. It is said that there was no journeyman printer who could set more type. From early boyhood he was a reader of books and, showing ambition to become a scholar, he entered Jefferson College when he was eighteen. It was a Presbyterian college, located at Canonsburg, Pa., and was afterwards merged into Washington and Jefferson College. He graduated as valedictorian of the class in 1844. The next year found him teaching at Mercer, Pa. Having become a member of the Presbyterian Church when a boy, there came to him during this year of teaching the imperative call to the ministry. "Here am I," was his response. To him a call to preach meant summons to obtain the best preparation. He gave one year to the study of theology at the Western Theological Seminary at Alleghany, Pa., and then had a year at Princeton. This year at Princeton broadened his general education and had lasting influence in shaping his style, as well as grounding him in his theological studies. Though licensed to preach, he was not to be ordained and have a pulpit for two years. In that period, he taught in the Steubenville Male Academy, while giving all spare time to study and reading. To Steubenville in those teaching days came Janet Woodrow, called "Jessie," of Chillicothe, Ohio, to school. She was the daughter of Rev. Dr. Thomas Woodrow, who was born in Paisley, Scotland, in 1793 and was a graduate of Glasgow University. The Woodrows trace their Scotch history for 600 years with numbers of men of scholarship and standing in the ministry. Dr. Woodrow sailed for Canada on October 21, 1835, with his wife and seven children. His wife, born Williamson, died shortly after landing. After a year as Presbyterian missionary at Brockville on the St. Lawrence, Dr. Woodrow accepted a call to the First Presbyterian Church at Chillicothe, Ohio. He preached there for ten years, then at Columbus, Ohio, where he died April 27, 1877. He was "a fine scholar, a good preacher and especially powerful in prayer"—say the records of the Presbytery at Chillicothe.

Joseph Ruggles Wilson and Janet Woodrow were married June 7, 1849, the bride's father officiating. Ordained by the Presbytery of Ohio as a Presbyterian preacher two weeks after marriage, the young preacher accepted a position as "professor extraordinary" of rhetoric (they had high-sounding names in small colleges in those days) in Jefferson College. After one year's service, he heard the call to the South, which made Woodrow Wilson a Virginia-born child of Ohio-born parents, and for four years he was professor of chemistry and natural sciences in Hampden-Sydney Presbyterian College, Virginia. In addition to his professional duties, he preached on Sundays to country churches in the vicinity of the college. Here two daughters were born, Marion and Annie Josephine. In 1855 he accepted a call as pastor of the Presbyterian Church at Staunton, Va. The town was in the heart of the Valley of Virginia, with a cultured citizenship, given to good works and to hospitality. The home where his distinguished son was born December 28, 1856, was the manse of the Presbyterian Church of which he was pastor. The boy was christened Thomas Woodrow Wilson. The elder daughter, Marion, married Rev. Ross Kennedy, a Presbyterian preacher, who died some years later in Augusta, Arkansas. The younger daughter, Annie Josephine, married Dr. George Howe, a physician in Columbia, S. C., who died, leaving one son, Dr. George Howe, Professor of Latin and Dean of the College of Arts in the University of North Carolina, and a daughter, who is Mrs. Frank Compton, of Chicago. Mrs. Howe, daughter, and child were frequent visitors at the White House until Mrs. Howe's death during President Wilson's presidential term. The youngest son, Joseph Ruggles Wilson, named for his father, was long member of the staff of the Nashville (Tenn.) *Banner*, and now holds a responsible position with the Fidelity and Deposit Company of Maryland and is making his home in Baltimore, Md.

In the spring of 1858, when "Tommy" Wilson was less than two years old, his father became pastor of the First Presbyterian Church at Augusta, Georgia. He soon took rank among the foremost preachers and leaders of the Presbyterian Church. In the division of the churches, caused by the War Between the States, Dr. Wilson cast his lot with the Southern branch of the church. He was chosen "Stated Clerk" of the Southern Presbyterian General Assembly, and held the position for forty years, resigning at the age of seventy-seven in 1899. He was Moderator of the Assembly in 1879. Upon his invitation, the first General Assembly of the Southern Presbyterian Church was held in his church at Augusta. It was here that Dr. Thornwell made the address, giving reason and justification for the Presbyterians of the South to withdraw and organize an Assembly, composed exclusively of Southern churches. Dr. Thornwell, of small stature, was, to quote Dr. Wilson, an "intellectual athlete." Twenty-five years afterwards, in a description of the occasion, he wrote: "Every eye was upon him (Thornwell) and every sound was hushed by a spell whilst for forty historic minutes this Calvin of the modern Church poured forth such a stream of elevated utterance as he of Geneva never surpassed; his arguments being as unanswerable as they were logically compact." The impression it made on Dr. Wilson may be appreciated when twenty-five years later he said, "The thrill of that hour is upon me now."

It was the blood of such forbears that ran in the veins of Woodrow Wilson and had much to do with his thinking and acting. His life illustrated the maxim, "A man's education should begin with his grandfather." He paid tribute to them when he visited England in 1918. At Carlisle, where his grandfather on his mother's side, Dr. Thomas Woodrow, was minister of the Independent Congregation from 1819 to 1835, he attended services at Lowther Street Congregational Church and on being invited to the pulpit said:

"It is with unaffected reluctance that I inject myself into this service. I remember my grandfather very well, and, remembering him, I can see how he would not approve. I remember what he required of me and remember the stern lesson of duty he spoke. And I remember painfully about things he expected me to know and I did not know.

"The feelings excited in me to-day are really too intimate and too deep to permit of public expression. The memories that have come of the mother who was born here are very affecting. Her quiet character, her sense of duty, and her dislike of ostentation have come back to me with increasing force as these years of duty have accumulated. Yet perhaps it is appropriate that in a place of worship I should acknowledge my indebtedness to her and her remarkable father, because, after all, what the world now is seeking to do is to return to the paths of duty, to turn from the savagery of interests to the dignity of the performance of right."

The boy was father to the man.

## Chapter III

# BOYHOOD DAYS OF TOMMY WILSON

**A VIRGINIAN BY BIRTH—AT SCHOOL IN AUGUSTA, GEORGIA; COLUMBIA, SOUTH CAROLINA; AND DAVIDSON COLLEGE, NORTH CAROLINA—CIVIL WAR DAYS—LIFE IN THE CAROLINAS—"PREP" SCHOOL DAYS—BALL PLAYER—THE BOY WAS FATHER TO THE MAN**

*"Go in and win. Go after their scalps. Don't admit for a minute that they can beat you."*—Wilson

PRESIDENT WILSON was born in the commonwealth long called "the Mother of Presidents." It was in the Presbyterian manse in Staunton, Virginia, on December 28, 1856, that the seventh Virginia-born President first opened his eyes. He "was bred a gentleman and a man of honor in the free school of Virginian Society" to quote the opening paragraph of Wilson's "George Washington," writing of the birth of the first Virginia President. He was given the name Thomas Woodrow Wilson and was called "Tommy" until he graduated at Princeton. He then dropped the "Thomas" and became Woodrow Wilson. Some years before, his predecessor, Stephen Grover Cleveland, dropped the "Stephen." It has been remarked that the only two Democratic Presidents in half a century were influenced to discard their first names because most Presidents had possessed but a single given name. The name he chose to keep was the maiden surname of his mother.

In 1858, the father having accepted a call to the

pastorate of the First Presbyterian Church in Augusta, the earliest recollection of Tommy was when he heard the shrill cry on the street: "Lincoln is elected and there'll be war." He watched the troops march away to fight under Lee in Virginia. His other recollections of the War Between the States were limited largely to the burial of many Southern soldiers, to the marching of the men in Augusta when the unfounded rumor came that Sherman's Army was approaching the city, and to a night vigil in his father's study. The scarcity of food lingered in his memory. When, as President, he was forced to food restrictions in the World War, he recalled, from experiences in his boyhood days, that people could live without distress on restricted diet. He had no patience in 1917–18 with those who were unwilling to conform to the reasonable regulations for conserving the supply of sugar and wheat so that there might be plenty for the fighting men. He would often remind those who complained that in the war of the Sixties the people of the South were very restricted in food products, but, with a little effort and ingenuity, housewives were able to prepare appetizing meals, citing his mother as one who thus made the best of the situation.

In the summer of 1865, Tommy saw Jefferson Davis pass through Augusta under guard on his way to Fortress Monroe. The next year found Federal soldiers sleeping in his father's church. He was nine years old when the war ended, and in those years play interested him more than war and reconstruction. In an address delivered at the University of North Carolina, January 19, 1909, he told his audience how as a boy he had stood by the side of Robert E. Lee and looked admiringly into the great man's face. Most of his mature years were spent in the Middle States and he was free from sectional bias, but the formative days in the South during and following the war of the Sixties, when that section suffered from poverty and reconstruction, gave him a sense of its struggles, which made him appreciate its problems and honor its leaders. He knew and shared their privations, borne with fortitude and without lowering their ideals or affecting their morale. He loved to pay tribute to these qualities and was himself a product of such environment.

He was a lithe and active boy. With his chum and playmate, Pleasant A. Stovall, later to be named by Wilson Minister to Switzerland, where he served the period of the World War, Tommy's favorite recreation was horseback-riding. Stovall says he had many a tumble from the saddle, while Tommy managed to keep his seat. The favorite resort of the boys in the neighborhood was the stable on the parsonage lot. They organized "the Lightfoot Club" and played with other baseball nines, but the club was more than an athletic organization. It was something of a debating society, with parliamentary procedure. The chaps understood "the previous question" and Tommy here mastered the rudiments of parliamentary law. It was about this time he printed some cards "Woodrow Wilson, United States Senator." Horseback trips and delightful week-ends to the country home at "Sand Hills" were the chief pleasure of Wilson and Stovall. The "Sand Hills" was the home of his aunt, Mrs. James Bones. Playing Indian one day, his cousin, Jessie Woodrow Bones, was hit with an arrow by Tommy. She came tumbling down from the top of a tree. "I am a murderer; it wasn't an accident; I killed her," he cried as he carried her limp body into the house. Fortunately she sustained no injury.

Tommy was nine years old before he was taught his letters. Reading aloud was a habit in the family. He was familiar with the stories of Dickens and Scott before he knew his alphabet and could enjoy the humor of those favorite authors in the Wilson home. There were no good public schools in Augusta when Tommy began his pilgrimage toward learning. His first teacher was John T. Derry, who had served four years in the Confederate Army, brave and beloved of all his pupils. Derry's school was called a "selected classical institution." He spent thirty-five years as teacher. Among his pupils besides Tommy Wilson was Joseph R. Lamar, later Associate Justice of the United States Supreme Court. Wilson always gratefully remembered his soldier instructor. But Tommy's real teacher, then and afterwards, was his father. They were constant companions, and to the day of his death, Woodrow Wilson quoted from his father and with affectionate pride. To him he chiefly owed the processes of education that were responsible for the perfection of his style. Sunday afternoon was looked forward to by the boy, for then his father discussed with him books and men and sciences. "You do not know a subject until you can put it into the fewest and most expressive words," he impressed upon the son.

In the autumn of 1870, Dr. Wilson became Professor in the Southern Presbyterian Theological Seminary at Columbia, S. C., succeeding Dr. James H. Thornwell, who was as well esteemed in the South as Henry Ward Beecher was in the North. Prior to that time, Dr. Benjamin M. Palmer, the distinguished New Orleans divine, had been professor of pastoral theology. Dr. Wilson was the third of this illustrious Presbyterian preacher-trinity. At Columbia, Tommy attended the school taught by

Charles Heyward Barnwell. His father here as at Augusta was school teacher as well as companion. It was here that Tommy buried himself in Marryat's and Cooper's tales of the sea and imbibed the knowledge of ships and sea-lore. He knew every class of ship and the location and name of every spar, sheet and shroud. That knowledge, broadened, often surprised naval officers when he cruised with them as Commander-in-Chief of the Navy.

It was in Columbia that his romantic fancy showed itself. He began to write. His youthful masterpiece was of the mysterious disappearances of ships setting sail for or expected at Pacific ports. He depicted himself as "Admiral Wilson," in command of a naval fleet sent out to discover and destroy a nest of pirates responsible for ravaging the sea. He wrote daily reports to the Navy Department of the progress of his fleet. In hot pursuit of the pirates, he was often eluded. Finally one night the piratical looking craft, with black hull and rakish rig, was overtaken. The chase had been exciting and carried Tommy's fleet to the neighborhood of an island uncharted and hitherto unknown. There was no visible harbor and it was uninhabited. There was a narrow inlet which seemed to end at an abrupt wall of rock a few fathoms inland. Should the fleet sail into the inlet? "Admiral Wilson" scented a trap, and he sent a boat on a scouting mission. The discovery was made that it was a cunningly contrived entrance to a spacious bay, the island being really a sort of atoll. There lay the ships of the outlawed enemy and the dismantled hulls of many of their victims. Heroic work by the American sailors gave succor to surviving victims and destroyed the piratical crew. It was a tale as dramatic as some of those of Marryat's. One privileged to read the manuscript says it recalls the art of Defoe. Tommy did not merely write a romance. He lived it and was himself the Admiral. The daily "reports" would pass muster in the Navy Department to-day and the chase of the pirates is so thrilling as to suggest that when books enticed Tommy Wilson from the sea, a skilled navigator and writer of sea tales was lost in the making of a teacher, college president, governor, and chief magistrate of the Republic.

In 1873, at the age of seventeen, Tommy matriculated at Davidson College, in Mecklenburg County, situated near Charlotte, N. C., where the Scotch-Irish patriots signed the Mecklenburg Declaration of Independence, May 20, 1775. His father was a trustee and it was the favored Presbyterian College of the Carolinas. The buildings were few; the teaching force was small, but they were good scholars. Living was so simple that every student cut his wood, made his fires, filled his lamp (kerosene), kept his own room, and carried water from the pump. It had then, as it has now, a reputation for good scholarship and high religious tone. The faculty embraced men of reputation in the South, such as Dr. Charles Phillips, Col. William Martin, of North Carolina; Blake and Anderson, from South Carolina; Richardson, from Mississippi; and Latimer, from Virginia. They were well grounded in the old curriculum and gave dignity to the profession of teaching. Some of them, like Lee and Hill and Albert Sidney Johnston, had served in the Confederate Army and had after Appomattox become teachers of the sons of their comrades.

Tommy became Secretary of the Eumenean Literary Society, and its records were models of neatness. He had debating talent, won honors as essayist, and stood well in his classes. But there was nothing which foreshadowed the future which was in store for him. He was a prodigious reader and walker. A tree planted by him on the campus stands as a living memorial. Outside class periods, when not found curled up in bed with his book in hand, he was exploring the surrounding country, often alone and seemingly absorbed in thought. A tradition still lingers at Davidson that he exhibited a record never equalled in the minimum time necessary to dress, cross the campus, and take his seat by the time the before-breakfast chapel bell, calling students to prayer, stopped ringing. His roommate was William Lecky, an Irishman, who was killed shortly after leaving college. When he became President he appointed a classmate at Davidson, the late Governor R. B. Glenn, of North Carolina, a member of the International Boundary Commission. He was not keen in athletics, but played indifferently on the baseball team. Afterwards he smiled as he related that one day the captain "balled" him out, saying, "Wilson, you would make a dandy player if you were not so damn lazy."

It was at Davidson he obtained his only nickname. In rhetoric class one day, studying the part of Trench's "English: Past and Present" which sets forth how beasts with good Saxon names take the Norman appellation when they come to the table as food, the professor asked Tommy:

"What is calves' meat when served at the table?"

"Mutton," he answered amid laughter, and he was called "Monsieur Mouton" as long as he remained at Davidson.

There was a persistent report for a time that he was expelled from college and that this was the real cause of his leaving before the close of the term. Investigation proved there was no foundation for the rumor, which doubtless grew out of the fact that another student by the name of Wilson was expelled that year.

"Wilson was my classmate for one year at the college," said Dr. David Mebane. "He was always afterward my friend, and the friend of every Davidson man who went to school with him. At the White House he was glad to talk over old times with Davidson students. He was seventeen when at school, a fine, graceful young man, brilliant in his studies, and an athlete. As shortstop on the college team, he was a handy player. I remember once I broke two fingers catching a fast ball in a game, and he was the first at my side to give me aid.

"He was extremely handsome, too, in those days, and many were the girls who cast admiring glances at him. They used to cheer him on the ball field. He was a good batter and could hit the ball a hefty clout."

Delicate health sent Wilson home to recuperate at Wilmington, North Carolina, his father having accepted the pastorate of the First Presbyterian Church there. For a year he was at home, with his super-teacher, his father. If they had been chums before, they now became the closest comrades and friends. They had kindred tastes. Both loved books and loved to talk of the meaning of words and the meaning of life as well. He was coached in Latin and Greek, preparatory to entrance to Princeton, by Mrs. Joseph R. Russell, an excellent teacher. "Some day you are going to be President of the United States," she said to him one day, when he showed more interest in questions of government than in Greek. She did not live to see her prediction fulfilled.

He is remembered in Wilmington by characteristic

activities—as he walked into church with his mother, as he strolled the streets with his father, as he talked to sailors on the water-front, as he played shortstop on the neighborhood baseball team and as he swam in the Cape Fear at the foot of Dock Street. The river and the ships fascinated the youth. Their color and associations of adventure and romance fed his imagination. He wrote sea-tales as at Columbia, but he tore them to bits. He had become more critical of his style. Sometimes he would board a ship bound for the other side of the world and come back in the pilot's boat. The lure of the sea was strong upon him, and it was in those days that he had his heart set on going to the Naval Academy. His father saw that he was meant for letters and teaching and politics and set his foot down upon a naval career. When the Navy lost Tommy Wilson as a future Admiral, it gained in 1913 a commander-in-chief whose marvelous grasp of naval matters made him real leader of the men who go down to the sea in ships. But Tommy is chiefly remembered in Wilmington as the first person who owned and rode a bicycle in North Carolina, and he rode it with calm indifference to the astonishment caused by the then unique method of locomotion. His father, looking to the restoration of his health so that he could enter Princeton, doubtless encouraged out-door exercise, and the bicycle fitted admirably into the program.

Tommy was quiet, reserved, self-reliant, partial to the company of older men, gentle and courteous, but he lived much to himself and, generally speaking, was less socially inclined than in later life. Society in Wilmington in the Seventies retained its ante bellum flavor and the people of that historic city had the flower and grace of culture and leisure. "There's not a girl in Wilmington who can carry on a conversation requiring wide reading or knowledge," he said one day to former Congressman John D. Bellamy, a college student with whom he played and with whom he talked about Walter Scott and others of their favorite authors. His indictment of the girls was not original or true, for serious-minded collegians have generally indulged in such assertions, though they change their minds in their senior year, as Tommy Wilson did. Wilmington society opened its doors, but his mind was on mastering the science of government. He did not fit in with its social life. He did not want to fit in. He was not unfriendly about it, but just calmly interested and absorbed in other things. He never argued about it. He just went his own way, content to be with his father and to be with his mother, whose health was delicate and who loved his quiet talk and believed in his star. Many still remember mother and son, during the vacations of the latter, as they walked slowly along the street late in the afternoons, the mother leaning heavily upon the arm of her son.

The mother was not to live long, and the son, soon to go to Princeton, resolved to bear no other given name than that of his mother. He shortly dropped "Tommy."

His education began with his grandfather.

## CHAPTER IV

# AT OLD NASSAU

RECEIVED STIMULUS IN STUDY OF POLITICS AND GOVERNMENT—EXCELLED IN DEBATE—EDITOR PRINCETONIAN—"KNEW EXACTLY WHAT HE WANTED"—ESTIMATE OF TEACHER AND CLASSMATE—"A FUND OF HUMOR INSIDE"—WOULDN'T SPEAK IN FAVOR OF PROTECTIVE TARIFF—A PRODUCT OF OLD NASSAU TRAINING—"NO ONE EVER DISLIKED HIM"

*"The college should seek to make the men whom it receives something more than excellent servants of a trade or skilled practitioners of a profession."*—WILSON

"YOU know nothing whatever about it."

These words, spoken with feeling by Thomas W. Wilson shortly after he matriculated at Princeton, showed his classmates how the tragedy of war and reconstruction had burned itself into his memory. They were talking about the trials that follow war. His classmates had never known the dire poverty that befell the South. Wilson had grown up in its shadow. So, without stopping to explain the intensity of his utterance, he made this brief assertion, and left the little gathering. That was all. "It was years afterwards," said one of his classmates, "as I was reading the tribute to General Lee in Wilson's 'History of the American People', that I understood what overmastered him that day."

Woodrow Wilson was one of twenty young men from the South to matriculate at Princeton in September, 1875. His father had found leading and learning at Princeton when he was preparing to teach and to preach. His scholar-son should have the opportunity which had meant so much toward his own scholarship. In the early days of the Republic, many Southern youths had been attracted to Princeton—Madison, the most distinguished, and Macon, called by Jefferson "the last of the Romans", among the number. The Witherspoon tradition attracted patriotic youths long after the passing of the great Signer. Wilson grew up with Witherspoon as a hero, and of his addresses, that on Witherspoon, upon the occasion of the unveiling of the statue opposite the Church of the Covenant in Washington, D. C., ranks among the best. Did the young "Tar Heel", as he entered Princeton, think the mantle of Witherspoon would one day fall on his shoulders?

Princeton gave Wilson what he had come after—fellowship with serious men preparing to do real work in life, instruction by professors who were happy to share what they had learned with youths on fire for knowledge, and companionship with young fellows who were later to make the class more or less famous. He was not in college long before his measure was taken and he was accepted as an upstanding youth of superior mental equipment, who was chiefly concerned with big questions. He even then spoke with the distinction of culture. "Tommy Wilson, upon his arrival at Princeton, rushed to the library and took out Kant's 'Critique of Pure Reason'." That was what "Pete" Goodwin wrote of him in the history of the class of '79. It was what the historian of the class thought of Wilson's zeal for knowledge. Only it was not Kant. Wilson's mind was toward politics—political economy, perhaps the presidency even then. He plunged into reading "Men and Manner in Parliament" in the *Gentlemen's Magazine*. It was what he wanted. The picture of the great leaders of Parliament in the days when there were giants appealed to young Wilson's imagination. Parliamentary history, followed by English history, gave him such knowledge of the way things were done in England that he turned with avidity to a study of how government is carried on in the United States. The result was that in 1879 the *International Review* carried an article on that subject by Thomas W. Wilson. The key to the paper was "Congress should legislate in the presence of the whole country, in open and free debate."

Wilson was not a "star" student. He ranked 41 in a graduating class of 122. He specialized in English, the Science of Government, and kindred subjects. His training under his father had made him accurate in his scholarship and felicitous in composition. The humanities appealed to him more than the sciences. He delved into treatises on Government, mastered the history of how free governments had been won in the past, and on class was soon the authority upon subjects in which he was deeply interested. He exercised himself in the literary society, and wrote and wrote and wrote on government, always how governments should respond to the popular demands and promote the welfare of the people.

Two years after entering college, Wilson became one of the editors of the *Princetonian*, the college newspaper, and in 1878 became its managing editor. He sang in the glee club, took some part in pranks; he had passive interest in athletics, being President of the Athletic Committee in '78–79, and again of the Baseball Association. But the library was his attraction, debate his recreation, and association was mostly with men of similar tastes. He was regarded as "high-brow" but had the regard and respect of his classmates, had perfect courtesy, and made deep friendships that were never broken. That was the way he had—a few friends without capitulation. "Though born in Virginia he was essentially a product of Princeton" is the opinion of his alma mater. "Whatever of tenderness there was in his nature was developed in the soft twilights of the campus." One of his schoolmates, Robert Bridges, truly said of him when he was chosen President of Princeton: "His education and training were cosmopolitan and he was the product of no section—he was a representative American." With Ohio-born parents, a native of Virginia, his boyhood spent in Georgia, North Carolina, and South Carolina, his mature life from the day he entered Princeton was all spent in Maryland, Pennsylvania, Connecticut, and New Jersey, the latter state making the deepest impression upon him and giving him its highest honors. "Wilson knew exactly what he wanted," said Mr. Bridges, "and he had very definite ideas as to what part of the curriculum would help him to do it." We are told that he worked hard at the thing he wanted and let the rest go. His rank in class did not bother him. He practiced the elective system in his own career ten years before Princeton had much of it in the curriculum.

What he was driving at was this—"to study government and write about it." His aim was to make "public affairs his life study, and in order to do so he must not only be a good writer but also a good speaker." His favorite authors were Bagehot and Burke. It was Wilson's habit often to go into the woods about Princeton, according to Mr. Bridges, to read aloud the writings of Burke, Brougham, Bagehot or Chatham. The newspaper reporters who followed his political campaigns frequently marveled at the endurance of his voice. Rarely, if ever, did he become hoarse. He spoke in an even tone, without inflexion, and therefore without great strain on his vocal cords. The man might become tired, but not the voice. And his speech was the more effective for its evenness. The early training he gave himself told afterwards.

Mr. Bridges recalled that in his student days at Princeton young Wilson was ever ready for a debate and he gathered around him a body of young men who were interested in public questions. But he would never argue in the set debates on a side in which he did not believe. In one of the greatest debates of the course he drew the side of Protection. He did not believe in it and promptly withdrew from the competition. "He was easily the best debater we had," records Bridges, "and it was giving up a certainty, but he never hesitated. He did not believe—and that was enough." Mental integrity of that kind characterized his whole political career.

A few days after Wilson's funeral, Dr. E. P. Davis, of Philadelphia, classmate and close friend and consulting physician, who spent a day with him in January, 1923, talking to a friend about Wilson's college days, said:

"In University days Woodrow Wilson was known as Tommy Wilson. His features were very plain, his dress simple, his living economical, his associates men of intellectual and moral worth. He abounded in humor, good fellowship, and was universally beloved. He was democratic by nature and absolutely uninfluenced by money or social position. He was on the editorial staff of college publications and fond of humorous writing. He excelled in debating and writing upon political economy, the history of the United States, the theory of government in general, and the interpretation of the Constitution of the United States.

*Photo, from Western Newspaper Union*

**WILSON AS PRESIDENT OF PRINCETON**

*Photo by Pacific & Atlantic Photos*

**WILSON AS A SENIOR AT PRINCETON**

Interesting photographs of the President's early days as student and educator

**WOODROW WILSON AND HIS FAMILY IN THE EARLY DAYS** © *Underwood & Underwood*

The family group at Columbia, S. C. Left to right: *Top row,* Woodrow Wilson; his sister, Mrs. Howe; his father, Rev. Dr. Joseph R. Wilson; Mrs. Joseph R. Wilson, Jr.; Mr. Joseph R. Wilson, Jr.; *bottom row:* Dr. Howe and his four children

"During his University days he wrote his book on Congressional Government which remains an authority and a classic upon the subject. He also contributed articles of similar nature to English periodicals. At that time his bent and bias in life were already pronounced. A democrat, he was devoted to the study of the development of his country. He cared nothing for the grades of college marks, and while he might easily have taken very high grades, he was a respectable student and desired to be nothing more. He did not take part in athletic sports, although he could have done so.

"His diversions were those of friendship, talking and walking with his friends, reading and studying the literature of the subjects to which he was devoted. His yearly expenditures would form one of the smallest items in the yearly allowances of the average young man in an expensive modern university. It cannot be remembered that anyone ever disliked him.

"He was formidable in argument. At a reunion after his first nomination, a leading Republican lawyer and politician of New Jersey asked him if he remembered sitting up all night in his Freshman year arguing concerning the causes of the War of 1861. He closed his question with the remark made to the class: 'Fellows, how homely he was.'"

Princeton had made its mark on him. He had left his mark on Princeton. The day was to come when the two names most illustrious in Princeton history were to be John Witherspoon and Woodrow Wilson—the first to lead for American Independence and to sign the Declaration; the second to give inspiration and leadership in the World War and to World Peace.

The only professor now living who taught at Princeton when Wilson was a student, Dr. Theodore Whitefield Hunt, of the English Department, said: "The impression he made upon me as he sat before me in the college classroom was that of an exceptionally mature student deeply interested in current events, often devoting to general reading hours that others were giving to regular academic schedules, willingly surrendering his academics to the attractions of general literature, history, and political writings." Books to him were his servants. He dominated them and was not ruled by them. He states that he often strolled about the campus with a bright-eyed freshman "in the person of President Hibben, idealism and pragmatism thus in company." Dr. Hunt added that his "undergraduate life and study were thus in a true sense a premonition of what he was to be and an evident preparation for it."

"He was always reading," he said.

Had Professor Hunt any notion that a future President sat before him?

"Not the slightest," he said, "there were two university Presidents before me in those days—Hibben, a freshman, and Wilson, a senior. My, my! if I'd only known! Why, I would have said: 'Look here, pardon me.'"

The old scholar shook his head contemplatively.

"History's a puzzling thing."

The young Woodrow Wilson was sober, he said; but later he admitted that his gravity was largely external. "He had a fund of humor inside."

"He has been called unsympathetic and even cynical, inclosed within the confines of his own thought and life," added Professor Hunt. "This is not true, for as a neighbor of his for years and familiar as few others have been with the everyday experiences of his home life, I never failed to find in his nature a marked degree of cordiality, of affectionate friendship, and a quick response to every generous impulse. And yet it must be confessed that there was a section of his composite being which he kept under lock and key, and into which sanctum no one outside of his family was ever allowed to enter."

It was this reserve, according to the men in the faculty who knew him well, that puzzled many people. Professor Hunt and Professor Christian Gauss have both remarked upon the oddity of seeing him so often walking through the campus under the elms alone. "People would frequently stop and talk with him," said Professor Gauss, "but invariably he would walk on alone, they turning off another way or staying behind."

"Living as his next door neighbor for a series of years," says Dr. Hunt, "it gives me unfeigned pleasure to emphasize the attractiveness of his home life, as son, as husband, and father. It was a home in which the tenderest experience of household affection prevailed and which was marked by that generous hospitality which is such a dominant characteristic in all families of Southern lineage. It was from his venerable father that he inherited his fund of humor, as it was from his father and distinguished uncle, Doctor Woodrow, that he inherited his theological views."

Nassau's mark was upon him.

## Chapter V

# FINDING HIMSELF

**STUDYING LAW AT THE UNIVERSITY OF VIRGINIA—INCIDENTS AND REMINISCENCES—STARTED LAW AS STEP TO POLITICAL CAREER—THERE WAS INCOMPATIBILITY OF TEMPERAMENT—TOOK HIS DEGREE AT JOHNS HOPKINS—MARRIED TO MISS ELLEN AXSON—BEAUTIFUL HOME LIFE—DEATH OF MRS. WILSON**

"*The man who knows the strength of the tide is the man who is swimming against it, not the man who is floating with it.*"—Wilson

LAW, particularly in the South, is the vestibule to a political career. For more than a century the University of Virginia has been the training school for many youths, especially of the South, who held to the Jeffersonian creed. Jefferson counted the founding of the University of Virginia as one of the three things worth being placed on the simple shaft which marks his grave in Monticello, hard by the University of Virginia.

In 1879, the lack of money among its clientele had reduced the attendance to 328, with standards well maintained. Great teachers, with salaries of $2,000, and sometimes less, emulated Mark Hopkins. The greatest of them at the period (September, 1879) when Woodrow Wilson went there to study law, was John B. Minor, head of the Law Department. His reputation among teachers of the law was of the best and embryonic lawyers from a score of states thronged his classroom. Thither went the Princeton graduate, attracted partly by Minor's fame and partly by the feeling which always possessed him that he was the real son of the commonwealth in which he was born. He entered into the life of the college circle. He was a frequent and brilliant contributor to the University magazine. Though not an athlete, he enjoyed sports and often acted as umpire. He was initiated into the Phi Kappa Psi. He joined the Jefferson Literary Society, of which he was secretary, and as at Princeton won rank among the best debaters. It is interesting that the two "star" debaters of the society were Woodrow Wilson and William Cabell Bruce, now Senator from Maryland. He won the orator's prize and Bruce the debater's medal in a debate April 2, 1880, upon the query: "Is the Roman Catholic Church a menace to American institutions?" Wilson took the negative, his associate being J. M. Horner, now Episcopal Bishop of Western North Carolina. The affirmative was taken by Senator Bruce and Benjamin L. Abney of South Carolina. The judges rendered the decision:

"The committee of the faculty selected by your society to judge of the debate for prizes of the society, beg leave to report as follows:

"While the general character of the debate in question has been very creditable to the speakers and to the society they represent, two of the contestants have shown remarkable excellence. Being requested to decide between these gentlemen our committee is of the opinion that the medal intended for the best debater should be awarded to Mr. Bruce.

"In deciding that the position of the orator to the society, with the other medal bestowed therewith, should be awarded to Mr. Wilson our committee desires to express very high appreciation of his merits not merely as a speaker, for which this honor is bestowed, but as a debater also."

At that time as he afterwards abundantly proved in crucial days, Wilson believed in righteous peace when it could be had with honor. With many other students, he went to a circus at Charlottesville. Mr. M. H. Caldwell, of Concord, N. C., tells of an incident growing out of it and the mass meeting which followed:

"Trouble began when the students were enthusiastic in applause of a show girl. Some yelled, others clapped their hands. This enraged a showman. He rushed into the ring, denounced all of us as ruffians, scoundrels and blackguards, and threatened to throw us from the tent. He reminded us of the showman that had been killed there in former years and declared that if any one was killed on this occasion it would be a student.

"Several of the students wanted to fight there, but some one came and got the showman. We went back to the campus and the fun was on. A mass meeting was called to determine whether or not all of the students should go to the show that night and compel the man to apologize or whether everyone should stay away. Leroy Percy, later United States Senator from Mississippi, was spokesman for the crowd that wanted to fight; Woodrow Wilson was champion of the other crowd. Fiery speeches were made, but the logic of Wilson prevailed and his side won by about ten votes."

Speaking of the same incident, N. C. Manson, Jr., of Lynchburg, Va., says:

"There was great excitement and a number of fiery speeches on both sides of the question. Mr. Wilson spoke against the attack; Mr. Percy for it. Mr. Wilson was well known to the students; was exceedingly popular, and his courage was recognized by all. I have always thought that his influence with the students, combined with his wonderfully frank discussion of the reasons for and against the attack which he summed up in the question, 'Is it worth it?' secured the defeat of the proposition by a small majority." In his speech Wilson had counselled against the attack, but declared if the majority decided against him he would be ready to fight with them.

"When Wilson reached the University," said Senator Bruce, "he was tall and lanky, correct in dress and a stickler for proper deportment. While he was not a goody-goody, he was never absent at chapel, and showed the deep religious training of his father, a Presbyterian clergyman. He was always a model among the students.

"He was not conceited, but always had much confidence in himself and was conscious of his superiority of intellect.

"He had a good sense of humor and used to tell the gang funny stories, often at the expense of his worthy father. To illustrate the condition of the family, he told this one of an encounter between his father and a parishioner down in North Carolina:

"The parishioner said:

" 'How come, Preacher Wilson, you have such a sleek horse and you're so skinny yourself?'

" 'Well,' answered Wilson's father, 'I feed the horse, but the congregation feeds me.'

"Woodrow did not then manifest qualities which appeared in later life. But he did have the spark of greatness. Gov. Hubbard of Texas recognized it at our graduation exercises. Wilson's speech was the second on the program and after it Hubbard said there was a young man whose name would go down in history."

M. B. Winder, of Richmond, another classmate, remembers Mr. Wilson "chiefly as the rather frail young man whose name immediately preceded mine on the roll call of the class. But I also remember him," Mr. Winder added, "as one of the most brilliant contributors to the pages of the University magazine and as one of the most interesting talkers in the old 'Jeff' hall, whither many of us were attracted by the desire to hear him."

Roswell Page, brother of Thomas Nelson Page, was among the classmates who remembered Mr. Wilson as one "ever appreciative of anything that savored of humor, though very reserved behind a pair of eye glasses that were always worn"; and virtually all of the 32 alumni of the classes of 1879–81 now living in Virginia recall Wilson, the singer. Mr. Wilson was a member of the University glee club in 1880 and 1881 and his friends said he possessed a tenor voice of marked qualities. He also was a member of the college quartet.

Wilson's chief absorption was the study of law and government, or rather law as it related to government. The days at the institution Jefferson founded helped in the shaping of Wilson's life and always afterward he looked back upon those years with gratitude, and the associations and interest did not wane. Shortly before he was chosen President of Princeton there were negotiations looking to his becoming the first president of the Virginia University when the Jefferson idea of a chairman of the faculty seemed no longer the best policy of administration. At that time he wrote: "What you say about the University of Virginia of course interests me very greatly. I think that the wisest thing that can be done is to take some man from the South, who has already had some experience as head of a university,

**PRESIDENT WILSON IN 1884**

The Glee Club of Johns Hopkins University, organized by Woodrow Wilson (*standing, second from left*) when he was a post-graduate student in 1884

*Photo. Brown Bros.*

**AN ACADEMIC PROCESSION AT PRINCETON**

Woodrow Wilson in the center in cap and gown as president of the university. At his left is Andrew Carnegie, on whom the university conferred the degree of LL.D.

and who can come to the University of Virginia with enthusiasm not only, but with a good deal of experience as well."

Wilson's advice in principle was followed and his warm friend, Dr. Edwin A. Alderman, was chosen. In the early days of his administration, when Alderman was ill, Wilson said to a member of the cabinet: "I wish he were strong. He would fill a great place admirably and be a tower of strength to the administration."

Wilson pursued his legal education under Professor Minor until the close of 1880, when, having been troubled by a long period of indigestion, he found it imperative to give heed to his health. The next twelve months found him in Wilmington, N. C., recuperating and reading and gaining strength, and helped by stimulating association with his father. Completing his law course, with collateral reading, Wilson obtained license to practice law and May, 1882, found him located at Atlanta. He formed a partnership with Edward Ireland Renick, somewhat older than Wilson.

RENICK AND WILSON

read the simple sign out of a window of a room on the second floor, facing the side street, at 48 Marietta Street. Both young men were strangers in the bustling city, with no influential connections necessary to insure clients in the first months of practice. Young men of character and learning, they studied, and Wilson wrote, and waited for the clients who did not come in sufficient numbers to give adequate income. It was while waiting in Atlanta for clients that he wrote the first chapter of his "Congressional Government." Study and preparation for its writing and the actual writing of the beginning of his great work engrossed his time so fully that the lack of clients did not distress him. He saw in these eighteen months in Atlanta that his life work was neither in the court room nor in advising clients. It must be in consecration to the thing that had long gripped him —teaching young men the road to better government and its just administration. It was more "incompatibility of temperament" than lack of clients that determined Wilson's quitting the law for teaching. He was disillusioned in Atlanta when he discovered "the depth and slime of the gulf that often separated the philosophy of law from its practice." If he could be said to entertain any deep-seated prejudice, it was against what he called "the legalistic" barriers that stood in the way of securing quick justice. The slow processes and miscarriages of justice, and particularly as to unlawful combinations in restraint of trade, were unbearable to him. He wished sound and prompt ways to prevent illegal practices. It was to this end, when he became President, he conceived the value of the Federal Trade Commission. He believed it could, without harassing business, check unfair practices, avoiding the years of litigation that ancient processes made possible.

In 1883, Wilson went to the Johns Hopkins University for two years to take the course in history and political economy, holding the Historical Fellowship the second year. Chiefly, he devoted himself to research work, under the guidance of such authorities as Richard T. Ely and Herbert B. Adams. His association with kindred spirits, not a few of whom attained distinction, made his days at Johns Hopkins always happy memories. With Charles B. Levermore (who recently won the Bok Peace prize), he organized a glee club, and frequent meetings of social enjoyment were held at the home of Prof. Charles S. Morris, of the Latin and Greek Department. That club had among its members Davis R. Dewey, Edward T. Ingle, David T. Day, B. J. Ramage, F. M. Warren, Albert Shaw, E. R. L. Gould, Arthur Yager, and others, some of whom won high place. He appointed Yager Governor of Porto Rico. The picture of that club, with Wilson wearing a mustache and "sideburns," still hangs in the room of the Historical Seminary. These were years of broadening study and inspiration. He wrote at that time "An Old Master," a study of Adam Smith. In 1886, he obtained his Ph.D. degree, his thesis being "Congressional Government." He had plowed in a virgin field, the book was well received, became an authority, and remains as marked a contribution to the study of government as Mr. Bryce's "The American Commonwealth."

Wilson's "Life of George Washington," published in 1896, bore this dedication to his wife:

To
E. A. W.
Without Whose Sympathy and Counsel
Literary Work Would Lack
Inspiration

It was in 1883, on a visit to his cousin, Jessie Woodrow Bones, at Rome, Georgia, that Mr. Wilson met Miss Ellen Louise Axson. The event had so large a place in his life that it may be well to say that the meeting was on the piazza of the Bones residence and that he took her to her home across the river that evening. It is tradition that, as he crossed the bridge, returning, he voiced the resolve that one day Miss Axson should be his wife.

On his eleventh visit she gave the answer which later made her Mrs. Wilson. She was the daughter of Rev. S. Edward Axson, prominent Presbyterian minister of Savannah. Her grandfather was Rev. Nathan Hoyt, long Presbyterian pastor at Athens, Georgia. It was an ideal union, for the two young people had been reared in like environment of culture and religious atmosphere. The venture in law at Atlanta had revealed to him that teaching and politics, not law, was his life work. There was no prospect of immediate marriage. He had decided upon two years at Johns Hopkins to take his degree and Miss Axson went to the Art Students' League, in New York, to perfect herself in painting, in which she had real talent. These days of preparation accomplished, the young couple were married at the home of the bride's grandfather in Savannah, on June 24, 1885. A honeymoon in the mountains of Western North Carolina, with Waynesville in the centre, was marked by rambles, with some pencil sketches by the bride and much reading by both. Then, Wilson having accepted a professorship in Bryn Mawr, they set up a home near Philadelphia. It was during these years that the two oldest children, Misses Margaret and Jessie Woodrow (now Mrs. Francis B. Sayre), were born, both at Gainesville, Ga. Thence to Wesleyan University, at Middletown, Conn., where their younger daughter, Eleanor, who later became the wife of the Hon. William G. McAdoo, was born.

Only one other home of long duration was known —that at Princeton—until the move to the White House. The Princeton house was a home of their own making, and the architecture and furnishings attested Mrs. Wilson's taste. It is said to have been designed after one in Keswick, England. The buff-and-black timbered house is approached through a closed porch. Steps led to a well-like room lined with tiers of brick that made an ideal library. Mrs. Wilson entered into all social affairs at Princeton and to that home came men of letters and distinction. It was a place of study, of companionship, of the finest flower of hospitality. Deeply religious, well read, and artistic, Mrs. Wilson was a leader in the social life of the college town, as wife of a professor of growing influence and later as the wife of the distinguished President. Her ambitions for her husband and her faith in his future made her keenly interested in all that concerned him. All his life he was a home-body, giving himself without reserve to those in the loved circle. The Wilsons never permitted the claims of society to deny the supremacy of the home life. The family group in Washington embraced the President, Mrs. Wilson, their three daughters, and Miss Helen Woodrow Bones, a cousin of Mr. Wilson.

To go ahead of the story: a few weeks prior to Wilson's inauguration to the Presidency, a visiting friend to whom she talked freely, was asked by her: "What do you think of the propriety of an inaugural ball when Woodrow is inaugurated?" (She never called him anything but "Woodrow.") The visitor thought these balls were garish and rather cheap, but it had so long been regarded as a necessary part of the inauguration, he supposed the Committee would wish to keep up the custom.

"I cannot bear to think of a ball, with the modern dances, when Woodrow is inaugurated," she said, carrying the impression that she regarded the occasion as a "dedication," not a social event. There was no inaugural ball. The Washington Committee protested without avail, and the belles and dressmakers of Washington stormed. Mrs. Wilson had her way and the President-elect shared her view. In the few short months Mrs. Wilson presided as "the first lady of the land," as the President's wife is always called, she won all hearts by her gracious receptions, her re-making and beautifying portions of the White House grounds, and her leadership in removing the squalor of the tenements and crowded alleys of the city of Washington. Welfare workers and artists and women with a purpose found her a co-worker.

Mrs. Wilson after a long period of declining health, died in the White House, August 6, 1914, and her husband and daughters tenderly carried her body to Rome, Georgia, to sleep beside her parents. She lives in the hearts of those admitted to the sacred precinct of her friendship and in her contribution to society and improving living conditions. She illustrated the best of Southern womanhood, happy and beautiful alike, as a girl in the home of the Christian minister, wife and mother in the quiet college campus surroundings, and as first lady in the White House. The dedication of his book, "George Washington," expressed his obligation for her sympathy and counsel. He would have added his "devotion" if he could have permitted any save "heaven and the One Ear alone" to hear the affection that blessed and steadied him.

Mrs. Wilson died seventeen months after becoming mistress of the White House. "Promise me," she whispered to Dr. Grayson as she was passing, "that when I go you will take care of Woodrow." Always her thought was of the husband in whom her life and ambition had been centered. And Dr. Grayson never forgot and never failed.

Finding himself, Wilson found home and happiness.

## CHAPTER VI

# EDUCATOR AND LECTURER

BEGAN TEACHING POLITICS IN BRYN MAWR, A COLLEGE FOR WOMEN—HIS HEART'S DESIRE DISCLOSED—TWO YEARS AT WESLEYAN—RETURNS TO PRINCETON AS PROFESSOR AND IS CHOSEN PRESIDENT—POPULAR ON THE PLATFORM

*"I have not read history without observing that the greatest forces in the world and the only permanent forces are the moral forces."*—WILSON

GRADUATING at Johns Hopkins, which he entered in September, 1883, Wilson received the Ph.D. degree in June, 1886. His thesis was "Congressional Government." Impressed with the failure of congressional government because it lacked direction, responsibility and action, the remedy proposed was responsible cabinet government. Steeped in the study of parliamentary leaders during his Princeton days, Wilson had reached the conclusion that the British system had advantages over the American system in giving quick effect to the mandate of the people. But he did not go so far as to recommend the British system for this country. Rather he contrasted the points of advantage with the disadvantages, not so much of American government, as in the actual workings of congressional government, where in virtual secret session most of the important measures were shaped with no public debate.

Concurrent with securing his degree came his marriage and entry upon his career as educator and lecturer. Accepting the position of associate professor of history and political science at Bryn Mawr, lately founded to give broader education to women, he established a home in the suburbs of Philadelphia. The young women privileged to come under his instruction went into life better citizens, as well as better scholars, even if they could not then vote. Thirty-four years later he stood before the Senate urging the ratification of the Nineteenth Amendment, conferring suffrage upon women. Did his early association at Bryn Mawr have influence that contributed to his leadership for women's political rights?

In his third year at Bryn Mawr he accepted a lecture engagement at Johns Hopkins, lecturing there once a week for twenty-five weeks. At Bryn Mawr and at Johns Hopkins he taught and lectured on political science, adding classical history and the history of the Renaissance in his Bryn Mawr classes. He loved his work, read prodigiously, and when he appeared before the classes, had a message. Neighbors observed that his student lamp burned far into the night, presaging the long hours and vigils in the White House. A number of his associates in the faculty at Bryn Mawr had been classmates at Johns Hopkins. Their comradeship was stimulating, the student body responding to the enthusiasm of the teacher, and a happy home life contributed to give the days fullness of content.

Professor Wilson entered upon his work at Bryn Mawr in the fall of 1885. Writing in November of that year to an old Princeton classmate, the late Charles A. Talcott, of Utica, N. Y., who was later Mayor and Congressman, Wilson disclosed what was his heart's desire. It revealed the spirit that actuated him as student, teacher, citizen, governor and president. He wrote:

"In the thinking and writing which I am trying to do, I constantly feel the disadvantage of the closet; I want to keep close to the practical and practicable in politics; my ambition is to add something to the statesmanship of the country, if that something be only thought, and not the old achievement of which I used to dream when I hoped that I might enter practical politics.

"I seek, therefore, in the acquaintances I make, not other professors, not other book-politicians, but men who have direct touch of the world; in order that I may study affairs rather than doctrine. But the practical men I meet have not broad horizons; they are not students of affairs; they learn what they know rather by friction than by rational observation; they are at the opposite extreme from men of books who are all horizon, and the one extreme is as fatal to balanced thought as the other.

"Now, you, Charlie, are both in affairs and studious of them; if ever I met a fellow with whose ways of thinking I could sympathize and from whom consequently, I could receive aid and comfort, thou art the man, and I need you. If you need me in any degree, the old compact between us is, therefore, *ipso facto* renewed.

"I believe, Charlie, that if a band of young fellows, say ten or twelve, could get together, and by getting together I mean getting their opinions together upon a common platform, and having gotten together on good solid planks with reference to the questions of the immediate future, should raise a united voice in such periodicals great and small, as they could gain access to, gradually working their way out by means of a real understanding of the questions they handled, to a position of prominence and acknowledged authority in the public prints and so in the public mind, a long step would have been taken towards the formation of such a new political sentiment as the country stands in such pressing need of, and I am ambitious that we should have a hand in forming such a group."

He showed then the faith he never lost in the people. "All the country needs," he says, "is a new and sincere body of thought in politics, coherently, distinctly and boldly uttered by men who are sure of their ground," and he asked why should not men animated for high and helpful purpose in politics meet the need better "than either of the present moribund parties can give?"

After three years, in 1888, a call to the chair of history and political economy in the Wesleyan University was accepted and brought him two happy years of residence at Middletown, Connecticut, a charming setting for such an institution. Established as a Methodist institution, Wesleyan attracted serious-minded teachers and students from other creeds. Its curriculum was broad and its instruction thorough and the life healthy. Its students were not generally from the homes of the rich. Wholesome and plain living, high thinking and noble ambition for service were the rule. It planned to turn out preachers and judges and legislators and missionaries and business men who had a larger conception of business than mere accumulation. Into this atmosphere, bringing a larger vision of public service, Wilson breathed a new sense of the responsibility of educated youth to civic betterment.

During his stay at Wesleyan the plan he afterwards urged in public utterances was put in practice. "Every university should make the reading of English literature compulsory from entrance to graduation," he wrote, adding: "It offers the basis of a common American culture for college men. It gives imagination for affairs and the standard by which things invisible and of the spirit are to be measured." It was at Wesleyan he wrote "The State."

At Wesleyan he was called upon for assistance in some of the administrative work of the institution. Among these duties was membership of an Athletic Committee. He devised for the Red and Black a series of "rotation plays," as he called them, in which various sequences of plays followed one another without signal. Traditionally, the Wesleyan boys had been well satisfied if they could merely keep down the Yale score when they played that college. Professor Wilson's admonition was: "That's no ambition at all, go in and win; you can lick Yale as well as any other team. Go after their scalps. Don't admit for a moment that they can beat you." He even planned an offensive football play which carried Wesleyan to victory over Pennsylvania and paved the way for a score against Harvard—a notable achievement for a Wesleyan team. At a Thanksgiving Day game against Lehigh in 1889, when the Wesleyan defense was being hammered down, a figure in black rubber coat, rubber boots and umbrella left the side line and stood in front of the Wesleyan crowd. Closing the umbrella and using it as a baton, the tall figure beat the air until he had co-ordinated the Wesleyan cheering into a mighty yell which so inspired the Wesleyan players that they swept down the field for a second touchdown, tying the score, which remained unbroken. It was Professor Wilson.

In 1890 the chair of jurisprudence in Princeton became vacant through the death of Dr. Alexander Johnson, and Wilson was chosen for the work at the place to which his friends believed he had been predestined. At any rate, agreeable as was his life at Wesleyan, the love and lure of his alma mater claimed him. From September, 1890, therefore, until he became Governor of New Jersey, he was professor and president of Princeton, and indeed lived in his own home until he took passage for the eight-year residence in the White House. He had an abiding love for Princeton, attested in his attempts to lift it to his ideals for a university. A university, he had said, was a place where men go "to hear the truth about the past and hold debate about the present with knowlege and without passion." He gave possibly his best expression of his feeling about the place when, in accepting the gift of a lake from Andrew Carnegie, he said: "I do not think that it is merely our doting love of the place that has led us to think of it as a place which those who love their country and like to dwell upon its honorable history would naturally be inclined to adorn with their gifts," giving vent to his devotion as he embraced all Princeton, when he added: "We could not but be patriotic here."

It was at Princeton in student days he had found the controlling impulse to his life work. Residence in the South in the seventies, where the people talked politics and government more than trade and industry, had awakened in him the sense of the duty of a citizen. But it was at Old Nassau he was born again. In his student days he had heard the clear call to leadership in politics.

He returned with the glow of enthusiasm and happiness of opportunity to open the door of service to those he was to teach. For twelve years here he studied government, its history, its development, its laws, its limitations and its literature. And he applied all he learned and hoped and thought and dreamed as to how government could be made the instrument of equality and happiness to mankind.

The spirit of Witherspoon was upon him. Tradition of the noble days when devotion to liberty and independence by Princeton's president caused Fox to exclaim, "Cousin America has run off with a Presbyterian parson" stirred within him. The simple dignity and love of learning that was incarnated in James McCosh held him in emulation. Every sacrifice and every noble tradition, as well as love of his calling, appealed to him as he returned to the old place. He had gone away to carry its best ideals. He had returned to live and to impart them. His lecture rooms were crowded with ambitious youths who followed him with a new understanding of what politics and citizenship meant to an educated American. He became at once easily Princeton's most popular professor. Students going into the world carried something of the compulsion of public service he stressed and imparted. The splendid diction and faultless structure and brilliant phrasing of his lectures were but the vehicle of the mighty political and social truths he was bent upon instilling. Then, as always, his ready flash of humor and wealth of illustration—from the classics and from the street—made the student body eager to hear his interpretation of the vital affairs of an increasingly complex system. They felt that he brought to them treasures new and old out of the reserves of a large storehouse of knowledge. He asked them to accept nothing upon his "say-so" and never led them into a blind alley. He had none of the vanity of dignity. He always had a remedy for every political ailment, or he frankly told his students, "my mind is in debate" and when debate was ended, gave the conclusion.

The class-room, however, was not permitted to monopolize his thought or circumscribe his deep interest in what concerned his countrymen. He brought to his class freshness of treatment of public questions that many professors thought might involve something political or partisan. He never concealed his convictions and never spoke as blind partisan. But he rang clear where his principle was fixed. It was in his teaching days that Professor Wilson revealed himself. The things that he pondered in his heart then he afterwards practiced as the leader of the Republic.

It was while Professor at Princeton that the one hundred and fiftieth anniversary of the College of New Jersey occurred. Professor Wilson was chosen as the commemorative orator. The address made a profound impression. He warned young men, while alert for what was new in science, against giving up "old drill, the old memory of times gone by, the old schooling in precedent and tradition, the old keeping of the faith as a preparation for leadership in days of social change," and he declared, "We must make the old humanities human again." He was no foe to science but welcomed its instruction. He stood against its monopoly in college life. Science, he said, "has given us agnosticism in the realm of philosophy and scientific anarchy in the field of politics."

The promotion from the most popular professor to the presidency of Princeton was the natural and easy step. When President Francis Landey Patton, in 1902, resigned, the selection of Woodrow Wilson was hailed alike by faculty, trustees and alumni of Princeton as the logical succession. Mr. Wilson was not quite forty-four years of age. He had won the place of distinction by superior fitness. Coming to it by the merit system of promotion, he insisted upon it in others when called to the highest public station. Not only did "Nassau men" welcome his election, but the liberal and progressive thought of America shared in approval. The subject of his inaugural was "The Relation of the University to the State." Wilson's reputation had traveled far and educators and public men saw in him a dynamic force. Great things were expected of him. The prophecies came true. He needed no period of the novitiate. Student and professor, he had spent his best years at Princeton. Its fine traditions were in his blood. He knew where it was weak. The exhibition of executive ability in university president foreshadowed successful administration at Trenton and Washington. He resolved to graft upon the old institution the vital principles Witherspoon had helped to secure for America when the young republic was born. He later outlined his policy, or his conception of education, in an address in which he said:

"We are upon the eve of a period when we are going to set up standards," which followed his statement to a body of teachers in another commonwealth: "You know that the pupils in the colleges in the last several decades have not been educated. You know that with all of our teaching we train nobody.

You know that with all our instructing, we educate nobody." If that statement had been made by one outside the teaching profession, it would have created a sensation. As it was, the teachers to whom he was speaking felt that he was making his declaration more to stir them up to better instruction than announcing a policy. He was doing both.

Wilson's term as President of Princeton was from 1902 until he was elected Governor of New Jersey in 1910. Life as head of the old institution, which had been his nourishing mother, gave promise of long years of happiness and usefulness, with time for study and summers abroad and lectures and addresses to his countrymen. These would have filled his full measure of happiness if the conditions at Princeton were such as his judgment approved. First, he must "set up new standards." And until "new standards" threatened to change social conditions and estrange rich donors, Wilson's incumbency as president was a continuation of his popular career as professor. If he had been content to insist upon the preceptorial changes, without his vigor in demanding democratization of university life, the days of stress and controversy might not have made the call to political office pleasing.

As professor and president, Wilson had become a prime favorite as a public speaker, often addressing gatherings of business men and public men, as well as educational bodies. His plain-speaking and dissection of evils, clear conception of remedies, and his original and clear-cut way of presenting his real views made him a leading figure among educators who felt the call to serve their country as well as their college. He had been speaking his mind since his graduation in his addresses, but the forum of President of Princeton gave him a national audience. Now the dramatic quality of his utterances, as well as his frank turning the light upon college problems, challenged public attention. He never spoke that he did not say something worth hearing, and something that he must say. He would not "sell the truth to serve the hour."

It was not a far cry from being President of the University, which gave Witherspoon as leader in forming the Republic, to becoming President of the United States in days of crisis and change.

The Schoolmaster in Politics outlined his policy in his inaugural as President of Princeton.

In Washington "The Relation of the University to the State" was translated from theory into practice.

He was on his way to Washington.

## Chapter VII

# HIS FIGHT FOR DEMOCRACY IN EDUCATION

"AMERICA WILL TOLERATE NOTHING EXCEPT UNPATRONIZED ENDEAVOR"—RAISING THE STANDARDS OF EDUCATION—BROADENING THE CURRICULUM—THE PRECEPTORIAL SYSTEM—THE CONTROVERSY OVER STUDENT CLUBS—COLLEGES MUST BE RECONSTRUCTED FROM TOP TO BOTTOM—THE "BATTLE OF PRINCETON"

*"It is service that dignifies, and service only."*—Wilson

"I HAVE told the authorities I will not be the President of a Country Club. Princeton must either be an educational institution or I will not remain."

With these words, spoken in telling of the long drawn-out contest at Princeton, Mr. Wilson, then President of the College, voiced his attitude against permitting the "side-shows", as he called the numberless activities of college social life, to crowd out the serious business of obtaining an education. "Too many college students," he went on, "give their initiative and enthusiasm to other things and bring a jaded mind to their classes." It was to such a young man that he made an oft-quoted retort. "This is a dull subject," said the student seeking to excuse his low marks, to which the College President replied, "The only dull thing about this subject is the mind brought to it."

His quarter of a century of teaching before he became an executive had given Mr. Wilson opportunity to know the defects of college life. The growing aloofness of the scholar from the problems of the world in which he lived was a matter that gave the new President concern. He had long been of the opinion that the air of superiority assumed by college graduates, which often blocked their way to service, was the result of a lack of democratic practice in the colleges and the universities. In his classes he had found men coming with the fag end of their powers to their studies. He debated with himself whether a college was primarily an educational institution or a social club. When, therefore, with practical unanimity, the trustees of Princeton in 1902 elected Dr. Wilson to succeed Dr. Patton as President, the opportunity came to put into practice the ideas he had long been evolving. The election of Dr. Wilson, with his lack of reverence for Things as They Are, was to cause much anxiety in the breasts of those who were well satisfied to permit Princeton to be a favorite of youths who enjoyed the pleasure of living in its clubs and cramming enough to skin through their examinations.

Wilson had made a reputation in the educational world. As early as 1900 suggestion had been made of his availability for President of the United States. But this was only by scholars and a few others who knew of his mastery of questions of government. It added to Princeton prestige to have its President highly regarded. The reactionary group, joining heartily in his election, were later to have a jar and regret their choice. Cradled in Presbyterianism and the child of the church, Princeton had had none but a preacher as its President. It was a departure to elect a lawyer, even though he was an elder and the son of a preacher. Disregarding ministerial succession broke a precedent, and the new President was to break many others.

Soon, before the end of the first year of his incumbency in fact, Wilson startled the students by letting them know that if they wished to remain at "the most charming Country Club in America", as Princeton had been called, they must pass their examinations. Social and all other kinds of "pull" were at an end, the new executive announced. The rule created a sensation. In addition to requiring scholarship, a new system of collegiate study was evolved. Students were required, if taking elective studies, to master the subjects they undertook. The next step was to bring students and faculty into nearer relationship by adopting the preceptorial system, which has since been adopted by a number of other colleges. Having taken these two progressive steps within a few years, President Wilson laid his hand on the system that was responsible for the lack of diligence in study—the social system. He proposed the quadrangle or dormitory, which should house a certain number of men from every class, with a young professor as the head of the house, so to speak. It was the logical next step in the preceptorial plan. There was everything to commend it except the fatal defect: it was too democratic and cut across the grain of the exclusive system of sumptuous club houses. The objection to the club houses was that only a portion of the student body was admitted and there grew up a feeling that those who were not chosen were ostracized. The ambition for selection to these exclusive clubs was such that young students sometimes devoted more time to electioneering for admission into the charmed circles than to preparing their lessons. It ministered to snobbery.

Because Wilson's "quad" system would have taken the place of the clubs, the intensity of feeling against him was greater than can be described. "He wants to make a gentleman chum with a mucker" was the cry raised by the club group, and they asked what the world was coming to when a man must be "compelled to submit to dictation as to his table companions." The clamor by certain of the alumni against the "quad" system influenced the trustees. The Board had approved the "quad" plan, but on account of the protests, requested President Wilson to withdraw it. He was not that kind of man. But the fight was so bitter that echoes of it remain to this day. President Wilson was not fighting clubs as such. He was the last man to wish to deny anyone the right to choose his own associates. All he was trying to do was to make Princeton a real educational institution. If the clubs stood in the way of a better educational development, so much the worse for them. The object was education. It was a contest between two principles—Privilege and Democracy. They have been at war for all time. When Wilson, solely in the pursuit of educational efficiency, became the champion of Democracy, the old order of Special Privilege fought him at Princeton as later it did when he was in the White House. He replied as President of Princeton as he did at Washington. He neither asked nor gave quarter.

The division at Princeton between President Wilson and his antagonists reached the crucial stage when a lady left $250,000, and William C. Procter, of Cincinnati, offered to give $500,000 for a graduate college. The conditions were the location of the graduate school at a certain site considerably removed from the undergraduate schools and that another $500,000 should be raised to match Mr. Procter's half a million. The trustees "looked a gift horse in the mouth;" informed Mr. Procter that the plan of a graduate college had been adopted only tentatively, and asked him if his gift was conditional upon permitting him and those at Princeton in touch with him to control the location, or whether he wished to make a donation and trust to the wisdom of the college authorities to use it in the wisest manner. He withdrew his offer of the money. President Wilson had before expressed his belief that in colleges there was "a strong tendency to glorify money" unduly, and that with the increasing wealth of the country this tendency would be accentuated and that we would "drift into a plutocracy." He said he believed that at Princeton, to which many sons of rich men came, the policy should be one that would "so impress those boys with ideas of democracy and personal worth that when they became, in the ordinary course of nature, masters of their fathers' fortunes, they would use their undoubted power to help, not hurt, the commonwealth."

President Wilson felt that the graduate school, as proposed, was more ornamental than necessary. He asked, "When the world is looking to us as men who prefer ideas even to money, are we going to withdraw and say 'After all, we find we were mistaken: we prefer money to ideas'?" He justified his position further by saying: "We should be forever condemned in the public judgment and in our own conscience if we used Princeton for any private purpose whatever." That seems so sound that at this distance it is remarkable that there was any sentiment among the trustees in opposition to President Wilson's views. However, fourteen out of the thirty trustees stood against him. Some wavered. The bulk of the faculty, the alumni, and student body approved his declaration when he said, "I cannot accede to the acceptance of gifts upon terms which take the educational policy of the university out of the hands of the trustees and faculty and permit it to be determined by those who give money."

The conflict was to the bitter end. It was not lessened by the plain speech of the fighting President. He loved peace—he believed there might be occasions when a man should be "too proud to fight"—but he was not the man to remain silent when he saw influences at work which he felt would undermine the spirit and scholarship of his beloved alma mater. He hurled defiance at his opponents in an address to the Pittsburgh alumni, saying:

"You can't spend four years at one of our modern universities without getting in your thought the conviction which is most dangerous to America—namely, that you must treat with certain influences which now dominate in the commercial undertakings of the country.

"The great voice of America does not come from seats of learning. It comes in a murmur from the hills and woods and the farms and factories, and the mills, rolling on and gaining volume until it comes to us from the homes of common men. Do these murmurs echo in the corridors of universities? I have not heard them.

"The universities would make men forget their common origins, forget their universal sympathies, and join a class—and no class ever can serve America.

"I have dedicated every power that there is within me to bring the colleges that I have anything to do with to an absolutely democratic regeneration in spirit, and I shall not be satisfied—and I hope you will not be—until America shall know that the men in the colleges are saturated with the same thought, the same sympathy, that pulses through the whole great body politic.

"I know that the colleges of this country must be reconstructed from top to bottom, and I know that America is going to demand it. While Princeton men pause and think, I hope—and the hope arises out of the great love I share with you all for our inimitable alma mater—I hope that they will think on these things, that they will forget tradition in the determination to see to it that the free air of America shall permeate every cranny of their college.

"Will America tolerate the seclusion of graduate students? Will America tolerate the idea of having graduate students set apart? America will tolerate nothing except unpatronized endeavor. Seclude a man, separate him from the rough and tumble of college life, from all the contacts of every sort and condition of men, and you have done a thing which America will brand with its contemptuous disapproval."

A windfall of three million dollars, and the renewal of Procter's gift, inclined the trustees to undertake the plans which they had declined and which Wilson had not approved. What college has trustees who could consistently throw a brick at the Princeton authorities? President Wilson, seeing fate and money had combined to give the victory to his old opponents, accepted the situation. He had made the bravest fight recorded to democratize university life. One of the queer slants of the contest was that in 1910, at the very meeting where the opponents of Wilson won as to site, thanks to three million arguments in the way of three million dollars, in the election of a trustee, the anti-Wilson candidate, Mr. Adrian Joline, was defeated for trustee. He was the same Mr. Joline to whom Dr. Wilson had written in 1907 that he wished "we could do something to knock Mr. Bryan once for all into a cocked hat."

The scars of that famed university contest were still fresh when Mr. Wilson went to Washington. Often, when he was assailed, he would refer to incidents and lessons from "the battle of Princeton." It cut deeper than political contests, for in the college town it affected whole families. The first Mrs. Wilson, who, in addition to her beautiful affection, was far more ambitious for her husband than he was for himself, had felt the strain of the differences in Princeton which the outside world thought of as quiet and serene classic shades far removed from clash and conflict. The turn of affairs, however, could not destroy the principles he enunciated at Pittsburgh. "Democratic regeneration in spirit" in college was not defeated. It was only deferred. College submission to the dictation of wealth always proves the undoing of the right kind of higher education. To-day few gifts are made conditional upon permitting the donor to determine what course the institution shall take. The democratization of colleges received an impulse from Dr. Wilson's courageous stand. Princeton, and all institutions, even if for a time the great issue was confused, have felt the blessing of the democracy in education proclaimed by Woodrow Wilson. With a brief period of redeeming New Jersey from the thraldom of trusts, opposing privilege and the power of wealth in the commonwealth as he had in college affairs, Mr. Wilson went to Washington to continue, on a larger scale, leadership in the age-old war between Democracy and Privilege.

He blazed the way.

## Chapter VIII

# WRITER AS WELL AS MAKER OF HISTORY

MAN OF LETTERS TO HIS FINGER TIPS—MADE HISTORY FASCINATING AND POLITICAL SCIENCE INTERESTING—HIS FATHER TAUGHT HIM TO THINK IN DEFINITIONS—THAT TRAINING AND WIDE READING RESPONSIBLE FOR HIS ELEGANT STYLE—MADE HISTORY AS PRESIDENT AS HE HAD WRITTEN IT AS CITIZEN

*"The historian needs consummate literary art as much as candor and common honesty."*—Wilson

LONG before he became President, Mr. Wilson had been elected to the American Academy of Arts and Letters whose constitutional qualification for membership is "notable achievement in art, music or literature." That honor came not because he was a professor of history and jurisprudence. It was awarded because his historical writings were literature in the highest sense of the word. He fully exemplified his own assertion that "the historian needs an imagination quite as much as he needs scholarship, and consummate literary art as much as candor and common honesty." "Whatever else he may be," said an English critic, "President Wilson is a man of letters to his finger tips—a man steeped in literary traditions, and possessed of fine literary gifts. He can make political science readable to the layman, and he can make history fascinating without imparting to it the cheap over-coloring of fiction or the hectic fervor of partisanship."

"Congressional Government," Mr. Wilson's first

published work, appeared in 1885, six years after his graduation. It had been prepared as the thesis required for his degree of Doctor of Philosophy at Johns Hopkins University. Most academic dissertations are soon buried in oblivion, but the brilliancy of this one raised it at once to the rank of a political classic, and brought its author an immediate reputation in the world of learning. It is an analysis of our legislative procedure, describing the American national system in contrast with the British. In vivacity and incisiveness of style it has often been favorably compared with Bagehot's famous work on the English Constitution.

Four years later came "The State: Elements of Historical and Practical Politics" (1889), a comprehensive manual tracing government to its origins and analyzing its ancient, medieval, and modern types. A pioneer work in the field of knowledge treated, it was one of the earliest examples of the new historical method applied to the subject of political science. Critics on both sides of the Atlantic gave it a warm welcome, a distinguished English scholar saying: "Mr. Wilson will be considered as the foremost of those who rendered possible an intelligent study of a department of sociology upon which the happiness and good government of the human race essentially depend."

"Division and Reunion, 1829–1889" (1893), is an able summary of the larger features of American public affairs from the election of Andrew Jackson to the end of the first century of the Constitution. As a general history of political development during the period covered it shows extensive knowledge, unusual power of summarizing, an acute political sense, fine impartiality of judgment, and an admirable sense of proportion. His insight into the tendencies of the times, the vivid manner in which the views of parties and contemporary political life are characterized show historical talent of a high order. The style is easy and flowing, striking phrases flash out brilliantly and often, and there are few if any other books on this important period which are so thoroughly enjoyable to read.

The "Life of George Washington" is a masterpiece of biography. The first President is shown in the proper setting of his own eighteenth century age and time—as the Virginia country gentleman, frontier-surveyor, and military commander. It is a history of the times written as an epic, the events being grouped about the personality of the hero but with the figures of the men who surrounded him also delineated with a sure and vivid touch. Again the narrative is one full of charm and the style singularly careful and polished.

President Wilson's best known and most widely read work, "A History of the American People" (1902), was written during the years of his Princeton incumbency. It originated in his desire to find a means whereby he might continue his study of governmental problems. The work is designedly popular in character and treatment of its subject, and was frankly intended for the general reader rather than for scholars and specialists in American history. But it is an able summary of American political history and none but a true man of letters could have given the book its fine literary flavor and form. The author sets forth the approved modern judgment of the great questions and great men of American origin; his frank democratic bias is never concealed, but it never disturbs his imperturbable fairness. Very few men, with his Southern antecedents, could have kept such an admirable balance between extreme Northern and Southern views. President Wilson showed himself almost wholly devoid of sectional prejudice of any sort. Good judges consider the chapters dealing with the Jacksonian period the best of all. The dominating presence of masterful men is everywhere felt, and one catches the spirit of the time and the very atmosphere of its life from the glowing, vivid word-painting. It was the frequently expressed opinion that this "History" does for the United States what J. R. Green's "Short History" did for England. Like Macaulay, Froude, Motley, Parkman, and Green, Mr. Wilson never forgot that written history must be, if possible, literature as well as accurate assembling of facts. The opening paragraph of the chapter entitled "The Swarming of the English" illustrates the ease and pictorial quality of his narrative style:

"It was the end of the month of April, 1607, when three small vessels entered the lonely capes of the Chesapeake, bringing the little company who were to make the first permanent English settlement in America, at Jamestown, in Virginia. Elizabeth was dead. The masterful Tudor monarchs had passed from the stage and James, the pedant king, was on the throne. The 'Age of the Stuarts' had come, with its sinister policies and sure tokens of revolution. Men then living were to see Charles lie dead upon the scaffold at Whitehall. After that would come Cromwell; and then the second Charles, 'restored,' would go his giddy way through a demoralizing reign, and leave his sullen brother to face another revolution. It was to be an age of profound constitutional change, deeply significant for all the English world; and the colonies in America, notwithstanding their separate life and the breadth of the sea, were to feel all the deep stir of the fateful business. The revolution wrought at home might in crossing to them suffer a certain sea-change, but it would not lose its use or its strong flavor of principle."

"Constitutional Government in the United States" (1908) exhibits Mr. Wilson's high quality as a thinker and is in many ways the most complete expression of his political ideas. Particularly in this work did he show his belief that the President of the United States, both by reason of the duties imposed upon him and by his relation to the rest of the government and to the people, must almost necessarily be the leader of his party as well as the leader of the nation. This carefully considered conclusion of Wilson the scholar should be borne in mind when judging the public acts of Wilson, party leader and president. In the latter capacities he was but following out the conclusions reached after prolonged study and thought in the quiet of his academic home.

Thoughtful readers will note another impressive and significant fact in the work of this scholar and historian. His "Constitutional Government," "Life of Washington," and "History of the American People" are all essentially studies in leadership, and throughout them all there runs a quiet consciousness of his own power. He writes, as afterwards he came to speak, as one having authority.

After entering public life he no longer had time or opportunity for sustained study and literary composition. As from time to time he was called upon to express himself upon the great political, social, and international questions of the hour, it was chiefly through the spoken word that he had to convey the conclusions and opinions formed in his richly stored mind. And yet, so thorough was his knowledge of the subjects dealt with and so perfect his command of English, that many of the stenographic reports of his extemporaneous speeches read like finished examples of carefully composed written work. This is notably true of the addresses contained in "The New Freedom" (1913). There is not a page in it that a man of letters might not be content to have written at leisure; there is not a suggestion that the flowing sentences were spoken in the glare and heat and excitement of public platforms. And the subject matter is as good as the form, for, as Mr. Wilson himself said, "they are an attempt to express the new spirit of our politics and to set forth, in large terms which may stick in the imagination, what it is that must be done if we are to restore our politics to their full spiritual vigor, and our national life to its purity, its self-respect and its pristine strength and freedom."

With the coming of the Great War all the resources of his scholarship, his knowledge of history, and his gift of expression were drawn on to the utmost. The writer who had long labored in the still air of delightful studies now became the inspired spokesman of a great nation, and indeed of the masses of the peoples of other nations. No other President, probably, has accomplished so much of his work through the successful use of written and spoken appeals to the Congress, to the American people and to the public opinion of the world. They aroused the attention and extorted the admiration of the leaders of thought and affairs in all the allied countries. They shaped contemporary events not only in the current sense but in the larger aspects of history. Their remarkable literary quality would alone be sufficient to insure their being read by generations yet unborn. His incisive, clear-cut, throbbing sentences and paragraphs helped to crystallize the vague longings of right-thinking men in all nations. They were the articulate expression of the hopes of the world, and for Americans the clarifying and vigorous definition of their national purposes and ideals in the war:

"Our object is to vindicate the principles of peace and justice in the life of the world as against selfish and autocratic power and to set up amongst the really free and self-governed peoples such a concert of purpose and of action as will henceforth insure the observance of these principles."

"We have no selfish ends to serve. We desire no conquest, no dominion. We seek no indemnities for ourselves, no material compensation for the sacrifices we shall freely make. We are but one of the champions of the rights of mankind. We shall be satisfied when those rights have been made as secure as the faith and freedom of nations can make them."

Convinced belief in democracy runs through all the messages and addresses like a golden thread. In his mind, the means of bringing about democratic government comes from within, not from without, by moral, not by physical force. "I have not read history," he said, "without observing that the greatest forces in the world and the only permanent forces are the moral forces." That was ever his keynote, and if it had its origin in his ancestry, it had been reinforced through wide historical study and keen observation of the men and events of his own time.

In the domain of pure belles-lettres, Mr. Wilson's finest efforts are to be found in the two volumes of his literary and historical essays, "An Old Master" (1893) and "Mere Literature" (1896). These essays indicate the wide range of his reading—"a thoughtful, brooding, vital kind of reading," Bliss Perry calls it—and show the windows from which he looked out upon the world and grew human by seeing all its play of force and folly. His pages breathe an intense love of literature and of the fine things of literature, the expressions of a broad and catholic humanity. The following is a significant passage: "There is more of a nation's politics to be got out of its poetry than out of all its systematic writers upon public affairs and constitutions. Epics are better mirrors of manners than chronicles; dramas oftentimes let you into the secrets of statutes; orations stirred by a deep energy of emotion or resolution, passionate pamphlets that survive their mission because of the direct action of their style along permanent lines of thought, contain more history than parliamentary pamphlets."

When he was fifty Wilson expressed regret that his style had not improved, though he had "sedulously cultivated" it. He knew, to quote from one of his own essays, that the ear of the world must be "tickled in order to be made attentive—that clearness, force and beauty of style are absolutely necessary to one who would draw men to his way of thinking; nay, to anyone who would induce the great mass of mankind to give so much as passing heed to what he has to say." Demosthenes would have made little impression on the Athenians but for his style; Cicero would not have been listened to in the Roman forum but for his style; it was the style of Burke that carried his words across the channel to France and across the ocean to America; the style of Rousseau started a revolution.

It was Wilson's style in which he dressed his appeals

for peace that helped him to reach the heart of men all over the world. To a remarkable style he added wit that was never lacking in appositeness and brilliancy. "For light on a dark subject," he said, "commend me to a ray of wit." He explained in "Mere Literature":

"Wit does not make a subject light, it simply beats it into shape to be handled readily. For my part, I make free acknowledgment that no man seems to me master of his subject who cannot take liberties with it, who cannot slap his propositions on the back and be hail fellow well met with them.

"Most of your solemn explanations are mere farthing candles in the great expanse of a difficult question. Wit is not, I admit, a steady light, but ah! its flashes give you sudden glimpses of unsuspected things such as you will never see without it. It is the summer lightning which will bring more to your startled eye in an instant, out of the hiding of the night, than you will ever be at the pains to observe in the full blaze of noon."

As a stylist few writers in his own field equal and none excel him. But that easy, graceful, unfaltering command of language that marked his middle and later years was the result of a long apprenticeship and assiduous practice in the art and craft of writing. President Wilson was accustomed to give his father the credit for his style of expression. "My best training came from him," he said. "From the time I began to write until his death in 1903 at the age of eighty-one, I carried everything I wrote to him. He would make me read my writing aloud, which was always painful to me. Every now and then he would stop me. 'What do you mean by that?' I would tell him, and of course in doing so would express myself more simply than I had on paper. 'Why didn't you say so?' would be his reply. And so I came to think in definitions."

But this, of course, was only part of his training. Another and principal part was his loving study of the best models of our language, especially his favorites—Burke, Lamb, Boswell's Johnson, Bagehot, Stevenson, and others. All combined to create that finished, sensitive, intimate style which he made such a masterly instrument of expression adaptable to any literary purpose. His language has all the elegance of classic English and yet it is shot through and through with the phrase and the feel of the man in the street. It was his books and his writings with which he was occupied when the lights in his Princeton study burned late, and the click of his typewriter was heard through the open window by neighbors and midnight wayfarers.

But those years of devoted labor gave back a rich fruitage. As scholar, historian, and man of letters his literary productions everywhere reveal a vigorous mind, a fine culture, high ideals, and a broad, sympathetic humanity, ideal qualities in the future leader of a great nation.

If Wilson's health had permitted, the volumes he intended to write would have made a history of his own times that would have been illuminating and invaluable. A few days before the war, speaking to an intimate friend, he outlined that after his term expired he intended to write. He sketched his plan with some detail and with enthusiasm. Some of the chapters, he said, would tell truths that "wouldn't be complimentary to some individuals."

Years before, visiting his father in Wilmington, N. C., during his illness, Mr. Wilson spoke freely and intimately to Dr. James Sprunt, a cherished friend, of his hopes and ambitions. They centered in the books he hoped to write and the faith he hoped to make living on the printed page. But when illness fell upon him, he knew that those long cherished ambitions could not be realized.

He died with his greatest book unwritten.

## Chapter IX

# GOVERNOR OF NEW JERSEY

VICTORY OVER THE BOSSES—THE SCHOOLMASTER IN POLITICS—GIVING THE POLITICIANS A NEW VIEW OF THE ADMINISTRATION OF THE PEOPLE'S AFFAIRS—NO FOE OF THE ORGANIZATION WHEN IT NAMED BEST MAN—CUT DOWN THE JUNGLES

*"Up from the common soil, up from the quiet heart of the people, rise joyously to-day streams of hope and determination bound to renew the face of the earth in glory."*—Wilson

IT was not a far cry from battling in ancient academic shades of Princeton for educational democracy to becoming Democratic candidate for Governor of New Jersey. Every now and then after Woodrow Wilson's "Congressional Government" appeared, college-mates and friends would say to political leaders: "Keep your eyes on Woodrow Wilson." When Parker was nominated, more than one journal suggested "For President—Woodrow Wilson," but it got no further. In 1910 it was evident to Wilson that his fight to democratize university life had made him *persona non grata* to many at Princeton. He was in a receptive mood for a call to public service. He had won victory at Princeton, but the call to official life gave opportunity to put in practice his long study of Government. It appealed strongly. How much of political history is influenced by what happens on the side-lines! If Princeton was in danger in the conflict of coming under the control of influences that were undemocratic, the State of New Jersey was hopelessly in the hands of the big corporations, particularly the public service companies and allied "big business." The Democratic party had long been out of power and "the interests" dominated the Republican state administration and New Jersey was regarded as "the home of trusts." If the Republicans were the agents of privilege, Democratic leadership held little hope for relief. The "bosses" of both parties were dominant, and there was no insistent and commanding note of revolt in either party, but there was a growing dissatisfaction in the ranks of both parties. Securely entrenched, the Republicans paid no heed to what the bosses contemptuously called a "visionary reformer." The Democratic bosses, out of power, were looking for an opportunity to win a long desired victory. At that time the name of Princeton's President was brought forward. Echoes of his fight for educational democracy had gone beyond the campus and had won approval. If this foe of privilege could fight and win for democracy in a college, why should he not be drafted to fight for the rule of the people in Jersey? That question was asked and the suggestion reached ex-Senator James Smith, the recognized leader of the Democratic party. The leaders were looking for a winning candidate. The need was for one who would make a popular appeal, a new man who would catch the imagination of those voters who wished to overthrow their machine-made government.

The idea of "the scholar in politics" or high-brow government was no more attractive to many Democratic than to the Republican bosses. But successive defeats and the desire for offices made the Democrats willing to take a chance with the Princeton scholar. They made overtures to him. Some one about that time asked Bob

Davis, the Jersey City boss, if he thought Woodrow Wilson would make a good Governor.

"How the hell do I know whether he'll make a good Governor?" the boss replied; but he put his foot on ground he knew how to tread when he said, "he'll make a good candidate, and that is the only thing that interests me."

The "bosses" wished to win the election and they saw many county and state offices coming if Wilson could lead them to victory. Still they feared the very thing that did happen to the Big Boss. It was that, if the college president should be elected, he would throw down the organization men. "The Princeton sage is the man of the hour," ex-Senator James Smith, the Big Boss, was quoted as saying, "and the medium by which the Democratic party is to have its hunger for the plums of victory appeased after so long a wait."

The bosses wished to have the glamour of a scholar at the head of the ticket, but wanted him to be a show-window Governor while they held the real direction of affairs for themselves. Therefore, they asked Mr. Wilson to meet them at a club in New York to talk over the matter of his possible acceptance of the nomination for the Governorship. A leading lawyer, afterwards and always influential as friend and supporter of Wilson, turned to Mr. Wilson in the meeting and said, "Dr. Wilson, there have been some political reformers who, after they have been elected to office as candidates of one party or the other, have shut the doors in the face of the organization leaders, refusing even to listen to them. Is it your idea that a governor should regard himself free of all obligation to his party organization?"

That was the crux with the organization men. They

were ready to go down the line for Wilson, but they wanted some assurance that when he was elected he would feel he owed them the right of conference and recognition. Mr. Wilson assured them on this point and enunciated his view of what course a party leader and chief executive (he regarded them as one and inseparable) should pursue. Moreover, it was the policy he marked out for himself as Governor of New Jersey and President of the United States. He said:

"Gentlemen: I have always been a believer in party organizations. If I were elected Governor of New Jersey, I would be very glad to consult with the leaders of the Democratic organization. I should refuse to listen to no man, but I should be especially glad to hear and duly consider the suggestions of the leaders of my party. If, on my own independent investigation, I found that the recommendations for appointments made to me by the organization leaders named the best possible men, I should naturally prefer, other things being equal, to appoint them, as the men pointed out by the combined counsels of the party."

That was on July 12, 1910. On July 15, Mr. Wilson issued a statement that if it were the wish "of a decided majority of the thoughtful Democrats of the State" that he should be their nominee, he would accept. He issued the statement and did not turn a hand to affect the result.

The "bosses," aided by those who felt confident Mr. Wilson would usher in a new day in government, nominated him. However, a large element of the anti-boss Democrats, seeing the bosses favored him, organized to nominate a man not acceptable to the organization. The speaker who presented Wilson for the nom-

© Keystone View Co.

GOVERNOR WILSON AND HIS FAMILY

A group portrait during his term as Governor of New Jersey. Standing beside the Governor is his first wife, and in the back row, from left to right, are his daughters Jesse (now Mrs. Francis Sayre), Eleanor (now Mrs. W. G. McAdoo), and Margaret

GOVERNOR WILSON AT SEA GIRT 

At Mr. Wilson's left is Champ Clark, Speaker of the House; and Senator Hughes, of New Jersey

ination said Wilson would accept "without any private obligations or undertakings whatever." Nominated by a small majority, when the news reached him at Princeton, he responded and drove to the Convention Hall and made a speech that thrilled his hearers and the State, and insured his election.

"I did not seek this nomination," he said. "I have made no pledge and have given no promise. Still more, not only was no promise asked, but, as far as I know, none was desired. If elected, as I expect to be, I am left absolutely free to serve you with all singleness of purpose. It is a new era when these things can be said."

Upon that he was elected. In 1908 the Republican candidate had carried the state by 82,000 majority. Wilson's majority was 49,150. The Democrats carried the Legislature also, and it had to elect a United States Senator. The story of Wilson's matchless campaign even now stirs the pulses when it is recalled. The "high-brow" candidate in his first campaign speeches captured the voters. It was a triumphal march of compelling oratory. It was in a speech to a packed house in Jersey City where his famous limerick was first given public applause. He was speaking with great earnestness, arousing enthusiasm, when a man in the gallery called out:

"Go it, Woody. You are all right. But you ain't no beaut."

Quick as a flash, Wilson quoted his limerick, and it made a hit:

"For beauty I am not a star;
There are others handsomer, far;
But my face, I don't mind it,
For I am behind it;
'Tis the people in front that I jar."

Soon the test came which caused Richard Croker, in answer to the question what he thought of Wilson, to say "an ingrate is no good in politics." New Jersey had a primary to select a Senator. James E. Martine was the only candidate and he received 54,000 out of 73,000 votes cast for Senator. Not long after the election ex-Senator James Smith called to see the Governor-elect. He stated that Martine lacked the qualifications, and said he himself would be candidate for Senator.

"The primary selected Martine," said Wilson, "and there is nothing for the Legislature to do but ratify that selection."

"The primary was a joke," replied Smith. "Martine received only 54,000 votes, while in the election you received 233,682 votes. Nobody regarded the primary as binding."

"It was very far from a joke," said Wilson. "The question of who is to serve as Senator one term is insignificant compared to whether the voters of New Jersey are to have the right to choose their Senator."

The fight was on. It can be truly said that no such issue was ever fought in an American commonwealth. Martine had no organization and only Wilson saved him. Smith had the "organization." Wilson had only the principle that a primary choice was sacred and should not be violated. The whole country looked on to see if the schoolmaster in politics, an amateur at the game, could defeat the ablest professional. The answer as to whether Wilson was an ingrate is complete, for before he consented to run for Governor he was given the assurance that Smith would not stand for Senator. Before he was nominated he had written a friend: "I have been asked by the men most influential in the Democratic party in New

Jersey whether I would accept the nomination for Governor if it came to me unsought, unanimously, and without pledges of any kind, and I have felt obliged to say that I would." He felt that Smith's candidacy before the people would defeat the party. Wilson had said when assured Smith would not run, "Were he to do so while I was Governor, I should have to oppose him. He represents everything repugnant to my convictions."

When legislators, desirous of ending Boss Rule in Jersey, seemed to waver under pressure, Wilson heartened them with this declaration: "Do not allow yourselves to be dismayed. You see where the machine is entrenched, and it looks like a real fortress. It looks as if real men were inside, as if they had real guns. Go and touch it. It is a house of cards. Those are imitation generals, those are playthings that look like guns. Go and put your shoulders against the thing and it collapses."

It collapsed. The conflict had attracted national interest. The bosses everywhere said: "Wilson is a dangerous man." The people who had been hitherto hopeless were cheered and strengthened. That victory turned thousands to him with admiration. It had large part in sending him to the White House. Immediately after the senatorial contest was won, Wilson presented a program of legislation. It was progressive and so radical as to make timid legislators hold their breath. "I am accused," he said, "of being a radical. If to seek to go to the root is to be a radical, I am. I tell you the so-called radicalism of our times is simply the effort of nature to release the generous energies of our people. The need of the hour is just that radicalism that will clear a way for the realization of the aspirations of a sturdy race."

Some legislators suggested that they were elected to pass laws, he to enfore them. He declared that the theory of "the three co-ordinate branches, as it had been pedantically exaggerated in practice" ought not to bring a stalemate to action. He asserted party leadership. By superior generalship he secured good legislation long desired, but which the bosses had thwarted. As party leader, he summoned the Democrats to the program to end the rule of special interests, and he challenged the Republican legislators to prove themselves true representatives of the people by giving aid. The executive office was open to all legislators who came in and out. Wilson attended conferences and caucuses. Questioned as to his right to be in a conference of legislators, discussing a pending measure—a conference he had called—Governor Wilson replied: "You can turn aside from the measure if you choose; you can decline to follow me; you can deprive me of office and turn away from me; but you cannot deprive me of power so long as I steadfastly stand for what I believe to be the interests and legitimate demands of the people themselves."

When the General Assembly adjourned, it had to its credit an entirely unprecedented range of progressive legislation. This included several splendid welfare laws, the best of regulatory measures for public service corporations—the "seven sisters," as laws to end trusts were called—measures of employers' liability and the most intelligent organization to regulate primaries and elections that any state had enacted in such a period, and other wise and necessary laws. Pressing for honest primaries and elections, he declared "back of all reform, lies the means of getting it," and he added: "The people are determined at last to take over the control of their politics. We are going to cut down the jungles in which corruption lurks." The victories were hard won. One rich concern, which had an employee in the Assembly, threatened him with reduction of pay, and there was a persistent lobby of the interests. One Senator, whose vote was essential for a reform measure, said:

"Governor, I would vote for the measure, but my constituents are against it."

"How do you know your constituents are against it? I will tell you what I will do. I will speak at your county seat next Thursday night for the measure. You speak against it. Then we will ask for an expression of the people. If they are for the measure, you will then vote for it. If they are against it, I will not ask you to vote for it. Do you accept my proposition?" The legislator voted for the measure without a debate with the Governor before his constituents.

The leader of the Democratic organization was invited by the Governor to come to his office to "talk things over." He had promised to call in the organization leaders. He was keeping his promise. Soon the leader lost his temper.

"I know you think you've got the votes," he exclaimed in a loud tone insultingly. "I know how you got them."

"What do you mean?" asked Governor Wilson.

"It's the talk of the State House that you got them by patronage," he flung out the insult.

"Good afternoon," said the Governor, pointing to the door.

"You are no gentleman," cried back the enraged political boss.

"You are no judge," was the answer as the angry leader made his exit.

Wilson had said that a political machine was "a house of cards." Soon his statement was proved. That boss, still Democratic State Chairman, who had tried to insult Governor Wilson, was a short time after, with some friends at a dinner in the same dining room with a party of officers of the New Jersey National Guard at Sea Girt. The chairman asked them to join his party in a toast. The diners at both tables rose to their feet.

"I give you," he cried, "the Governor of the State of New Jersey"—and all glasses were raised—"a liar and an ingrate."

Those who had risen to drink the toast upon his invitation lowered their glasses, stupefied by the suggested toast.

"Do I drink alone?" he asked. He did. The following day a Wilson supporter was chosen State Chairman. He had "licked the gang to a frazzle." A study of the record of Woodrow Wilson as Governor of New Jersey convinced the American people that he was the type of man needed in the White House.

It was only 163 miles from Trenton to Washington, but there were many bridges to cross before like policies on a larger scale were to have a national application.

He had won promotion.

## Chapter X

# THE BALTIMORE CONVENTION

WILSON OWED HIS NOMINATION TO HIS PROGRESSIVE PRINCIPLES AND TO HIS APPROVAL OF THE FIGHT TO ORGANIZE THE CONVENTION BY PROGRESSIVES—BRYAN'S MAGNIFICENT LEADERSHIP ROUTED THE REACTIONARY FORCES AND THE BOSSES—WILSON WOULD MAKE NO PROMISES

*"No man can be just who is not free."*—Wilson

"WHAT do you think of the resolution?" asked William Jennings Bryan of a friend as they started to the Armory in Baltimore for the Thursday night session of the Democratic National Convention of 1912. He had read to the friend a resolution he intended to introduce at the evening session.

"I think," was the reply, "that it is full of dynamite."

"Whom will it blow up?" asked Bryan.

"That is in the lap of the gods," was the reply. "It may blow up the man who offers it, and it may blow up those at whom it is aimed."

It was an open secret that the bosses were resolved to eliminate Bryan once and for all. Their plan also embraced unforgiving and unrelenting warfare upon what called itself, for want of a better name, "progressivism." That element had been man-handled and defeated by the Old Guard in the Republican Convention at Chicago. The Democratic bosses aimed to do likewise at Baltimore. The real fight at Baltimore was not between candidates. It was between opposing ideals of government.

Bryan was in his happiest mood. He always is when he is fighting against political control by the "interests." But his heavy jaws were set for "a fight or a funeral." For days, even before the Convention met on the 25th day of June, 1912, he had been concerned, not about candidates, but to prevent bosses or Big Business naming the President or writing the platform. The Progressives had staged a fight against the selection for temporary chairman of Judge Alton B. Parker, supported by Tammany and called by Progressives "reactionary." Bryan sought in vain to defeat Parker's selection. It looked as if the " Conservatives " or " Reactionaries" would gain control of the Convention. Bryan felt that they could be unhorsed only by arousing the country to the danger. He resolved on firing a gun that would startle the "embattled farmers" and others whose hearts were set upon making the Democratic party the vehicle of undoing Privilege. He succeeded.

That was a brilliant scene in the Armory as Bryan was recognized. Every seat was occupied. Diplomats and Senators from Washington had come over. Ladies in the gallery in summer costumes in tiers behind the presiding officer lent beauty to the scene. It was no ordinary convention, though the quadrennial conventions of the major parties are always the most notable gatherings in America. Here there was unwonted confidence that the delegates were naming, not merely a candidate, but the next President.

The Nebraskan was cheered as he moved to the platform. There was some objection to his recognition. There would have been more if the delegates had known the character of the bomb concealed on his person. He

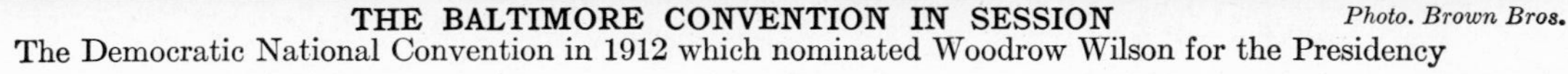

**THE BALTIMORE CONVENTION IN SESSION** *Photo. Brown Bros.*

The Democratic National Convention in 1912 which nominated Woodrow Wilson for the Presidency

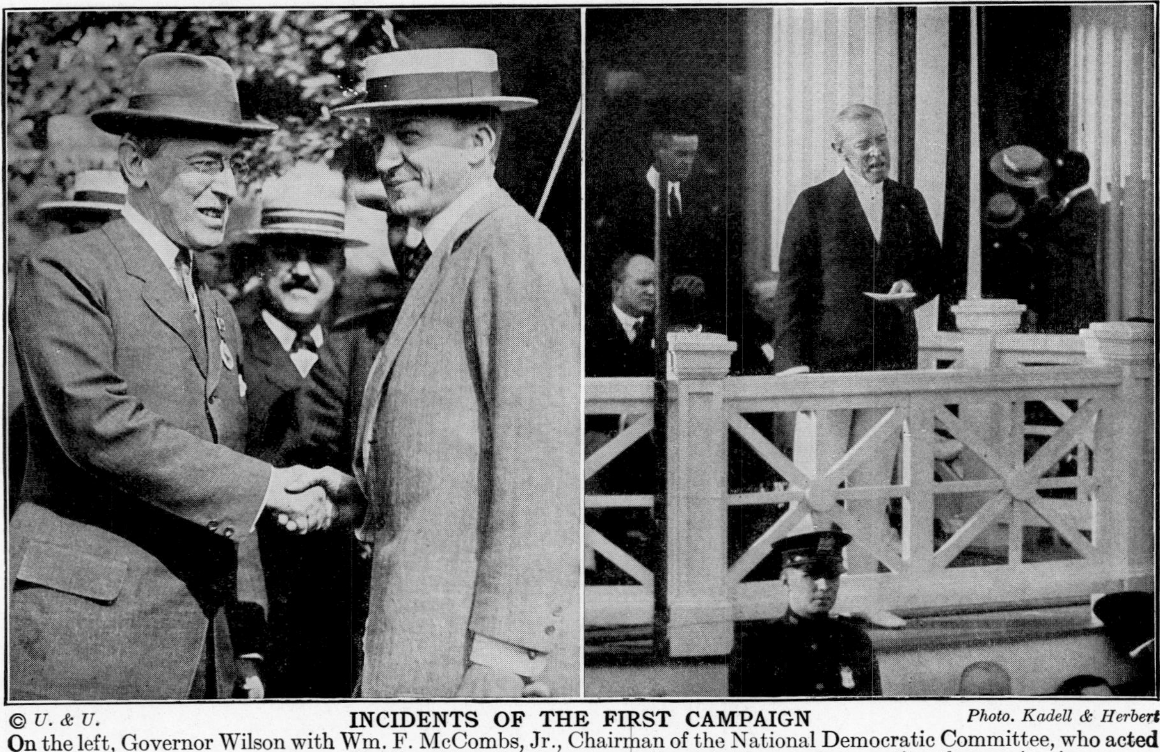

*© U. & U.* **INCIDENTS OF THE FIRST CAMPAIGN** *Photo. Kadell & Herbert*

On the left, Governor Wilson with Wm. F. McCombs, Jr., Chairman of the National Democratic Committee, who acted as his campaign manager. On the right, the Governor delivering his speech accepting the nomination

read his resolution, first in silence. As he proceeded the delegates, or some of them, gasped in consternation, and as he finished with the demand for the "withdrawal of any delegate under any obligations to J. Pierpont Morgan, Thomas F. Ryan, August Belmont, or any other member of the privilege-hunting and favor-seeking class," pandemonium broke loose. Ryan and Belmont were both sitting on the floor as delegates. For minutes, so great was the uproar and bitter feeling that many feared Bryan would suffer violence. The partisans of Bryan were cheering, opponents were howling insults, and friends of both Ryan and Belmont were vociferous in their denunciation. During the raging storm Bryan stood unmoved. The debate that followed has rarely been equalled in vigor of attack on what Bryan called "the privilege-seeking" class; in the defense of Ryan and Belmont; and in the hostility to Bryan's injecting the resolution into the Convention.

Bryan's resolution was as follows:

"*Resolved*, That in this crisis in our party's career and in our country's history, this convention sends greetings to the people of the United States and assures them that the party of Jefferson and of Jackson is still the champion of popular government and equality before the law. As proof of our fidelity to the people, we hereby declare ourselves opposed to the nomination of any candidate for President who is the representative of or under any obligation to J. Pierpont Morgan, Thomas F. Ryan, August Belmont or any other member of the privilege-hunting and favor-seeking class.

"*Be it further Resolved*, That we demand the withdrawal from this convention of any delegate or delegates constituting or representing the above-named interests."

The debate turned chiefly upon argument by Bryan's opponents denying the right of a Convention to demand the withdrawal of delegates whose credentials had been approved by the Convention. Just before the vote was taken, Bryan withdrew that part of his resolution asking withdrawal of Ryan and Belmont, and the remainder was then adopted by a large majority. Bryan yielded only when satisfied the first and more important resolution would meet the case.

Before the Convention met, Mr. Bryan sent an identical telegram to Clark, Wilson, Underwood, and Harmon, all the candidates for President, asking their co-operation in selecting as temporary chairman some well-known Progressive acceptable to the leading progressive candidates. "Eight members of the sub-committee have, over the protest of the remaining eight," he said in his telegram, "agreed upon not only a Reactionary, but upon the one Democrat who, among those not candidates for the Presidential nomination, is, in the eyes of the public, most conspicuously identified with the reactionary element of the party." The reference was to Alton B. Parker, who had been the Democratic candidate for President in 1904. Bryan and Parker were brought together. Bryan said to Parker, "I have not the slightest objection to you personally, but I do object to the faction which has chosen you to preside." He had wired the Presidential candidates, "I shall be pleased to join you and your friends in opposing his selection by the full committee or by the Convention."

Bryan's telegram was published far and near. It was the crux of the situation. What candidate would take his stand with the militant Progressives? It was a serious question to propound, but the answer of Wilson and the failure to answer by the other candidates had a large influence on the result. Wilson's friends were divided. His manager, W. F. McCombs, who had been his student at Princeton, saw no hope for Wilson's nomination, except by obtaining the vote of New York. If Wilson agreed with Bryan it was a repudiation of New York's candidate for chairman, and would make it impossible for Wilson ever to receive the vote of the New York delegation. McCombs therefore advised a telegram to Bryan that was in substance a rebuke to Bryan, including the statement, "I have neither the right nor the desire to direct the organization of a Convention of which I am not even a member." It was the belief of many of Wilson's friends that if he sent such a telegram it would end the possibility of selection to leadership for progressive action and would be fatal to his chances.

Wilson rose to the occasion. The reply to Bryan, which he wrote with his own hand, began with "You are quite right." He added that the Convention was composed of "men who are progressive in principle and by conviction." He went on to say, "It must, if it is not to be put in a wrong light before the country, express its convictions in its organization and in its choice of the men who are to speak for it." He added further that he felt sure his friends would act to secure such result.

The managers of the other candidates were already lined up for Parker. Parker won in the committee with 31 votes; James, supported by Wilson's friends, received 20 votes, and O'Gorman 2. Wilson's friends would have been satisfied with either James or O'Gorman. Though James was a supporter of Clark, the Wilson forces favored him because they knew he was truly progressive and eminently fair.

The issue had been clear cut—Wilson was the only man in the field ready to win or lose in boldly taking his stand with the militant Progressives. If Clark had repudiated his managers, as Wilson refused to follow McCombs, there are many who then believed that the twenty-eighth President would have been Champ Clark. One thing is certain; the issue Wilson met so promptly and courageously attracted to him the enthusiastic support of the progressive and forward-looking people of the Republic.

He lacked the votes to be nominated, or even to control the election of a temporary chairman, but from that moment his ultimate nomination was assured. His boldness and courage attracted the approval of the country, which made public sentiment set so strongly toward Wilson that delegates instructed for others were deluged with telegrams to vote "for Wilson and rebuke Reactionary Bosses." They poured into Baltimore by the thousands and the tens of thousands.

But it was days before the consummation, and Wilson at Sea Girt did not know the telegrams were going to stampede Clark delegates who voted for Clark steadily. During the balloting, the report reached Wilson that McCombs was promising offices for votes for Wilson. He immediately issued a public statement saying that no one was authorized by him to offer any position to any one. This angered McCombs, who called Wilson up on the 'phone and told him his nomination could only be brought about if he would promise not to appoint Bryan as Secretary of State.

Wilson refused to make such a promise and said to Tumulty, his private secretary, "I will not bargain for the office. It would be foolish for me at this time to decide upon a Cabinet officer, and it would be outrageous to eliminate anybody from consideration now, particularly Mr. Bryan, who has rendered such fine service to the party in all seasons."

The fight over the temporary chairmanship was carried to the Convention, where Bryan presented Senator Kern, a progressive. Kern, in his speech, urged Parker to withdraw, said he would do likewise, and in the interest of harmony suggested several names. He made challenge to New York to withdraw Parker. New York would not do so. Then Kern nominated Bryan for temporary chairman, saying, "There is only one man to lead the hosts of progress, and that is William Jennings Bryan."

Parker won, receiving 579 to Bryan's 510. But it was a Pyrrhic victory.

Bryan's defeat for the temporary chairmanship was hailed as his final retirement from the counsels of his party. "Incidentally," wrote a newspaper correspondent who had not sensed the real situation, "his downfall appears to have seriously endangered the Wilson boom, and present indications are that the recently glowing prospect of Wilson's victory in November has been sent a-glimmering." Parker tendered the olive branch by declaring that Bryan ought to be chosen Chairman of the Platform Committee.

The second big battle of the convention was over the unit rule, Mayor Newton D. Baker, of Cleveland, making the most convincing speech of the debate. Ohio had sent a mixed delegation, some delegates elected and instructed in district primaries and others appointed and instructed by the State Convention. The unit rule, had it been applied, would have denied the district-named delegates the power to carry out the mandates of their constitu-

8

encies. By a vote of 565½ to 491½, the Convention abrogated it in all states where the law did not specifically provide that it should apply. This was a victory for Wilson, for if the unit rule had prevailed, he would have received no votes from Ohio. It was a demonstration of the devotion of the delegates to the right of the people to representation, all the more surprising because it showed that the anti-Wilson leaders did not control the Convention. They had opposed it because it gave Wilson important strength. In the South Dakota contest the Wilson delegates also won. Those on the inside believed these two test votes indicated that there were a number of delegates instructed for other candidates who were at heart for Wilson. But this did not appear in the balloting for president until several days intervened.

On the first ballot, taken on Friday, the vote stood: Clark 440½; Wilson 324; Harmon 148; Underwood 117½. By midnight Clark's vote had risen to 556 and Wilson's to 350½. The Clark forces believed victory was in sight. Never before had a candidate, receiving a clear majority of all the votes, failed on subsequent ballots to secure enough to give him the two-thirds necessary to secure the nomination. On Saturday sixteen ballots were taken, the vote on the last being Clark 463½; Wilson 407½; Harmon 29; Underwood 112½. The adjournment over Sunday turned the scales. Hundreds and thousands of telegrams poured in from all parts of the country, particularly from sections where progressivism was strong, demanding that delegates "vote for Wilson and Progress." Many of them asserted that was "the only way to defeat Privilege and the bosses." The appeal to Cæsar had been made by the Progressives, defeated in their effort to organize the Convention. They responded. The spectacle was witnessed of voters thousands of miles away changing the voting in the Convention—in fact controlling the nomination. The Clark forces did not realize the influences at work in the country until it was too late. In fact, after support of Parker, the damage done could not be repaired. The remarkable thing was that the enthusiasm for Wilson was almost wholly spontaneous. Many Clark supporters "back home" were disappointed when his managers lined up for Parker instead of James. They grew colder still when they tried to uphold the unit rule. They were astounded when the report went over the country that the bosses were supporting Clark. Clark's legislative record in the line of progress was sound and consistent. His supporters in the West, or many of them, felt that his managers were responsible for the situation and not Mr. Clark himself.

Bryan's charge that the reactionary forces were behind Clark's candidacy was bitterly resented by the Missourian. Ex-Senator Dubois, his campaign manager, on Saturday had represented to Speaker Clark that his candidacy had suffered by what he called "Bryan's attack upon his honor," and advised Clark that he should come to Baltimore and make answer. The Speaker took the first train for Baltimore, but the Convention had adjourned before he arrived. Many of his supporters advised him not to appear before the Convention, and he returned to Washington without asking to be heard. They told him no candidate for the presidency had ever appeared before a Convention and his appearance might be misunderstood and would do more harm than good. Speaker Clark accepted their advice and issued a statement in which he challenged Bryan for "proof or retraction." Bryan followed with a statement in which he said he believed Speaker Clark was "right at heart, but had been misled"; and added that the only criticism he had made was not that Clark "had acted wrongfully, but that he had failed to act." "The contest is not personal," he said, and added "it is between Progressive Democracy on one side and Reactionary Democracy on the other," and in such a contest it was Clark's duty to take one side or the other.

Monday's ballots showed the decided drift to Wilson. The telegrams pouring in were getting in their perfect work. The Clark forces held firm in the early ballots, but when the last ballot of the day (41st) was taken, Wilson was in the lead. The vote stood Wilson 499½; Clark 424; Harmon 27; Underwood 106. The tide had turned and was setting strongly to Wilson. Five ballots were taken on Tuesday. The certainty of Wilson's nomination becoming apparent, the opposition melted. After the forty-fifth ballot Underwood's name was withdrawn, and on the forty-sixth ballot Wilson was nominated, receiving 990 votes. Clark received 84 and Harmon 12. The nomination was made unanimous. Thomas R. Marshall, of Indiana, was nominated for Vice-President.

The gavel fell on the historic Baltimore Convention. The "schoolmaster," not even a political factor in July, 1910, had on July 2, 1912, been called to the leadership of the Democratic Party.

The Democrats of the Republic celebrated the Fourth of July, 1912, in the firm belief that they had named as heir to Jefferson's mantle another native of the Commonwealth of Virginia. They believed also that they had named the next President of the United States.

They had done both. And Wilson led.

## CHAPTER XI

# THE CAMPAIGN OF 1912

WILSON'S DIRECTING HAND AT THE START—MADE FEW PROMISES—WILSON AND MARSHALL HAD POPULAR RECORDS—NO DEMOCRATIC DIVISION—ROOSEVELT'S VIGOROUS AND EFFECTIVE ONSLAUGHT—"THOU SHALT NOT STEAL"—PART TAKEN BY LA FOLLETTE AND GOMPERS—WILSON'S BIG ELECTORAL MAJORITY

*"In the affairs of a great nation we plan and labor, not for the present only, but for the long future as well."*—WILSON

WOULD Mr. Wilson have been elected in 1912 if there had been no split in the Republican party that year? That question has been answered both ways. The best way to answer it is to compare 1892 with 1912. The Harrison administration had not met with popular approval. Harrison was one of the ablest lawyers who has served as chief magistrate in the nation's history. He obtained the reputation of being cold. The revolt of the farmers in the West he regarded as a temporary sympton of agrarian discontent. He lacked the power to deal successfully with the labor troubles in the East. There was no foreign issue to divert the attention of the people from hard times. The Democrats carried the House in 1890 by a large majority. That presaged the Democratic victory in 1892. No third party, except in a few small Western states, affected the result. History repeated itself twenty years later. Taft's administration did not make a popular appeal. Held in high esteem for his lovable qualities and regarded as an able lawyer, the Payne-Aldrich Tariff Act and Ballingerism caused the people to regard it as a reactionary administration. As a result in 1910, the large Republican majority in the House was wiped out and the Democrats controlled the House by a big majority. The Republicans of the West were in revolt. If there had been no Roosevelt and no Progressive Party, Wilson would have been elected in 1912 and for much the same reason that brought about the election of Cleveland in 1892. To be sure the majority in the electoral college would have been much smaller. When a President fails to win popular favor and the people are bent on a change, the question of a third party seldom affects the result. This is far from saying, however, that the Progressive Party in 1912 was not one of the most significant and militant political revolutions in the history of America. Led by one of the most remarkable men, it had the impulse of a great moral force. It called itself a party, but it was an organized protest and an army with banners seeking a new order. It has been treated as a mere temporary division of the Republican party. It was more than that, for Mr. Roosevelt drew to his support hundreds of thousands of Democrats who had long admired the qualities for which he was distinguished.

Mr. Wilson had the good judgment to understand that many of the supporters of Roosevelt had cut loose from the Republican party because they wished a new day. He recognized that real Progressives, whether supporting him or Roosevelt, were animated by the same aims. Therefore, though urged thereto by some of his supporters, he refrained in his letters and speeches from controversy with Mr. Roosevelt or other Progressive leaders and raised no issues except upon tariff and the trust problem. Even then he refrained from any personalities. Indeed, seldom did he at any time inject or take notice of personalities in his campaign. The exceptions were when he felt impelled to do so by some strong circumstance. The wisdom of his policy toward the Progressives is seen in the fact that, when he came to the Presidency and presented his program, most of the measures were supported by Progressives in Congress.

A few days after the nomination, the members of the Democratic National Committee visited the presidential candidate at Sea Girt, N. J., to confer with him about the conduct of the campaign. They found that he had already given it thought. The suggestion of a national chairman gave concern. Hon. W. F. McCombs had been the pre-convention chairman of the Wilson forces, zealous and active. Mr. Wilson evidently doubted his ability to do teamwork and hesitated to see him in command. And yet he held him in esteem and was appreciative of all he had done. He gave thought to the make-up of the Executive Committee and vetoed some suggestions for its membership. It was agreed that McCombs should be chairman and W. G. McAdoo should be vice-chairman. McCombs did not approve but acquiesced. His strength was not equal to the strain, and McAdoo was compelled for a time to take the lead until McCombs could resume active management. The tension in the campaign due to the ill health and inability of McCombs to do teamwork was to be a thorn in the side when Wilson went to Washington and in making up his Cabinet.

Governor Wilson's hand was seen quickly in the direction of the campaign, selecting only progressives as the real managers. The League of College Voters, with yells and cheers, was an inspiring force in the campaign. "The schoolmaster in politics" attracted collegians, and Princeton men were notably active. Samuel Gompers, the veteran labor leader, was an early visitor to Sea Girt, with approval of platform. He left an enthusiastic supporter. He was to be a distinguished co-worker in advancing humane legislation. When war came he was to crown his career as member of the Advisory Committee of the Council of National Defense, and prove himself inspiring, influential, and effective in efforts to win the World War. Wilson told his campaign managers he could not consent for them to accept any large campaign contribution from any source, and under his inspiration the popular appeal for small sums was remarkably successful.

Mr. Wilson believed a candidate ought to make few promises and religiously keep every pledge made. He did not wish to arouse hopes that could not be fulfilled. The responsibility of leadership he took seriously and never surrendered to the temptation of promising the millennium. In a heart-to-heart talk to some newspaper men at Sea Girt, before he had written his speech of acceptance, Wilson said, "When messages are brought to me by friends, of what is expected of the next President, I am sometimes terrified at the task that would await me in case I should be elected. For instance, my daughter, who is engaged in social-welfare work in Philadelphia, told me of a visit she paid a humble home in that city when the head of a large family told her that her husband was going to vote for me because it would mean cheaper bread." He paused and said, "Think of the responsibility such expectation creates. I can't reduce the price of bread. I can only strive in the few years I shall have office to remove the noxious growths that have been planted in the soil and try to clear the way for the new adjustment which is necessary."

The Baltimore platform in its treatment of leading issues made instant appeal to the country. Even greater appeal was made in the personnel of the Democratic nominees. Wilson's spectacular and successful victory over New Jersey bosses, and the record of humane and advanced legislation he had secured, made him a popular hero. This was particularly true as to the young and independent voters of the country. They welcomed the opportunity to get rid of old guard and well-greased party manipulation. The nominee for Vice-President, Thomas R. Marshall, of Indiana, had a record second only among American Governors to that of Wilson. The voters studied what he had achieved as Governor of his State and found it progressive and humane. While he had been called upon for no such combat with Boss Rule as Wilson, he had shown the highest quality of independence and leadership. He had opposed the decree of "the organization" to sidestep the direct selection of a United States Senator. His wise leadership opened the door for the election of Kern to the Senate. The Indiana Senator was chosen majority leader, and he gave proof of the wisdom of the selection.

The Democratic leaders did not need to make promises. Their supporters said: "A Governor is President on a small scale. You can tell what will be done in Washington by reading what has been done in Trenton." Fortunately what had been done by Wilson had been blazoned on the front page of every paper for a year. The laws he had sponsored were fought at every step by the trusts, public service corporations, and other intrenched interests, for New Jersey was called "the mother of trusts." Under the old rule, the combinations in restraint of trade had flocked there as chickens gather under a mother's wing. Before the national issues were brought to the front, Wilson leaders paramounted his achievements in New Jersey and his fight for democratization at Princeton. With that background, appealing to the admiration and imagination of patriotic voters, the campaign progressed from victory to victory. To be sure Roosevelt attracted hundreds of thousands of young men, who, like Wilson's supporters, were tired of the old grandmother's leading strings which made Taft's campaign a procession from the funeral chapel to the cemetery. Roosevelt's cohorts were enthusiastic, militant, and strenuous. The same was true, with more moderation of expression and deeper conviction, of the same type of Wilson's supporters. The Roosevelt hurrah was for the man, rather than the new issues he championed, and which later he saw go into innocuous desuetude. But how he did move and stir millions as he called men to battle! The Wilson hurrah lacked the abandon of enthusiasm, but made up in deep devotion to the principles and faith in the candidate. Against two such attractive candidates, the able and undramatic Taft, weighted down with the Aldrich Tariff and Ballingerism (a 1912 prophecy of the Teapot Dome scandal of 1924), could make no headway. He was also handicapped by money-bags campaign blundering. As early as September a member of the Democratic Executive Committee said, "Taft will not carry over four States." The Taft press derided the prophecy. The committeeman was too generous, for the Republican candidate received only the electoral vote of Utah and Vermont. Mr. Taft had won the nomination at Chicago on the first ballot over Roosevelt. The nomination to the vice-presidency went to James S. Sherman, of New York, who died October 30. Herbert S. Hadley, of Missouri, with Progressive leanings, was named for Vice-President. There was gossip that the Taft forces had offered to nominate Hadley, a Roosevelt supporter, for President at Chicago, as a compromise candidate, but Theodore Roosevelt put his foot down on any compromise with what he called "the thieves" and "porch-climbers."

There was no delay after the selection of the campaign committee in organizing the Wilson forces. Whatever disappointment grew out of the contest at Baltimore was not visited on Wilson. Clark and Harmon and Underwood gave whole-hearted support. As Speaker and leader of the House respectively, Clark and Underwood were to co-operate in the progressive legislation that marked the days to come at Washington, and Harmon was to give wise counsel. It is a matter of history that the attitude of the Democrats in the House in 1909–10 contributed in large measure toward the victory of 1912. Asked if he intended to take the stump, Mr. Bryan said, "Take the stump? I should say I will." Not even when he was a candidate for President was the Nebraskan more abundant in labors or in convincing brilliancy on the stump. In fact, as he said, it was the first presidential campaign for years in which he could praise the candidate as much as he desired without opening himself to the charge of self-praise.

All elements of the party co-operated. "We are for Wilson," declared Hearst's papers, though they were never partial to him as candidate or chief executive. As the campaign progressed, the Roosevelt hope of creating an imposing Democratic defection from Wilson faded, though he did poll a large Democratic vote in November.

Charging unfair tactics on the part of the Old Guard Republicans in control of the Chicago Convention, the supporters of Roosevelt withdrew from the convention and organized the Progressive Party with the red bandanna as its oriflamme, the bull-moose as its symbol, and "Onward, Christian Soldiers" as its marching song. With Roosevelt as candidate for President, Hiram Johnson for Vice-President, and George W. Perkins as the "angel", the party was born full panoplied, with abundance of enthusiasm and "ample funds" for conducting the wonderful campaign that followed. After the climax of 1912 all other campaigns in comparison have been dull and spiritless. Mr. Roosevelt, a veritable Rupert, was first to arrive on the field. He literally made a centre rush, so rapidly did he charge. Leaving Chicago, he plunged into the campaign and kept the country alternately gasping and applauding at the picturesqueness of his vocabulary and the vigor of his denunciation coupled with the earnestness of an evangelist. He early sensed that the contest was to be between him and Wilson. Though in his seven years in the White House he had not advised tariff legislation, Roosevelt warned the people against the evils Wilson's position on the tariff would inflict. He told the voters that "if the Democratic platform (on the tariff) was not repudiated" the party under Wilson would "bring every industry in the country to a crash which would make all the panics in our past history like child's play."

Popular as his campaign was, it was a year when the people would not think in terms of an old issue. They wanted something new, with "pep" in it, and, aside from his tariff speeches, Roosevelt supplied that demand. The best analysis of the political trend of the times was presented by Prof. John B. Clark in an article in the *Outlook*. A Republican and descended from a long line of Republicans, he contended that the real issue was the treatment of great business corporations. He contrasted the proposed treatment of them by the candidates greatly to the advantage of Mr. Wilson and his party. High protective duties could mean only continued exorbitant prices, he held, while Colonel Roosevelt's proposal to let the "good trusts" alone was proof that under him relief from monopolistic oppression could not be had. The Democratic Party, he said, offered the single solution—reasonable reform of abuses in the tariff, necessity of preserving competition and prevention of monopoly. Colonel Roosevelt declared his plea for high tariff duties was made to help wage workers. Governor Wilson availed himself of the Lawrence (Massachusetts) textile strike where it was brought out that operatives were getting only eight dollars a week, and pointed out that this great industry was always seeking tariff favors on the ground that they were needed "to pay good wages to employees." The Democratic candidate declared that the best wages were being paid by the unprotected industries.

Colonel Roosevelt, who was contributing editor of the *Outlook*, carried, in the issue of July 13, an article headed "Thou Shalt Not Steal", in which the "theft" charge against the Taft wing of the Republican Party was reiterated and elaborated. Colonel Roosevelt's trust plank was attacked with considerable effect. He had proposed a commission to regulate trusts expressly providing: "Any corporation voluntarily coming under the commission should not be prosecuted under the anti-trust law so long as it obeys in good faith the orders of the commission." Years afterwards, when the Federal Trade Commission was created under Wilson, Roosevelt's supporters said it was in line with his platform pledge. Wilson did not agree, but referred to it as an agency, not to regulate, but to prevent the practices of combinations.

Governor Wilson was progressive enough to suit many progressives, and so cool-headed and sure-footed and audacious (when convinced he was right) in all of his positions, that many independents were attracted to his standard. He made it clear that he would advocate no governmental change just for the purpose of change, but would seek change only as it meant necessary reform and restoration of the right of the people to govern their affairs. Speaking in Connecticut, where conservative sentiment was especially strong, he said:

"We ought to go very slowly and very carefully about the task of altering the institutions we have been a long time in building up. I believe that the ancient traditions of a people are its ballast. You must knit the new into the old. If I did not believe that to be progressive is to preserve the essentials of our institutions, I for one would not be a progressive."

Mr. Wilson's attitude and magnanimity also won him many friends. Speaking at Minneapolis, where anti-Taft sentiment was very strong, and, doubtless mindful of the harsh things Colonel Roosevelt had said about the President, Mr. Wilson said: "I do not believe that any man in the United States who knows his facts can question the patriotism or the integrity of the man who now presides at the executive office in Washington," and it brought from many sources the comment: "This is a magnanimous campaigner and a gentleman."

A conspicuous figure in that campaign was Senator La Follette, of Wisconsin. He fought Roosevelt for the control of the Progressive Party. When Roosevelt charged that the Taft nomination by the Republican convention was stolen, La Follette retorted that nobody had been more ready to "steal than Roosevelt." The Wisconsin Senator said in his weekly that Bryan at Baltimore was "a towering figure of moral power and patriotic devotion to civic righteousness" and that Roosevelt had "as great an opportunity to serve the progressive cause as Bryan had at Baltimore, but would not accept it because he was serving himself only." Such criticism by La Follette—a genuine progressive, even radical in progress—was Roosevelt's most serious handicap in uniting all progressive forces under his banner. But, in spite of it, his ability to attract the Republican Progressives was evident in the overwhelming vote given him.

October 14, Colonel Roosevelt, while bowing to a cheering crowd in front of a hotel in Milwaukee, was shot in the breast by John Shrank, of New York. Although badly wounded, Roosevelt showed the "stuff" of his courage when he insisted on being driven to the auditorium, where he spoke for an hour and a half. Governor Wilson, reluctant to fight a stricken antagonist, cancelled many of his speaking dates and waited for Colonel Roosevelt to resume. The assault on Roosevelt removed some of the asperities of the campaign, but upon his recovery it was carried through with vigor, resulting in what most political prognosticators declared it would—the election of Woodrow Wilson as the twenty-eighth President of the United States. Wilson received 435 electoral votes; Roosevelt 81; and Taft 15. The popular vote was: Wilson, 6,293,154; Roosevelt 4,119,538; Taft, 3,484,980.

And the first "schoolmaster in politics" to be chosen chief executive, made ready to move to Washington.

Would he use the Rod, the Big Stick, or Persuasion? Taft had used the last. Roosevelt had used the Big Stick. Did Wilson have the Rod ready? That was the question when a perfect day ushered in the new administration, auspicious of what promised to be a new Era of Good Feeling.

Baltimore's choice was ratified.

## CHAPTER XII

# PRESIDENT AND THE PRESIDENCY

"LET THE PEOPLE IN"—A KINDLY THOUGHT FOR THE PEOPLE WHO WANTED TO HEAR THE INAUGURAL ADDRESS—LOOKING FORWARD TO A "WORK OF RESTORATION"—"NOT A DAY OF TRIUMPH, BUT A DAY OF DEDICATION"—HIS CONCEPTION OF THE OFFICE OF CHIEF MAGISTRATE—ADDED EXECUTIVE INITIATIVE TO INSISTENCE THAT THERE BE NO INFRINGEMENT UPON THE RIGHTS OF THE EXECUTIVE

*"The President is at liberty, both in law and conscience, to be as big a man as he can."*—WILSON

"LET the people in."

As Woodrow Wilson turned his eyes to the upturned sea of faces on that perfect fourth of March, 1913, before he began his inaugural, he issued his first presidential order to the soldiers in charge of the arrangements. They had roped off a vacant space just in front of him from which the people were excluded.

"Remove the ropes and let the people in," was his low spoken direction. It was obeyed. He paused to acknowledge the acclaim as the people passed into the space, crowding near him. Interpreting the occasion, the new President said, "It means much more than the success of a party," which he declared the nation was using "to square every process of our national life again with the standard we so proudly set up at the beginning and have always carried in our hearts." He pointed out how our "great system of government" is, "in many respects, a model for those who seek to set liberty upon foundations that will endure against fortuitous change, against storm and accident." But he saw that "evil has come with the good, and much fine gold has been corroded." His next words seem an indictment of the recent spoliation of the naval oil reserves and like disregard of true conservation which aroused the white heat of the American people in 1923–24. He said, "With riches has come inexcusable waste. We have squandered a great part of what we might have used, and have not stopped to conserve the exceeding bounty of nature." That was the pledge that no Teapot Dome scandal would tarnish his administration. He called what had been done "shamefully prodigal." In our pride in our industrial achievements he said the country had not "stopped thoughtfully enough to count the human cost, the cost of lives snuffed out, of energies overtaxed and broken, the fearful physical and spiritual cost to the men and women and children upon whom the dead weight and burden of it all has fallen pitilessly the years through." Here was prophecy of his securing the eight hour law, protection of the child, and humane legislation. He went on, "The groans and agony of it all had not yet reached our ears, the solemn, moving undertone of our life, coming out of the mines and factories and out of every home where the struggle had its intimate and familiar seat." The indictment of preceding administrations was in these words: "The great government we loved has too often been made use of for private and selfish purposes, and those who used it had forgotten the people." He proceeded with his specifications: "There has been something crude and heartless and unfeeling in our haste to succeed and be great. Our thought has been, 'Let every man look out for himself, let every generation look out for itself.'" The duty to be done? "Ours is a work of restoration," he declared amid the applause of the multitude that literally hung upon his words. He enumerated among the things to be altered:

1. "A tariff which cuts us off from our proper part in the commerce of the world, violates the principle of just taxation and makes the Government a facile instrument in the hands of private interests."

2. "A banking and currency system based upon the necessity of the Government to sell bonds fifty years ago and perfectly adapted to concentrating cash and restricting credits."

3. "An industrial system which, take it on all its sides, financial as well as administrative, holds capital in leading strings, restricts the liberties and limits the opportunities of labor, and exploits without renewing or conserving the natural resources of the country."

4. "A body of agricultural activities never yet given the efficiency of great business undertakings or served as it should be through the instrumentality of science taken directly to the farm or afforded the facilities of credit best suited to its practical needs."

5. "Water courses undeveloped, waste places unreclaimed, forests untended, fast disappearing without plan or prospect of renewal, unregarded waste heaps at every mine."

6. We have not "perfected the means by which our government may be put at the service of humanity, in safeguarding the health of the nation, the health of its women and its children, as well as their rights in the

struggle for existence," and he pointed out in his pledge of "alteration" the need for sanitary laws, pure food laws and laws determining conditions of labor which "individuals are powerless to determine for themselves," and this fundamental truth that guided all he proposed: "The first duty of the law is to keep sound the society it serves."

These comprehensive six specific pledges of change, he said in his inaugural, were "some of the things we ought to do, and not to leave others undone, the old-fashioned, never-to-be-neglected fundamental safeguarding of property and of individual right." But these measures demanded by "justice, and only justice" were not to be secured by "cool process of mere science." The "nation had been deeply stirred," he told the multitude, "by a solemn passion, stirred by the knowledge of wrong, of ideals lost, of government too often debauched and made an instrument of evil." How should the task be approached? "It is inconceivable we should do this as partisans" or "in ignorance of the facts as they are or in blind haste." The call was to "restore, not to destroy." The attitude of approach he defined in these lofty words: "The feelings with which we face this new age of right and opportunity sweep across our heart-strings like some air out of God's presence, where justice and mercy are reconciled and the judge and the brother are one." Then came the climactic appeal which gripped his hearers and challenged American co-operation in the great task:

"This is not a day of triumph; it is a day of dedication. Here muster, not the forces of party, but the forces of humanity. Men's hearts wait upon us; men's lives hang in the balance; men's hopes call upon us to

*Keystone View Co.*

**THE NOMINEES FOR THE PRESIDENCY AND VICE-PRESIDENCY**

This photograph, taken on the lawn of the Governor's mansion at Sea Girt, in 1912, shows the Democratic nominees, Woodrow Wilson and Thomas R. Marshall, surrounded by prominent committeemen

**FIRST INAUGURAL** *© Harris & Ewing*

On March 4, 1913, the "Scholar in Politics" began his career as President of the United States which was to last for eight years and embrace the stormiest period which the world had ever known. He is here seen delivering his inaugural address on the steps of the Capitol at Washington

say what we will do. Who shall live up to the great trust? Who dares fail to try? I summon all honest men, all patriotic, all forward-looking men, to my side. God helping me, I will not fail them, if they will but counsel and sustain me!"

Wilson had a conception of the Presidency very different from that of most of his predecessors. In 1879, when a student in Princeton, he had written for the *International Review* an article with the subject, "Cabinet Government in the United States," in which he had revealed, although he was only twenty-three years old at the time, the definite conviction that the Presidency had not ordinarily been what the framers of the Constitution had intended it to be. In that article, Mr. Wilson declared that the Committees of Congress exercised too much power and the President possessed too little or, rather, too little that he used. He held that the trouble was not with the organic law but with the men who filled the office of President. He expressed the same views in amplified form in his book, "Congressional Government," published six years later. He regarded government by Congressional Committee as vicious. He hammered on this subject all through the book, saying, "This is the defect to which, it will be observed, I am constantly recurring; to which I recur again and again because every examination of the system, at whatsoever point begun, leads inevitably to it as a central secret." He argued that such a system destroyed responsibility and made efficient government impossible. "Nobody stands sponsor for the policy of the government," he wrote. "A dozen men originate it; a dozen compromises twist and alter it."

Calling attention to the low estate into which the Presidency had fallen, in 1907, he said: "From 1865 to 1896 no President except Mr. Cleveland played a leading and decisive part in the quiet drama of our national life. Even Mr. Cleveland may be said to have owed his great rôle in affairs rather to his own native force and the confused politics of the time, than to any opportunity of leadership naturally afforded him by a system which had subordinated so many Presidents before him to Congress."

Mr. Wilson thus went into office, holding that the man makes the Presidency and not the Presidency the man. Coming into the Presidency is an experience given to but few men and all so honored must enter upon their exalted duties with feelings of intense satisfaction tempered, of course, by a sense of the weighty responsibilities of the office. But no President probably ever took up his work with quite the satisfaction and relish that marked Woodrow Wilson's assumption of the loftiest position in the gift of the people. Had he not been saying that the office afforded opportunities which those who filled it had mostly overlooked? It was incumbent upon him now, in the popular parlance of the day, to "make good," and he was glad of the chance. "It is certain," says A. Maurice Low, an able foreign observer, "that no man ever came to the Presidency who was less awed by it than he. Most Presidents, as we gather from their correspondence and biographies, in their humility, a humility perhaps sometimes assumed as becomes the humble servant of the people, were fearful because they were so insignificant and the office was so vast; to Mr. Wilson it never assumed the aspect of a tyrant. It did not terrify him because it was a giant only in imagination. The wand was in his hands. As he willed, the Presidency had the stature and strength of a giant, of whom he was always the master, or shrank into the insignificance of a dwarf." The same writer, dwelling upon Mr. Wilson's discussions of the Presidency and the significance of those discussions in the light of subsequent events, says, "Read what Mr. Wilson has written and then see what he has done, and it is as if writing always with the calm air of philosophical detachment he is saying for all men to hear: 'This is the portrait of the perfect President; this is the President I shall be when I am given the opportunity.'"

In the very recent past, Congress almost unanimously passed a resolution that the naval oil reserves had been leased illegally and with evidence of corruption and directed the President "immediately to cause suit to be instituted and prosecuted for the annulment and cancellation" of the leases. It was followed by a Senate resolution requesting the President to call for the resignation of the Secretary of the Navy. President Coolidge asserted the right of the executive. He declined to admit that, after confirmation of members of the Cabinet, the legislative branch had any right or power to control his actions, but the resignation followed. It has been the almost unbroken position of executives and authorities on constitutional law to deny the right of Congress to direct executive action. Mr. Wilson supported such position at the time when thirty-seven Senators, long before the Treaty of Peace had come before them, sent a round robin to Paris, undertaking to forestall his action in foreign affairs. The action of other executives, with reference to their prerogative, was rather negative. They were content to fight invasion of their powers. Wilson believed in executive initiative, regarding the President as the chosen leader of the nation. One conspicuous example was his appearance before the Senate, October 1, 1918, urging concurrence in the Constitutional Amendment for woman suffrage.

It is not strange that such a man should overshadow the law-making body. A Congress is no greater than the greatest man in it and there was nobody in either of the Congresses of Wilson's administrations who approached him in knowledge of government or in clarity of thinking, and certainly none was more disinterested in asking only the best for the American people. It is inevitable that a strong man in the White House will make himself felt in Congress—if it is made up of reasonable men as it usually is—and if that strong man has what Wilson on one occasion, with somewhat more color than he usually injected into his writings, described as "the eight horses that draw the triumphal chariot of every leader and ruler of free men." As named by him these are:

Force of character,<br>
Readiness of resources,<br>
Clearness of vision,<br>
Grasp of intellect,<br>
Courage of conviction,<br>
Earnestness of purpose,<br>
Instinct, and<br>
Capacity for leadership.

And he had all eight.

## Chapter XIII

# CABINET MAKING AND BREAKING

PICKING THE CABINET—"I AM SWEATING BLOOD OVER CHOICES," HE WROTE—THE CABINET A PLACE OF COMMON COUNSEL—TEAM PLAY UNDER SOUND LEADERSHIP—BRYAN'S RESIGNATION THE FIRST BREAK—WHY BRYAN AND GARRISON RESIGNED, AND WHY LANSING WAS ASKED TO RETIRE

*"I summon all honest men, all patriotic, all forward looking men to my side. God helping me, I will not fail them."*—Wilson

THE election over, the first duty was the selection of a Cabinet. The leisure to make ready for Washington duties was denied him. He was still Governor of New Jersey and had pledged himself to a continuation of reforms. He did not feel free to resign until these measures became laws. He was hampered because the new Legislature was of an opposite political party, but in his message he said of his recommendations: "They are matters which we can approach without party bias or prejudice." The Republicans responded in equally fine spirit and gave aid in the measures Wilson had most at heart. His last work as Governor of New Jersey was to demand and secure the selection of juries free from political influence. He found time before the Legislature for a brief vacation with his family. A sea trip to Bermuda—he always loved the sea—brought needed rest.

The business of selecting a Cabinet and planning his inaugural afforded enough work to give zest to his play.

He was not long in coming to a conclusion as to the two ranking members of his Cabinet. He had not believed in Bryan's free coinage of silver plank when the Nebraskan was candidate for President in 1896. He had shared his views against imperialism in 1900. Later, in 1907 he had written to Joline, expressing the wish that Bryan should be "knocked into a cocked hat." He had, however, come to have genuine respect for Bryan and admiration for his patriotism. In an address at the Jackson Day dinner in Washington, Mr. Wilson had paid high tribute to Bryan. He had wired, "You are quite right," in his telegram to Bryan on the eve of the Baltimore Convention, when the Nebraskan was demanding that only Progressives be put on guard in the organization of the Convention. When urged by McCombs, who thought such promises would bring support to Wilson for the nomination, to promise he would not invite Bryan to become a member of his Cabinet, Mr. Wilson had refused to make that or any pledge as to his advisers if he should be nominated and elected. Almost immediately upon his election he found, particularly in the East, advisers and supporters who thought Bryan's selection would be a mistake. Wilson listened, sent for Bryan, and asked him to become Secretary of State.

The second selection was quite easy. He had tested the ability and capacity of William G. McAdoo and found that in fiscal policies McAdoo's mind "ran along with" his. He was resolved that his Secretary of the Treasury should be a man of initiative, independent, courageous, and able to lead in revenue and fiscal reform that would end control of the fiscal policy by the few great bankers of the money centres. The unfounded jealousy of

McCombs was the only dissent, and it did not weigh. The portfolio of the Secretary of War was tendered to A. Mitchell Palmer, of Pennsylvania, who had been the brilliant floor leader of the Wilson forces in the Baltimore Convention, and a leader in Congress. "I am a Quaker," answered Palmer, "and I could not consistently accept."

It was only a few days before March 4 that Mr. Wilson tendered the portfolio of Secretary of War to Lindley M. Garrison, Vice Chancellor of New Jersey, an able lawyer, who resigned after a service of thirty-five months. Palmer would have accepted the Attorney Generalship, to which he was later appointed to succeed Gregory. Mr. Wilson was hard to satisfy in securing an Attorney General. He wished a learned lawyer, who had no corporate leanings and who would be guided by the philosophy of law rather than precedent. J. C. McReynolds, of Tennessee, who was afterwards named as Associate Justice of the Supreme Court, was tendered the Justice portfolio. Perhaps the fact that turned the scale in his mind to McReynolds was that, after the tobacco combination had been found guilty of violating the anti-trust laws, McReynolds, counsel for the Government, declined to approve the sham penalty of division into separate companies.

The Secretaryship of the Interior was offered to Newton D. Baker, who declined because he felt impelled to carry out the reforms for which he had been chosen as Mayor of Cleveland. Later, in 1916, he came into the Cabinet as Secretary of War and served during the World War, winning the admiration of Pershing and Foch and Haig. It was not until a few days before the inauguration that Mr. Wilson named Franklin K. Lane, of California, who had made reputation as a member of the United States Commerce Commission. "I am your Secretary of the Interior," said Lane to President Wilson, as they entered the White House. They had never met until that hour. The Postmaster Generalship went to Albert S. Burleson, of Texas, long member of Congress, able parliamentarian. Colonel House is credited with having had influence in that selection, but Wilson had himself known Burleson's qualities and valued him. Josephus Daniels, of North Carolina, was named Secretary of the Navy. For Secretary of Agriculture, David F. Houston, college president and staunch friend, was selected. Later, as the best proof of Mr. Wilson's confidence, Houston was made Secretary of the Treasury. For Secretary of Commerce, Mr. Wilson is said to have had in mind the selection of Louis D. Brandeis, of Boston, later named by him as Associate Justice of the Supreme Court, but certain Massachusetts Democrats urged that instead a well-known party leader be named if New England was to have a representative in the Cabinet. Mr. Wilson named W. C. Redfield, of Brooklyn. As a member of Congress, Mr. Redfield had won reputation as an authority upon the tariff. He was a successful business man. For Secretary of Labor President Wilson had early selected William B. Wilson, of Pennsylvania. He had served in Congress and as an officer of the American Federation of Labor. He had the confidence alike of employer and employee. Thus officered the Ship of State began its new voyage, March 5, 1913. "Whether strong or weak in its various elements, this is no cabinet of political trade and barter," said the New York *World*. "It was fashioned to placate neither sordid political interests nor sordid financial interests. Every member stands on his own merits."

**WILSON'S THREE CABINETS**

Top, the first cabinet: Around the table, left to right: President Wilson, William G. McAdoo, J. C. McReynolds, Josephus Daniels, D. F. Houston, W. B. Wilson, W. C. Redfield, F. K. Lane, A. S. Burleson, L. M. Garrison, and W. J. Bryan. Center, the war cabinet: Robert Lansing has succeeded Mr. Bryan; T. W. Gregory has succeeded McReynolds; Newton Diehl Baker has succeeded Garrison. Bottom, the last cabinet: with Bainbridge Colby succeeding Lansing, John Barton Payne succeeding Lane, D. F. Houston succeeding Carter Glass, who took McAdoo's place in 1918; A. Mitchell Palmer succeeding Gregory; and E. T. Meredith succeeding Houston

**PRESIDENT WILSON AND SECRETARY OF THE NAVY, JOSEPHUS DANIELS** © *U. & U.*
Taken in the Presidential box at the Army and Navy football game in New York, on November 29, 1913

The first change in the Cabinet was the appointment of Robert Lansing as Secretary of State when Bryan resigned. Upon Lansing's retirement he was succeeded by Bainbridge Colby, of New York. When McAdoo resigned as Secretary of the Treasury, Carter Glass, of Virginia, was called to that portfolio until he resigned to accept a seat in the United States Senate. Thomas W. Gregory, of Texas, held the portfolio of Attorney General during the World War. He was succeeded by A. Mitchell Palmer, of Pennsylvania. Joshua W. Alexander, of Missouri, succeeded Redfield as Secretary of Commerce. John Barton Payne, of Illinois, succeeded Lane as Secretary of the Interior, and Edwin T. Meredith, of Iowa, came into the Cabinet as Secretary of Agriculture when Houston was promoted to the Treasury. Only Burleson, Daniels, and Wilson retained their original portfolios during the entire eight years, Houston remaining the entire period, though shifted from Agriculture to Treasury.

If Wilson "sweat blood," he but shared the fate of Lincoln, who had said that if the Twelve Apostles had again to be chosen, the principle of locality would determine their selection. Lincoln chose his competitors for the nomination and only his patience and greatness stood the strain of their feeling of superiority until by sheer evidence of commanding ability Lincoln converted them into a harmonious unit. Wilson regarded his Cabinet, as he said a Cabinet should be, "executive counselors."

The selection of a Cabinet was not easy. "I have been sweating blood over Cabinet choices," the new President wrote to one of the gentlemen who was invited and accepted a seat in the Cabinet. From the inception Mr. Wilson gave the members of his Cabinet free rein in the management of the affairs of their department. No President refrained so much from hampering them by naming their subordinates. Holding them responsible, he gave them liberty, confidence, and co-operation. More than that: he stood back of them when criticized and held up their hands. However, when for any reason a member of the Cabinet tendered his resignation, it was accepted without question. President and Cabinet members alike felt that if there were differences upon great policies, resignation was the only course. Mr. Lincoln, who did not always have harmony in his Cabinet, read this memorandum at one of its meetings:

"I must myself be the judge how long to retain and when to remove any of you from his position. It would greatly pain me to discover any of you endeavoring to procure another's removal, or in any way to prejudice him before the public. Such endeavor would be a wrong to me, and, much worse, a wrong to the country. My wish is that on this subject no remark be made nor question asked by any of you, here or elsewhere, now or hereafter."

Cabinet meetings were places of common counsel. Wilson did not, like Jefferson, submit questions to the body and let the majority rule. He did not, as Lincoln is said to have done, permit one member, like Seward, to monopolize his time. He did not, like Grant, leave to Cabinet ministers direction of policies that a President should control. The usual plan at these semi-weekly meetings was, after the greetings (he was always the soul of courtesy) something like this: The President would bring forward the chief matter that was on his mind—state the situation. If he was to send a message to Congress, he would read it and invite comment. With pencil in hand he would note suggestions of change. The members gave their opinions, and debate followed. Discussion ended, he would often say, "To quote a Quaker, presiding at a yearly gathering, I take it to be the sense of this meeting," stating it. Every Cabinet member by turn, one time beginning with the Secretary of State, and the next time with the Secretary of Labor, was invited to bring up any matter of public or department interest. "I have never," said a member of the Cabinet, "known any man in responsible authority on public affairs who sought and valued counsel as much as Mr. Wilson. He was fond of telling of a conference at Princeton to which he went with certain views and to which others came with opposing views. The whole matter was threshed out fully in discussion and a unanimous conclusion reached, different from any one of those entertained before the discussion. That happened often in our Cabinet meetings. He made his own decisions, of course, and properly, for the responsibility was his alone, but he always eagerly sought for light."

The first break in Wilson's Cabinet came on June 8, 1915, when Mr. Bryan tendered his resignation as Secretary of State. It was not attended by any lack of cordial relationship and the separation gave regret to both the President and Mr. Bryan. It was a wrench on both sides. The reason that prompted the resignation was plainly and frankly given by Mr. Bryan in these words: "Obedient to your sense of duty and actuated by the highest motives, you have prepared for transmission to the German Government a note in which I cannot join without violating what I deem to be an obligation to my country, and the issue involved is of such moment that to remain a member of the Cabinet would be as unfair to you as it would be to the cause which is nearest my heart, namely, the prevention of war." The letter breathed warm friendship. In accepting, President Wilson said in part: "I accept your resignation only because you insist" and "with a feeling of personal sorrow." He referred to the fact that their judgments had "accorded in practically every matter of official duty and public policy until now." "As to the cause," he said, "even now we are not separated in the object we seek, but only in the method by which we seek it." For that reason his feeling was "deeper than regret—I sincerely deplore it."

In all the annals of official correspondence, there could not be found two letters so free from all that is formal or one so permeated by genuine admiration, each for the other. Very different in temperament, each admired the other for recognized sterling qualities. The resignation created a national sensation and was followed by much gossip. Those on the inside knew that the letters contained the true sentiments. Attempts were made to give an air of mystery where none existed. Mr. Bryan hated war—he believed the course of Mr. Wilson would bring war. He could not consistently sign or approve a note that he believed would eventuate in war with Germany. As a conscientious man and official, he felt the only honorable course was to retire to private life when he was not in harmony with his chief. He did so with genuine regret. On the President's part, he hated war. He had been derided for his long-continued attempts to "keep us out of war." But he believed it better to have war, if war should come, than to fail to assert the demands he made upon Germany. He felt then, as he said in his war message, "the right is more precious than peace," and he was so convinced he was right he could "do no otherwise."

The separation did not affect their mutual esteem. As Mr. and Mrs. Bryan were leaving Washington ten days after the resignation, the President called at their home to say "good-bye." Mr. Bryan took an active part in the 1916 campaign, helping in the winning of the West, and Mr. Wilson wrote him a letter of appreciation. After that campaign, Mr. and Mrs. Bryan were luncheon guests of the President and Mrs. Wilson in the White House.

Mr. Wilson never changed the opinion to which he gave expression at the Jackson Day dinner, 1912, in Washington: "I, for my part, never want to forget this: That while we have differed with Mr. Bryan upon this occasion and upon that in regard to the specific things to be done, he has gone serenely on pointing out to a more convinced people what it was that was the matter. He has had the steadfast vision all along of what it was that was the matter and he has not, any more than Andrew Jackson did, based his career upon calculation, but has based it upon principle."

The second break in the Cabinet came suddenly. It was upon disagreement over "fundamental principles." On February 10, 1916, Judge Lindley M. Garrison, Secretary of War, tendered his resignation. The reasons given were differences with the President over "preparedness" and the Philippine question. These were the real reasons, but beneath them was a radical difference in the point of view of the two men. Garrison looked at questions from the standpoint of what Wilson called "legalistic." He was first of all a lawyer, an able and honorable one, and approached the consideration of public questions from that standpoint. Wilson was never fully controlled by precedent in such matters. Moreover, Garrison, as he himself asserted, was not cut out for teamwork. He was an individualist of the most pronounced type. In an interview published April 20, 1913, he said:

"I never could obey orders in the matter of opinion. Universal belief carries no weight with me. Another man's convictions are heard through politeness or interest, but they utterly fail to convince. I claim no moral or intellectual credit for the peculiar qualities of my mind any more than I can claim responsibility for my height or the color of my eyes. I was born as I am, and the case ends so far as I am concerned. Orders always irritate me. A program of conduct can never be carried out. It was so when I was a boy at school. I became a rebel the moment the teacher said the lesson would be so and so the next day. Going home I would study something else. I wasn't obstinate, but a task was odious and a command made me an outlaw at once."

In presenting his resignation, Garrison wrote Wilson:

"It is evident that we hopelessly disagree upon what I conceive to be fundamental principles. This makes manifest the impropriety of my longer remaining your seeming representative with respect to these matters."

Garrison's program included a considerable enlargement of the regular army and the formation of a reserve body of about 400,000 men to be known as the continental army and to be made up, for the most part, of men taking a brief but thorough training to the number of about 133,000 each year. Mr. Wilson, though his mind was open and he was looking for the plan which best met the needs of the nation, was not willing to back Garrison in fighting the plan proposed by the House Committee on military affairs, the distinctive feature of which was an increase in the number of the national guard, and the payment of these troops out of the national treasury and making them subject to the call of the President.

Garrison had written: "I consider the reliance upon the militia for national defence an unjustifiable imperiling of the nation's safety." Mr. Wilson replied: "I am not yet convinced. . . . I feel in duty bound to keep my mind open. . . . This is a time when it seems to me patience on the part of us all is essential." Agreement with Garrison meant a hopeless break with Congress and a contest and conflict over what Wilson regarded as methods. He had just returned from his Preparedness Tour in the West. He had won the people to a big program. "I am urging Congress," he told them, to adopt a "system by which we may give a very considerable body of our fellow citizens the necessary training if danger comes." He was unwilling to dictate to Congress, over the protest of the Military Affairs Committee of the House, the exact "system".

The second difference was over the Philippine question. Senator Clarke, of Arkansas, a month before had introduced a resolution giving the Philippines their independence in not less than two nor more than four years at the discretion of the President. Mr. Garrison wrote that he considered "the principle embodied in the Clarke amendment an abandonment of the duty of this nation and a breach of trust toward the Filipinos." Wilson's position on Philippine legislation was in keeping with the American position taken at the time the Philippines were purchased from Spain and the pledges of the Democratic party in all its platforms since 1898. Mr. Wilson in his correspondence with Mr. Garrison said he considered the Clarke amendment unwise.

Writing months afterwards, P. W. Wilson made this comment, applicable to the resignation of Bryan and Garrison: "Like Louis XIV, Wilson was his own Foreign Minister. He lost from his Cabinet, therefore, two men of strong personality. One was Lindley Garrison, his Secretary of War, who in 1916, when the country was still neutral, wanted military preparation. The other was William Jennings Bryan, the Secretary of State, who was still for peace. Between the Scylla of preparedness and the Charybdis of pacifism, the President had to steer the Ship of State: and the prophets of both evangels left him."

The third resignation, aside from the normal retirements, was the dramatic one of Robert Lansing, who had succeeded to the portfolio upon Bryan's resignation. When appointed Mr. Lansing was an unknown figure to the general public. He was an "up state" New York Democrat. He had lived for years in Washington, where he practiced law. His practice was largely confined to international law. He had married the daughter of Hon. John W. Foster, a Republican, who was appointed Secretary of State when Blaine resigned. Residing in Washington, Lansing had taken no part in politics, and it was incorrectly supposed by many that he was a Republican when his appointment was announced. At the beginning of the Wilson administration, he was named Counsel of the State Department. In that post he was capable and efficient to a high degree. The President and Bryan felt every confidence in him. His well prepared opinions and recommendations were received with favor. When Bryan resigned, the President, who, as the reason for Bryan's resignation showed, felt it his duty to conduct the negotiations with Germany himself, wished the least change possible in the continuity of diplomatic policy. He, therefore, named Lansing. It was not a popular appointment, nor unpopular. Many people said "the President is resolved to be Secretary of State in all big affairs, and wishes an international lawyer to assist him, and he has chosen wisely."

The President felt that Lansing might incline too much to accepted diplomatic practice, but he was confident, with all the legal questions fully stated by his Secretary of State, that he himself could determine the policies. When Lansing advised the President not to go to Paris, Wilson probably regarded it as presuming, but he said nothing. He wished his official family to be free with their advice.

Paris saw the beginning of the break. Lansing regarded his office as entitling him to primacy. The diplomats and press representatives in Paris regarded Colonel House as ranking next to Wilson. This was not agreeable to the Secretary of State. But that was only a pin-pricking incident. Wilson had his heart set upon a Covenant for Permanent Peace to be inseparably bound up in the peace treaty. He had promised that to the boys as they went to France. He had pledged it in his War Message and in almost every utterance before and during the war. He regarded any other treaty as no better than the miserable war-breeding Vienna treaty. The armistice had been agreed to by the Allies and Germany on the basis of the Fourteen Points and his addresses that pledged a League of Nations. It was his belief that only such an association could avert the debacle into which the world has fallen.

Not long after reaching Paris it began to be talked by the newspaper men gathered there that Lansing was not in harmony with incorporating the League covenant with the Treaty. "When we were in Paris I found that Lansing and others were constantly giving out statements," the President is quoted by Tumulty as saying to him a few days before he was stricken, "that did not agree with my viewpoint. When I had arranged a settlement, there would appear from some source I could not locate, unofficial statements telling the correspondents not to take things too seriously; that a compromise would be made, and this news, or rather news of this kind, was harmful to the settlement I had already obtained and quite naturally gave the Conference the impression that Lansing and his kind were speaking for me, and then the French would say I was bluffing." That statement was made, so Mr. Tumulty says, after Bullitt had testified that Lansing had told him that "the League Covenant was thoroughly bad and in his belief, if the Senate thoroughly understood, it would reject it."

When that statement appeared, just a few days before Wilson was stricken, he was heroically, and despite physical weakness, engaged in seeking to arouse the people to the supreme importance of ratifying the treaty. Lansing sent a telegram which was regarded as a virtual admission he had said in substance what Bullitt quoted him as saying. That angered Wilson. He had suspected Lansing's lack of co-operation and support and of opposition. "Lansing's own statement is a verification of the very thing (disloyalty) I have suspected," Tumulty quotes Wilson as saying. Tumulty says he was convinced that "only the President's illness a few days later prevented an immediate demand for the resignation of Mr. Lansing." That was the middle of September. The next week (September 26) the President was stricken and returned to Washington. For some weeks he was very ill.

On October 3, Lansing went to the Executive office to talk to Tumulty about the President's condition. Tumulty thus describes the interview: "He informed me that he had called diplomatically to suggest that in view of the incapacity of the President, we should arrange to call in the Vice-President to act in his stead as soon as possible, reading to me from a book which he had brought from the State Department, which I afterwards learned was 'Jefferson's Manual,' the following clause of the United States Constitution:

"'In case of the removal of the President from office, or his death, resignation, or inability to discharge the powers and duties of the said office, the same shall devolve upon the Vice-President.'"

Tumulty says, "I coldly turned and said: 'Mr. Lansing, the Constitution is not a dead letter with the White House. I have read the Constitution and do not find myself in need of any tutoring at your hands of the provision you have just read.'" Tumulty says he told Lansing that he would be no party to certifying to the President's "disability," and that Dr. Grayson came in at that time and "left no doubt in Mr. Lansing's mind that he would not do as Mr. Lansing suggested." Tumulty adds that he also told Lansing that "if anybody outside of the White House circle attempted to certify to the President's disability, that Grayson and I would stand together and repudiate it."

Mr. Lansing's statement differs. He says that on October third, "the newspapers under 'scare' headlines carried alarming reports concerning the President," and he went over to the White House to see Mr. Tumulty.

"He told me that on Wednesday, October 1, the President had become much worse," says Lansing. "I asked him in what way. He did not answer me in words, but significantly put his right hand to his left shoulder and drew it down along his left side. Of course, the implication was that the President had suffered a stroke and that his left side was paralyzed." Grayson came in, Lansing goes on, but "was extremely reticent as to the President's malady, giving no indication of any trouble other than a nervous breakdown." Lansing adds, "We decided (Lansing, Grayson and Tumulty) that the Cabinet ought to meet and confer about the matter." Later, Lansing says, he talked to Secretaries Baker and Lane who approved of calling a meeting of the Cabinet; the call was issued, and it met October 6. He continues, "Admiral Grayson and Tumulty were present during the early part of the meeting, and Grayson gave a very encouraging report on the President's condition, which, he said, showed decided improvement and seemed to indicate a speedy recovery." Lansing added: "We, therefore, asked Grayson to convey to the President our felicitations and best wishes." Nothing else was heard of "disability" of the President in his official family, though Senators later visited the White House and satisfied themselves that the President was able to discharge the duties of the office.

Though the Cabinet met weekly, Secretary Lansing did not bring before it his ultimatum sent to the Mexican government November 20, 1919, in connection with the arrest of W. O. Jenkins, who was a consular agent at Puebla, Mexico. It was reported that he was captured by bandits who demanded a ransom of $150,000. While payment of the ransom was reputed to be in process of arrangement, Puebla state authorities arrested Jenkins on the charge that he was in collusion with the bandits. There was conflict of testimony and much uncertainty. In the midst of it all Secretary Lansing sent a note "demanding the immediate liberation of Mr. Jenkins."

The President had not been consulted. When the tenor of the note became known to him, he took the matter out of Lansing's hands and virtually repudiated his warlike demand. That was the moment when Mr. Lansing ought to have resigned, if he had not felt constrained to do so in Paris or when the Bullitt incident disclosed his attitude of opposition to the cause dearest of all causes to the heart of his chief.

On February 7, President Wilson addressed a letter to Secretary Lansing and asked: "Is it true, as I have been told, that during my illness you have frequently called the heads of the executive departments of the government into conference?" He went on to say that "under our constitutional law and practice, as developed hitherto, no one but the president has the right to summon the heads of the executive departments into conference." Lansing answered, February 9, that it was true, that "certain members of the Cabinet, of which I was one, felt that, in view of the fact that we were denied communication with you, it was wise for us to confer informally together." He said it had never entered his mind that such action was "unconstitutional or contrary to your wishes," and that he had "no intention to assume powers and exercise functions exclusively confided to the President." He added that it had been his "constant endeavor to carry out your policies" and "to act in all matters as I believed you would wish me to act."

Concluding, Lansing said: "If, however, you think

that I have failed in my loyalty to you and if you no longer have confidence in me and prefer to have another to conduct foreign affairs, I am, of course, ready to relieve you of any embarrassment by placing my resignation in your hands." Wilson answered, February 11, that he was "very much disappointed" by the answer, said "no action could be taken without me by the Cabinet," and went on to say:

"This affair only deepens a feeling that was growing upon me. While you were still in Paris I felt, and have felt increasingly since, that you accepted my guidance and direction on questions with regard to which I had to instruct you with increasing reluctance, and since my return to Washington I have been struck by the number of matters in which you have apparently tried to forestall my judgment by formulating judgment and merely asking my approval when it was impossible for me to form an independent judgment because I had not had an opportunity to examine the circumstances with any degree of independence."

He would, therefore, says Wilson, "take advantage" of the suggestion of resignation, saying it "would relieve me of the embarrassment of feeling your reluctance and divergence of judgment" and "afford me an opportunity to select some one whose mind would more willingly go along with mine." He added, "I need not tell you with what reluctance I take advantage of your suggestion, or that I do so with the kindliest feeling. In matters of transcendent importance like this the only wise course is a course of perfect candor where personal feeling is as much as possible left out of the reckoning." Usually the President ended his letters "Faithfully yours." This ending was "Sincerely yours."

In formally tendering his resignation, February 12, Lansing denied he had attempted to "forestall" the President's "judgment" or "usurp" power in calling informal meetings of the Cabinet. He said "ever since January, 1919," he had "been conscious of the fact that you no longer were disposed to welcome my advice pertaining to the negotiations at Paris, to our foreign service, or to international affairs in general," and that he would have early in 1919 resigned, but wished "to cause you no embarrassment in carrying forward the great task in which you were then engaged." Later, in the latter part of July, 1919, he withheld his resignation only because "I felt loyalty to you and my duty to the administration compelled me to defer action." He closed by saying he left the office "with only good will toward you and a profound sense of relief, forgetting our differences and remembering only your kindnesses in the past." The President in accepting the resignation said his "best wishes will always follow you" and that "it will be a matter of gratification to remember our delightful personal relations."

The President was well within his rights in asking Mr. Lansing to retire from the Cabinet, but the ground upon which the resignation was called for was not regarded by the public as justifying the President's demand. The act (calling the Cabinet) he specified was, doubtless, in the President's mind an inseparable part of Lansing's suggestion to Tumulty of the President's "disability" to perform the duties of his office. Seeing that the call for the first meeting of the Cabinet followed the suggestion of "disability," the President evidently regarded the two as one joint act. In the words of his letter, however, the President named only the calling of the

Cabinet as the reason for desiring Mr. Lansing's retirement.

The people, who had known for weeks that the Cabinet was meeting regularly and had approved their coming together, could not understand why this course of Lansing's warranted a demand for his resignation. They did not know of his visit to Tumulty to suggest that the Vice-President should exercise the duties of chief executive. If the President had given the Bullitt incident or the Jenkins incident or the lack of co-operation at Paris, or if he had given no reason at all, he would have been in a position that would not have justified the severe and widespread criticism that followed.

When Mr. Lansing's book appeared, disclosing how widely he was at variance with the President upon the one issue that meant more than all others to Mr. Wilson, it was seen that he ought long before to have withdrawn from the Cabinet.

"In other countries there are cushions upon which such men fall," wrote P. W. Wilson, former member of Parliament. "The United States usually offers the pavement, and in the case of Mr. Lansing the blow of the boot was heard throughout the planet. What Wilson in health would have managed with a smile, Wilson from his sick bed only accomplished with the mailed fist."

Cabinets were made for unity!

## Chapter XIV

# TARIFF REFORM, FIRST STEP

TARIFF LEGISLATION AND EFFECT ON POLITICS—DID NOT MAKE CLEVELAND'S MISTAKE—DRIVES OUT TARIFF LOBBY—ABOLISHES "EVERY SEMBLANCE OF PRIVILEGE"—INCOME TAX INTRODUCED—REFUSES TO SANCTION GOLD BRICK FOR RELIEF OF FARMERS

*"We must abolish everything that bears even the semblance of privilege or of any kind of artificial advantage."*—Wilson

TARIFF changes have been held responsible for political successes and failures. To go back no further than September, 1890, when the McKinley Act was passed, the party responsible for it met a disastrous defeat in the November election. Its author, Mr. McKinley, who owed his subsequent promotion as President to issues not related to his tariff bill, was defeated. The Democrats carried the house in 1890 by a majority of 148, the Republicans electing only 88 members. "The women shoppers did it," explained Thomas B. Reed, Speaker of the House, alluding to the increased prices charged by retail dealers immediately following the passage of the McKinley Tariff. It not only gave the Democrats control of the House of Representatives, but presaged the election of Cleveland in 1892 and the control of the executive and legislative departments of the government for the first time since 1856. Even earlier, the friends of Grover Cleveland asserted that his famous tariff message of 1887, "it is a condition and not a theory that confronts us", was responsible for his defeat in 1888. They also attributed his second election to the fact that the people had, in the four years between his message and his re-election, decided he was right, as McKinley's friends asserted of his position when he became President in 1896. When Cleveland was inaugurated in 1893, he made a tactical mistake in postponing tariff legislation. If he had called Congress in session in April, 1893, to reduce the tariff in accordance with his great message of 1887, the abortion known as the Wilson-Gorman Tariff Act, which became a law without his signature, would not have called forth his statement that it represented "party perfidy and party dishonor." When, afterwards in his term, Mr. Cleveland's party had become hopelessly divided on the money question, he had lost the opportunity to obtain the sort of tariff measure upon which he had set his heart.

On the very day that he was elected, the matter of early tariff legislation was discussed by the President-elect with two friends, who afterwards became members of his Cabinet. Wilson was advertent to the disappointment of Mr. Cleveland. A short time after the election, and weeks before his inauguration, Mr. Wilson made a public statement that he would call a special session of Congress to reduce the tariff. It heartened the tariff reform forces of the country and guaranteed the victory which followed that summons.

It was said to be a theory of Theodore Roosevelt's that the party which meddled with the tariff would meet defeat at the next election. Whatever his reason, it is certain that during the seven years that he was in power the tariff schedules were not changed and he made no move to have them changed. Mr. Wilson would have used all his influence for the revision of the tariff downward even if it had been definitely known that it would mean his defeat. He was as far as the poles from holding that platforms are made to get in on rather than to stand on. The first plank in the Democratic platform upon which he had been elected read in part:

"We favor the immediate downward revision of the existing high, and, in many cases, prohibitive tariff duties, insisting that material reductions be speedily made upon the necessaries of life. Articles entering into competition with trust-controlled products and articles of American manufacture which are sold abroad more cheaply than at home, should be put upon the free list."

Mr. Wilson early had strong convictions about the effect of a high tariff, as was shown when, having drawn the "Protection" side in a debate at Princeton, he declined to advocate a doctrine he did not believe sound. He said in his speech of acceptance that the rank and file of the people found life very hard to sustain and he was convinced that mistaken government policies had something to do with the fact. In his inaugural address he had renewed his own pledge and given further approval to his party pledge to seek to cure defects in government policies. He often said that of the possessions of mankind justice was the most precious. A protective tariff was, in his eyes, rank injustice to the great body of the people. A tariff which "cuts us off from our proper part in the commerce of the world, violates the just principles of taxation and makes the government a facile instrument in the hands of private interests," found in him a sincere and effective opponent.

Moved by his own convictions and with his personal and party pledges as further incentive, Mr. Wilson went into the tariff struggle with all his might. He saw reduction of the rates as a practical means of proving his party a real servant of sound economics. There was such a strong sentiment in Congress for tariff reform that the compelling and driving force of the President did not have to be invoked to as great a degree as in some matters afterwards. But it was incumbent upon him to keep his party keyed up to its task and ready at all times to turn a deaf ear to the siren song of the interests which wanted a continuance of special privilege. Indeed, every one was familiar with the conditions at Washington, when the sugar, steel, and other lobbies came down on Washington "like the wolf on the fold." The scattering of the tariff lobby by Wilson was as wholesome as it was sensational. It freed legislators from the importunity of paid men and insured the writing of tariff schedules by the legally elected agents of the people rather than by those who were to be the beneficiaries of high rates. All records of tariff-legislation were broken. Mr. Wilson displayed genius of leadership in carrying out this first big policy of his administration. Instead of any division in the party, or the predicted "shipwreck on the tariff rock" which had come to so many administrations, Mr. Wilson emerged with high prestige.

It was on April 8, 1913, a month after his inaugural, that Congress met in extraordinary session. On that day Mr. Wilson broke the precedent of executives sending their messages and appeared in person to deliver the first message Congress had heard a President deliver since 1796. That fact, added to the distinction of the occasion, helped to emphasize the significance of the message. He compressed into that message the philosophy and wisdom of tariff reformers of all time—John Bright, William L. Wilson, John G. Carlisle, William J. Bryan, Grover

Cleveland, Roger Q. Mills, David A. Wells, and a host of others who had sounded the clear note against public taxation for private profit.

Mr. Wilson declared "a duty was laid upon the party now in power, at the recent election, which it ought to perform promptly, in order that the burden carried by the people under existing laws may be lightened as soon as possible, and in order that the business interests of the country may not be kept too long in suspense as to what the fiscal changes are to be, to which they may be required to adjust themselves." He continued: "The sooner the tariff is altered, the sooner our men of business will be free to thrive by the law of nature—the nature of free business—instead of by the law of legislation and artificial arrangement." He went on to say:

"We have seen tariff legislation wander very far afield in our day—very far, indeed, from the field in which our prosperity might have had a normal growth and stimulation. No one who looks the facts squarely in the face or knows anything that lies beneath the surface of action can fail to perceive the principles upon which recent tariff legislation has been based. We long ago passed beyond the modest notion of 'protecting' the industries of the country and moved boldly forward to the idea that they were entitled to the direct patronage of the Government. For a long time—a time so long that the men now active in public policy hardly remember the conditions that preceded it—we have sought in our tariff schedules to give each group of manufacturers or producers what they themselves thought that they needed in order to maintain a practically exclusive market as against the rest of the world. Consciously or unconsciously, we have built up a set of privileges and exemptions from competition behind which it was easy by any, even the crudest, forms of combination to organize monopoly; until at last nothing is normal, nothing is obliged to stand the tests of efficiency and economy, in our world of big business, but everything thrives by concerted arrangement. Only new principles of action will save us from a final hard crystallization of monopoly and a complete loss of the influences that quicken enterprise and keep independent energy alive.

"It is plain what those principles must be. We must abolish everything that bears even the semblance of privilege or of any kind of artificial advantage, and put our business men and producers under the stimulation of a constant necessity to be efficient, economical, and enterprising, masters of competitive supremacy, better workers and merchants than any in the world. Aside from the duties laid upon articles which we do not, and probably cannot, produce, therefore, and the duties laid upon luxuries and merely for the sake of the revenues they yield, the object of the tariff duties henceforth laid must be effective competition, the whetting of American wits by contest with the wits of the rest of the world."

Wilson was no iconoclast, who would fail to recognize conditions. "It would be unwise," he said in that message, "to move toward this end headlong with reckless haste, or with strokes that cut at the very roots of what has grown up amongst us by long process and at our invitation. It does not alter a thing to upset it and break it and deprive it of a chance to change. It destroys itself. We must make changes in our fiscal laws, in our fiscal system, whose object is development, not revolution or upset or confusion." He declared that the remedies must be "genuine" but also said, "Remedies may be heroic."

He signed the measure at the White House on October 3, 1913, and upon attaching his signature, in the presence of the Chairmen and members of the committee, cabinet and others, Mr. Wilson felicitated them upon their first step toward unfettering business.

It was hailed as the best tariff measure since the one enacted in 1846 of which James G. Blaine in his "Twenty Years of Congress" said it yielded "abundant revenue" and "the business of the country flourished under it, and seemed, for the time, to be so entirely vindicated and approved that resistance to it ceased."

The average rate of duties was reduced from forty to twenty-six per cent. The measure reduced or abolished tariff duties on practically all the articles entering into the cost of living. On all such articles the Payne-Aldrich Tariff Act, which it replaced, levied heavy duties with the effect of discouraging any competition from abroad and enabling home manufacturers, by combination and otherwise, to exact exorbitant prices.

Naturally relieving the people of part of the tariff tax resulted in a reduction of the treasury receipts. The platform on which Mr. Wilson had been elected had demanded an income tax. Provision for such a tax had been incorporated in the Wilson-Gorman tariff in Cleveland's last administration. It had been declared unconstitutional when, as Senator Vest stated, "a judge changed his mind over night." From 1896 until it was adopted, there had been an organized fight for the adoption of an amendment to the constitution authorizing the levying of an income tax. Its advocates believed that the expenses of national government ought not to be borne entirely on the basis of consumption, as the tariff tax imposes its burdens, but the cost of government ought to be apportioned in accordance with ability to pay. Of the $627,000,000 the Government received from the tariff and internal revenue taxes in 1913, only a comparatively small part was paid by those in receipt of large incomes. The income tax afforded the best measure of ability to pay. On February 25, 1913, an amendment to the constitution was adopted, giving Congress the power to levy a tax on incomes. This power the framers of the Underwood-Simmons Act availed themselves of and a graduated income tax was incorporated in the measure. When the demands of war called for the raising of billions of dollars, the basis for securing taxation from incomes was ready at hand.

Professor Taussig, a tariff expert and impartial critic, gave this statement on the tariff measure: "The pertinent sections of the tariff were rewritten. That they were substantially improved was the judgment of specialists competent on this intricate subject." Wilson had never claimed perfection for them, much less that there was anything in schedules too sacred to be changed. In fact, a non-partisan tariff commission was later created with ample power to obtain and report to Congress the facts essential to tariff making. This was to be no executive usurpation of the exclusive power of Congress to levy taxes. That was not the Wilson conception of the way to go about securing changes. A new agency, composed of competent specialists, was given the duty of ascertaining the facts by scientific investigation, and these were to be available to the executive for recommendation and to Congress in levying taxes for the support of government. It was recognized in 1916 that two years of war brought about economic changes and that the government should be ready to wisely alter its tariff and other revenue laws to meet changed or changing conditions. The facts obtained by the commission, to quote Wilson, were "for the guidance alike of our business men and our Congress." "For," he added, "American energies are now directed toward the markets of the world."

"Laws explicitly to remove any ban supposed to rest upon co-operation among exporters in seeking and securing their proper place in the markets of the world" opened the way for the marvelous expansion of foreign trade. "We have barred monopoly," he declared, and insured "peace in the business world, and, with peace, revived confidence and life."

The attempt in 1920 to relieve agricultural distress with the gold brick of high tariff, after the Senate had definitely kept the United States out of the concert of world powers, received no countenance from President Wilson. Farmers had made their crops at large expense. When the "bottom dropped out", they petitioned Washington for relief. The Republican leaders said, "A high tariff on wheat will insure you profitable prices. We will give it to you." They hurried through the Fordney Emergency Tariff, levying a tax of thirty cents a bushel on wheat and increasing the rates on other agricultural products. Wilson, in substance, said: "A high tariff on farm products the price of which is fixed in foreign markets, will bring no relief."

On March 4, 1921, on the last day he was chief executive, President Wilson sent one of the very few veto messages he ever wrote to Congress. "The situation in which many of the farmers of the country find themselves," he said in this message, "cannot be remedied by a measure of this sort. There is no short way out of existing conditions, and measures of this sort can only have the effect of deceiving the farmers and raising false hopes among them. The farmer needs a better system of domestic marketing and credit, but especially larger foreign markets for his surplus products. Clearly, measures of this sort will not conduce to an expansion of the foreign market. Actual relief can come only from the adoption of constructive measures of a broader scope, from the restoration of peace elsewhere in the world, the resumption of normal industrial pursuits, the recovery particularly of Europe, and the discovery there of additional credit foundations on the basis of which her people may arrange to take from farmers and other producers of this nation, a greater part of their surplus production."

On the same day an ineffective effort was made to pass the measure over his veto, but it lacked 21 votes of the necessary two-thirds. Upon his inauguration, President Harding called an extra session of Congress and the emergency tariff was passed. It substantially increased the duties on farm products. The increases were maintained in the Fordney-McCumber tariff enacted the following year. The farmers were told that an era of better prices would result from higher tariff rates. The bitter experience of the wheat farmers, who were to be the chief beneficiaries, has proved that President Wilson in his last message was right when he refused to be a party to giving, in the emergency tariff measure, "the promise to the ear" which has been "broken to the hope."

Wilson's tariff barred privilege.

## CHAPTER XV

# THE CURRENCY SYSTEM

THE FEDERAL RESERVE ACT—"BANKS TO BE MADE THE INSTRUMENTS, NOT THE MASTERS OF BUSINESS AND OF INDIVIDUAL ENTERPRISE AND INITIATIVE"—THE "INTERESTS" IN OPPOSITION—WOULD NOT SEE MONEY KINGS WHO HAD VAINLY FOUGHT HIM—IMPORTANCE OF THE FEDERAL RESERVE SYSTEM IN THE WAR—RURAL CREDITS—HOW WILSON CONVERTED GLASS

*"The duty of statesmanship is not negative merely. It is constructive also."*
—WILSON

IT would have been impossible to finance the war and loan millions to allies if provision had not been made by a sound currency system, demonstrating its flexibility, before the event. The Secretary of the Treasury, from taxation and bonds, obtained thirty-seven billion dollars to pay the expenses of America's part in the World War and to loan to allied and associated European nations. It was obtained easily. Bankers and people gave enthusiastic co-operation, bought bonds liberally and paid taxes cheerfully. It is, perhaps, the first time in history when raising billions to carry on a war became an inspiration for mobilization and patriotism. This plain statement of how the Federal Reserve System met the unprecedented demands of war without a strain is proof of its wisdom in that emergency as well as in normal times.

Long before he was thought of for the Presidency, when he was teaching his classes in political economy, Professor Wilson made a study of the currency and banking system, and pointed out the need of change. The defects of the old currency system had been seen for a generation, and there had been endless talk of reforming it, but the matter ended in talk. Following the panic of 1907, a committee headed by Senator Nelson W. Aldrich was appointed to study the banking and currency question. Experts were employed, and the commission visited Europe and held many hearings and conducted many inquiries. A program, the chief feature of which was a central bank, was worked out. But ever since Andrew Jackson smashed the central bank of his day, popular sentiment has been hostile to such a system and the Aldrich plan was dropped. The country was to worry along for seven more years, with ever-present danger of panic with all its train of unhappiness, until there should emerge a "head", a leader with the vision to see and the power and the will to do. In shaping the new legislation, the idea was to get away from anything like a central bank. The members of Mr. Wilson's party were particularly hostile to such a bank.

In his inaugural address, President Wilson placed the currency system second among "the things that ought to be altered." Briefly, he gave as the reason for proposing a change, that we had "a banking and currency system based upon the necessity of the Government to sell bonds fifty years ago and perfectly adapted to concentrating cash and restricting credits."

As soon as the first item of "the things to be done," reforming the tariff, had passed the House, President Wilson took up the second item, reforming the currency. On the very evening at the White House that he signed the tariff bill, President Wilson told the little company assembled that "we are about to take the second step."

Answering in advance the suggestion ready to be made that this should wait for the December session, Wilson asked: "For what do we wait? Why should we wait to crown ourselves with consummate honor? Are we so self-denying that we do not wish to complete success?"

On June 23, 1913, President Wilson, on a sweltering day, so hot that members of Congress longed to get away from Washington, read his message, urging early action on currency reform. He said, "Personal comfort, perhaps, in the case of some of us, considerations of personal health even, dictate an early conclusion of the deliberations." But he added: "There are occasions of public duty when those things that touch us privately seem very small," and he declared, "We are in the presence of such an occasion." He told Congress that, following setting business free by removing the trammels of a protective tariff, there "will follow a period of expansion and new enterprise, freshly conceived." He lucidly set forth the legislation needed: "We must have a currency, not rigid as now, but readily, elastically responsive to sound credit, the expanding and contracting credits of every day transactions, the normal ebb and flow of personal and corporate dealings. Our banking laws must mobilize reserves; must not permit the concentration anywhere in a few hands of the monetary resources of the country or their use for speculative purposes in such volume as to hinder or impede or stand in the way of other more legitimate, more fruitful uses. And the control of the system of banking and of issue which our new laws are to set up must be public, not private, must be vested in the Government itself, so that the banks may be the instruments, not the masters, of business and of individual enterprise and initiative." The legislation when enacted was in line with this admirable chart which he gave to those who were to frame it and pilot it through Congress.

President Wilson did not, of course, write the Federal Reserve Act. But Senator Glass said: "The one man more responsible for the Federal Reserve System than any other living man is Woodrow Wilson. It was his infinite patience, it was his clear prescience, it was his unsurpassed courage, it was the passion of Woodrow Wilson to serve humankind that overcame every obstacle, that surmounted every difficulty, and that put the Federal Reserve banking system on the federal statute books of this country." After its preparation, but before final conferences with the leaders in Congress, he submitted it to Mr. Bryan for his suggestions and indorsement. As drawn, the measure would have permitted the banks to issue their notes. Mr. Bryan quoted the declarations of several Democratic platforms to the effect that the issuing of money was a government function and should not be exercised by banks. Wilson and Bryan went into the matter fully. Wilson examined the evidence which Bryan presented. He was convinced that the change suggested by the Secretary of State was wise. It was made, and the bill, as introduced and passed, provided for the loaning of Government notes to the banks instead of the issuing of bank notes. This agreement on the Federal Reserve System by the two leaders of the party insured a practically solid support in Congress.

Looking back upon the benefits of the Federal Reserve System and the universal approval of the policy (criticism has been heard only of its administration, and the people must be careful to see that those who administer it carry out the spirit of the system as stated by Wilson when it was proposed), it might be supposed there was the same unanimity of sentiment when it was under consideration. Far from it. There was no such visible lobby in evidence fighting it as had gathered in Washington when the tariff was in the making. Wilson had driven them out as with a whipcord as polluters of the civic temple. But if the lobby was not so much in evidence, it was none the less present and active.

During the long-drawn-out fight in the Senate, a few of the most influential big bankers of the country arrived in Washington one night. There was no announcement of their arrival. They found quarters at the Army and Navy Club. Senators and others called for conferences. Why were these magnates at the Army and Navy Club? That question interested a young naval officer. He casually mentioned their presence to a member of the Wilson administration holding an unimportant position. The names of all the visitors and the length of their stay were reported to the White House. Soon the big men, accustomed to dictate national financial policies, saw that in Wilson they had measured swords with the victor in the contest—the contest to determine whether the Government or private financiers should rule. Sensing defeat, and hoping to secure some change in the measure, they requested a conference with the President. It was declined. He sent them a studiously polite and frigid reply that he knew of their futile efforts to defeat the measure, that he had the fight won, and did not care to discuss the measure with them. It was in rather more crisp language. Perhaps the words were curt. They meant: "You tried to lick me. I have licked you to a frazzle and will accept nothing but complete victory."

The favorite weapon in legislative antagonism to a measure is to "kill it with kindness"—that is, to propose some unobjectionable amendments along with a battalion of amendments that are barbed with destruction. That was the plan of opposition determined upon by the foes of currency reform. Some excellent amendments, afterwards incorporated in the measure, were offered by Senators seeking sincerely to perfect the bill. But in some great banking houses, where a Reserve system, with twelve Federal Reserve headquarters in all parts of the country to decentralize financial operations, was not received with favor, men were busy writing amendments calculated to cut the heart out of the Wilson plan. They were fired down to Washington. Some of them found their way into the hands of Senators and were offered on the floor.

Ex-Senator Aldrich, whose measure had been turned down by a previous Congress, came to Washington to oppose it. Appearing before the Senate Committee, he declared the Glass-Owen measure was "an important step toward changing the government from a democracy to an autocracy." Senators who had defeated the Aldrich plan had declared they opposed it because it would give to Wall Street dominance of the financial life of the nation—an autocracy of unregulated private wealth controlling the currency and banking of the country. If they were in any sense right, and if Aldrich had any right in his contention, the difference was this: The Aldrich measure practically created an autocracy of finance by bankers not governed by law, whereas the Glass-Owen measure placed the entire control of the currency of the nation in the hands of officials selected and paid by the Government. If it should become "autocratic", the people's representatives can regulate and change.

Heads of strong banking institutions voiced opposition. For example, Frank A. Vanderlip, of the National City Bank of New York, speaking before the American Bankers' Association, October 30, said: "It starts the country on an issue of fiat currency. There is no case in our history when a nation has started an issue of fiat money but the result has been a complete breakdown of the financial system of the country." That expressed the attitude of most of the heads of the big banking institutions and that point of view was voiced by Senators in long continued debate.

Experience proves they were wrong and Wilson was right. Vanderlip, on the last day of the Victory Loan, taking him by the hand, said to Carter Glass, then Secretary of the Treasury: "Glass, I want to say to you, that but for the Federal Reserve System we would never today be consummating a Victory Loan."

Wilson's guiding and determining hand was seen from the writing to the passage of the measure. Senator Carter Glass, of Virginia, Chairman of the House Committee on Banking and Currency, gives an illuminating statement of Wilson's superior wisdom. Glass originally believed the banks of the country should have minority representation on the central board at Washington which supervises the entire system. "I thought," he said, "that inasmuch as the banks owned the system, the government not being required to put up one dollar of government funds, the stock-holding banks should have the right to name minority representation on this central board."

Glass thus describes Wilson's contrary point of view and the result of a conference in the White House:

"But the President of the United States did not think so. I regarded his decision in that respect for a while as politically inexpedient and fundamentally wrong. I thought it was politically inexpedient because I conceived the notion that it would be impossible to get the legislation through if we did not let the banks have representation upon this central board. It was hard enough to get it through anyhow; it was the most terrific fight that ever was had. We got it through in the face of the opposition of nearly every bank in the United States.

"The President did not agree with me. I did not sleep any that night, and before I dressed the next morning I wrote him a letter telling him exactly what I thought about it. I don't reckon he ever got such a letter before in his life. His reply was that he was 'not at all disturbed about the political inexpediency of the proposition'; he did not propose to apply politics to the problem at all. But if I could convince him that it was 'fundamentally wrong,' then he would change his mind. And I tried to convince him.

"About two days afterwards I arranged for an interview with him with seven of the greatest bankers of the United States, and headed the procession to the White House to convince Woodrow Wilson that he was wrong about this thing. They stated their case with great fervor, force and persuasiveness. I said nothing, because I had written all I had to say on the subject. When we were through, Mr. Wilson quietly turned in his chair and said, 'Gentlemen, I challenge any one of you to point to a government board, in this country or anywhere in any other civilized country, upon which private interests are permitted to have representation.'

"In other words the Federal Reserve Board is an

altruistic body representing all the people of the United States, put there for the purpose of supervising this great banking system and seeing that no section and no class is discriminated against in its administration. Its members are not permitted to have any banking affiliation or connection at all. They are not permitted to own bank stock of any description. There is no single element of acquisitiveness in the whole formation of that board or in its operation. The Board is there to represent the people of the United States; and you might as well talk about giving the railroads of this country the right of minority representation on the Interstate Commerce Commission, appointed to supervise the railroads, as to talk about giving the banks minority representation on the Federal Reserve Board—and I didn't have sense enough at first to see it."

The fact that, after the measure carrying all the essential provisions Wilson insisted upon was enacted, leading financiers in the country co-operated to make it the great success it has been demonstrated, is proof of the best American spirit.

The long-drawn-out fight consumed three whole months. The measure reached the Senate on September 18. It was not until December 23, at 6 o'clock, that the President signed the epoch-making measure. "It is a Christmas present for the American people," its supporters declared as the chief executive attached his name to the act. During all the hot days of summer and the long contest that ran through the autumn and into the winter, President Wilson never yielded in his determination to secure legislation that would put an end to the concentration of reserves, a policy which had been found to operate to the advantage of the speculative interests at the expense of the farming and commercial interests.

For a long time there had been demand for better credit facilities for farmers. Under Wilson's leadership the Congress met this need by enactment of the Federal Farm Loan Act. Under it the farmer could for the first time negotiate loans on a long-term basis. By the terms of the act twelve Federal land banks were created, loans to be made to farmers for productive purposes only, through national farm-loan associations. Provision was also made for private land banks under government supervision. The new rural credits system is directed by a Federal Farm Loan Board on which President Wilson appointed capable officials. It has been calculated that if fully availed of, the rural credits legislation would save the farmers of the country sixty-six million dollars a year.

Credit was set free.

## Chapter XVI

# THE WILSON POLICY IN MEXICO

"IF I AM STRONG, I AM ASHAMED TO BULLY THE WEAK" —TAFT HAD "NO SYMPATHY WITH EXPLOITATION" —WILSON REFUSED TO APPROVE ELECTION BY ASSASSINATION—NO RECOGNITION FOR HUERTA—VERA CRUZ LANDING FOLLOWED BY HUERTA'S FLIGHT —POLICY OF "WATCHFUL WAITING" BORE FRUIT IN BETTER SITUATION IN MEXICO

*"We are glad to call ourselves the friend of Mexico."*—Wilson

"THERE is one thing I have got a great enthusiasm about, I might say a reckless enthusiasm, and that is human liberty. I want to say a word about our attitude toward Mexico. I hold it as a fundamental principle that every people has the right to determine its own form of government; and until this recent revolution in Mexico, until the end of the Diaz reign, eighty per cent of the people of Mexico never had a 'look in' in determining who should be their governors or what their government should be. Now, I am for the eighty per cent. It is none of my business, and it is none of your business, how long they take in determining it. It is none of my business, and it is none of your business, how they go about their business. The country is theirs. The liberty, if they can get it, and God speed them in getting it, is theirs. And so far as my influence goes while I am President nobody shall interfere with them."

This was the defiance Mr. Wilson hurled at the

critics of his Mexican policy in his celebrated Jackson Day speech at Indianapolis, January 8, 1915. He went on to say: "I am proud to belong to a strong nation that says: 'This country which we could crush shall have just as much freedom in her own affairs as we have.' If I am strong, I am ashamed to bully the weak. In proportion to my strength is my pride in withholding that strength from the oppression of another people." He took this shot at his critics: "When some great dailies thunder at watchful waiting, my confidence is not shaken for a moment. I know the temper and principles of the American people."

Mr. Wilson inherited the Mexican problem. When he came into office he found that his predecessor had sent war ships to Mexican waters where they remained. The revolution in Mexico that ended the long sway of Diaz had given hope that Francisco Madero, elected president October 2, 1911, would be able to organize a democratic government for the weal of the Mexican people. The usurpation of Gen. Victoriano Huerta and the proclamation on February 18, 1913, by the troops under his control that he had been made Provisional President, was followed next day by a military-controlled election by the Mexican Congress. Four days thereafter, Madero and Suarez, deposed president and vice-president, were assassinated—shot dead "while attempting to escape," as the assassins caused it to be stated. These events occurring upon the eve of the expiration of his term of office, President Taft deemed it just to the incoming administration to leave it a free hand. In a statement made February 26, a few days after Huerta had caused the assassination of Madero, President Taft said: "We must avoid in every way that which is called intervention, and use all patience possible, with prayer that some power may arise there to bring about peace throughout that troubled country," and added, "But I have no sympathy —none at all, and the charge of cowardice does not frighten me—with that which prompts us for purposes of exploitation and gain to invade another country and involve ourselves in a war, the extent of which we could not realize, and the sacrifice of thousands of lives and of millions of treasure." That utterance of Taft's was in line with Lincoln's when he declared for the same "forbearance and generous sympathies" toward the Mexicans which Wilson later exercised.

In a message to Congress, August 27, 1913, President Wilson reviewed the circumstances existing in Mexico, and told how he had in May, 1913, sent ex-Governor John Lind, as his personal spokesman and representative, to the City of Mexico, with instructions to endeavor to secure a satisfactory settlement on these terms:

"(a) An immediate cessation of fighting throughout Mexico, a definite armistice solemnly entered into and scrupulously observed;

"(b) Security given for an early and free election in which all will agree to take part;

"(c) The consent of General Huerta to bind himself not to be a candidate for election as President of the Republic at this election; and

"(d) The agreement of all parties to abide by the results of the election and co-operate in the most loyal way in organizing and supporting the new administration."

President Wilson had refused to recognize Huerta though Henry Lane Wilson, the American Ambassador, appointed by Taft, favored recognition. Later he had declared, "So long as the power of recognition rests with me, the Government of the United States will refuse to extend the hand of welcome to any one who obtains power in a sister republic by treachery and violence." The proposals were rejected by "the iron-handed" Huerta, as he was termed. Mr. Wilson said the rejection was probably due to misunderstanding of our position, and so long as it continued, "we can only await the time of their awakening to a realization of the actual facts. We cannot thrust our good offices upon them," though it was "our duty to offer our active assistance." He declared that "impatience on our part would be childish." He believed "we should earnestly urge all Americans to leave Mexico at once, and should assist them to get away in every way possible—not because we would mean to slacken in the least our efforts to safeguard their lives and interests, but because it is imperative that they should take no unnecessary risks when it is physically possible for them to leave the country."

As to Americans remaining in Mexico, "we shall vigilantly watch their fortunes" and "shall hold those responsible for their sufferings and losses to a definite reckoning." He said he would "see that neither side to the struggle now going on receives any assistance" by "forbidding the exportation of arms or munitions of war of any kind from the United States." He concluded his message with these words: "The steady pressure of moral force will before many days break the barrier of pride and prejudice down, and we shall triumph as Mexico's friends sooner than we could triumph as her enemies—and how much more handsomely, with how much higher and finer satisfaction of conscience and honor!"

In his message to Congress, December 2, 1913, he declared "There can be no certain prospect of peace in America until General Huerta has surrendered his usurped power." Huerta had "declared himself dictator." A popular election had been set in Mexico for October 23, to elect a Constitutional President. On October 10 Huerta had sent a strong force of soldiers to the halls of Congress in Mexico City and arrested 110 members of the lesser chamber, making himself supreme and rendering the election farcical. "Every day," said Wilson, "Huerta's power and prestige are crumbling and the collapse is not far away." He followed that review by saying, "We shall not, I believe, be obliged to change our policy of watchful waiting." His critics seized upon these last words to seek to destroy his policy by ridicule but that policy continued without change. Early in 1914, after a number of conferences with John Lind, President Wilson was more than ever convinced that the force opposing Huerta represented the popular will in Mexico, and he made known to the Senate Committee on Foreign Relations that he intended to raise the embargo on the shipment of arms into Mexico. March 14, 1912, President Taft had issued an order forbidding all export of arms except to the government of Madero. President Wilson, on assuming office, had issued an order for a complete embargo. He had made up his mind, after that careful and searching study which marked all his decisions, that the time had come to deliver a stroke that would hasten the coming of better times in Mexico. He lifted the embargo. His statement accompanying the order is interesting as showing how the President's sympathy was always enlisted when he saw what he regarded as a real movement toward a government based on "consent of the governed." "There is now no constitutional government in Mexico," he said in this statement, "and the existence of this order (the one forbidding the shipment of arms) hinders and delays the very thing that the government of the United States is now insisting upon; namely, that Mexico shall be left free to settle her own affairs and as soon as possible put them on a constitutional footing."

On April 9, Paymaster Copp of the U. S. S. *Dolphin* landed at the Iturbide bridge at Tampico with a whaleboat and crew to get supplies for his ship. While engaged in loading the boat the Paymaster was arrested by an officer and squad of men of General Huerta's army. Neither the Paymaster nor any of the crew was armed. Two of the men were in the boat when the arrest was made, and were obliged to leave it and submit to being taken into custody, notwithstanding the boat carried, both at her bow and her stern, the flag of the United States. The officer who made the arrest was proceeding up the street of the town with his prisoners when met by an officer of higher authority; he was ordered to return to the landing and await orders. Within an hour and a half from the time of arrest, orders were received by the commander of the Huertista forces at Tampico for the release of the Paymaster and his men. The release was followed by apologies from the commander and also by an expression of regret by General Huerta himself. General Huerta urged that martial law obtained at the time at Tampico, that orders had been issued that no one should be allowed to land at Iturbide bridge, and that our sailors had no right to land there. Our naval commanders at the port had not been notified of any such prohibition, and, even if they had, the only just and free course open to the local authorities would have been to request the Paymaster and his crew to withdraw and lodge a protest with the commanding officer of the fleet. Admiral Mayo regarded the arrest as so serious an affront that he was not satisfied with the apologies offered, and demanded that the flag of the United States be saluted with special ceremony by the military commander of the port.

After thus recounting the situation, President Wilson, in a special message to a joint session of Congress, April 20, said, "The incident cannot be regarded as a trivial one, especially as the ten men arrested were taken from the boat itself—that is to say from the territory of the United States; but if it had stood by itself, it might have been attributed to the ignorance or arrogance of a single officer," and he went on to say that "Unfortunately, it was not an isolated case" and he proceeded to relate a series of incidents showing that "the Government of the United States was being singled out, and could be singled out with impunity, for slights and affronts in retaliation for its refusal to recognize the pretensions of General Huerta to be regarded as the Constitutional President of the Republic of Mexico." He pointed out that "such offenses might grow from bad to worse until something happened of so gross and intolerable a sort as to lead directly and inevitably to armed conflict." The President said he had felt it his duty to "sustain Admiral Mayo in the whole of his demand and to insist that the flag of the United States should be saluted in such a way as to indicate a new spirit and attitude on the part of the Huertistas." The President said, Huerta having refused, he had come to Congress "for approval and support in the course I now propose to pursue." He asked and received (April 22) approval of his request "to use the armed forces of the United States in such ways and to such extent as may be necessary" to enforce the demands. He said "there can be no thought of aggression," and he reiterated that "the people of Mexico are entitled to settle their own domestic affairs in their own way, and we sincerely desire to respect their right," and he added his belief that "the present situation need have none of the grave complications of interference if we deal with it promptly, firmly, and wisely." The Congress having approved the policy of force when necessary, President Wilson was therefore authorized to prevent Huerta's successful defiance. The next attempt of the dictator to strengthen his power, and to be in position to defy America, was seen in his importation of ammunition from Europe.

Two hours after midnight, April 21, 1914, the news came to Washington that the *Ypiranga*, carrying munitions for Huerta, had sailed from Havana for Vera Cruz. When this message was communicated to Secretaries Bryan and Daniels, the former called the President up on the telephone, read him the message and recommended that the Navy be directed to prevent the landing. "What do you think, Daniels?" asked the President, for the Secretary of the Navy was on the other end of the phone. "The munitions should not be permitted to fall into Huerta's hands," was the answer. "I can wire Admiral Fletcher to prevent it and take the custom house. I think that should be done." Mr. Bryan had urged the danger of letting such supplies reach Huerta. The President hesitated, but after further exchange of views with the Secretary of State, gave the order for the Navy to land. The thing that determined the action, as well as the recommendation of both Secretaries, was the feeling that if the ammunition was landed it would strengthen the usurping president and increase the loss of life in Mexico, and that the guns might later be turned upon American youths. "There is no alternative but to land," said the President. The guns in 1333 boxes had been shipped from Hamburg and the cargo transferred at Havana to the *Ypiranga*.

This message was sent immediately after the telephone conference:

"Washington, D. C., April 21.

"Fletcher, Vera Cruz, Mexico:

"Seize custom house. Do not permit war supplies to be delivered to Huerta government or to any other party.

"Daniels."

The message went swiftly. Admiral Fletcher landed at Vera Cruz in the presence of sniping. Eighteen Americans were killed. The loss of that important port was a severe blow to Huerta. There was severe criticism of the taking of Vera Cruz and it was incorrectly broadcasted that it had been done "to compel a salute of the flag." The armed forces, after the first sniping, had little trouble. They treated the people well, interested themselves in sanitation, and as soon as the Mexicans understood there was no thought of occupation, friendly relations prevailed. A short time after Huerta's flight, and the orderly election of a President, the American forces withdrew. The incident, as regrettable as it was necessary, showed the Mexican people that the President was resolved that Mexicans should control their own country and he had no selfish thought in the policy to which he was committed. The purpose of the landing was accomplished in the weakening and undoing of Huerta's reign of terror.

The success of Wilson's policy of "watchful waiting," with force where imperatively demanded, in the long contest with the Mexican dictator, was recognized when on July 15,1914, shortly after the Vera Cruz occupation, Huerta quit his office and fled the country. Prior to his flight in disgrace and defeat, there came into existence a mediating agency that was known as the ABC Conference, the Ambassadors from Argentine, Brazil, and Chile undertaking to bring Mexico and the United States into accord. All along in his dealings with the Mexican situation Mr. Wilson kept in mind his policy announced in an address in Mobile, Alabama, October 27, 1913, with reference to "our neighbors, the Latin-American States," which was summed up in "We must prove ourselves their friends and champions upon terms of perfect equality," emphasizing the statement by the assertion: "You cannot be friends upon any other terms than upon the terms of equality. You cannot be friends at all except upon the terms of honor. We must show ourselves friends by comprehending their interest whether it squares with our interest or not." Nothing pleased Mr. Wilson so much, therefore, as to welcome the participation of the representatives from great Latin-American nations in securing the best relations with Mexico. He named Justice Joseph R. Lamar and Frederick W. Lehmann to represent the United States in the conference that consumed the summer of 1914. In accepting the offer of the ABC powers, Mr. Wilson said: "This Government will be glad to take up with you for discussion in the frankest and most conciliatory spirit any proposals that may be authoritatively formulated, and hopes that they will be feasible and prophetic of a new day of mutual co-operation and confidence in America." The decamping of Huerta simplified the task of the ABC commissioners. It was their opinion that Carranza should be recognized, and President Wilson's recognition in pursuance of their view was hailed as the first fruits of the closer co-operation which Mr. Wilson had proposed in his Mobile address—it was a precedent having good promise. The independent press recognized its significance. "It is worth a dozen Pan-American Conferences," said the Springfield *Republican*. "For an act like this crystallizes fine words and eloquent periods into a landmark of Pan-American diplomacy. It establishes a precedent; possibly opens a new era." This was complete answer to the jeremiads charging that Wilson's course was a blow to national prestige.

Carranza was an improvement on Huerta but left much to be desired as a chief magistrate. He was suspicious and opinionated and some of President Wilson's most anxious moments over Mexico came while Carranza was in authority. These were caused in part by the raiding activities of Francisco Villa, who fought Huerta along with Carranza but turned on the latter when he became the Mexican executive. Conditions on the border became so bad that tremendous pressure was brought on Wilson to intervene. Matters reached the crisis stage when Villa raided Columbus, New Mexico, and killed a number of American soldiers while they were asleep. But even then President Wilson would go no further than to send troops into Mexico with instructions, in the common vernacular, to "get Villa." His critics were most severe. He heard their arguments patiently, but budged not an inch from his position. He was thinking about the tragedy of war. "The thing that daunts me and holds me back," he is quoted as saying, "is the aftermath of war, with all its tears and tragedies. I came from the South and I know what war is, for I have seen its wreckage and terrible ruin. It is easy for me, as President, to declare for war. I do not have to fight, and neither do the gentlemen on the Hill who now clamor for it. It is some poor farmer's boy, or the son of some poor widow away off in some modest community, or perhaps the scion of a great family, who will have to do the fighting and the dying. . . . I know they will call me a coward and a quitter, but that will not disturb me. Time, the great solvent, will, I am sure, vindicate this policy of humanity and forbearance. Men forget what is back of this struggle in Mexico. It is the age-long struggle of a people to come into their own, and while we look upon the incidents in the foreground, let us not forget the tragic reality in the background which towers above this whole sad picture."

In a review of his first administration made in the campaign in 1916, Mr. Wilson gave this additional striking defense of his position: "The people of Mexico are striving for the rights that are fundamental to life and happiness—fifteen million oppressed men, overburdened women, and pitiful children in virtual bondage in their own home of fertile lands and inexhaustible treasure! Some of the leaders of the revolution may often have been mistaken and violent and selfish, but the revolution itself was inevitable and is right. The unspeakable Huerta betrayed the very comrades he served, traitorously overthrew the government of which he was a trusted part, impudently spoke for the very forces that had driven his people to the rebellion with which he had pretended to sympathize. The men who overcame him and drove him out represent at least the fierce passion of reconstruction which lies at the very heart of liberty; and so long as they represent, however imperfectly, such a struggle for deliverance, I am ready to serve their ends when I can. So long as the power of recognition rests with me the government of the United States will refuse to extend the hand of welcome to any one who obtains power in a sister republic by treachery and violence. No permanency can be given the affairs of any republic by a title based upon intrigue and assassination. I declared that to be the policy of this administration within three weeks after I assumed the presidency. I here again avow it. I am more interested in the fortunes of oppressed men and pitiful women and children than in any property rights whatever. Mistakes I have no doubt made in this perplexing business, but not in purpose or object."

It turned out that the President's Mexican policy was not only humane and Christian but the best policy that could have been adopted in view of developments in the early part of 1917, when it became known that the German government was actively at work to embroil Mexico in a war with this country. German propaganda undoubtedly accounted for a part of the pressure on Mr. Wilson to intervene in Mexico. With a war on Mexico on hand of course the United States would have been handicapped in the effort it was to make to aid the Allies in putting down the German menace in Europe. The Zimmermann note (dated Berlin, January 19, 1917) proposed an alliance with Mexico "to make war together and together make peace" on the basis "We shall give general financial support and it is understood Mexico is to reconquer the lost territory in New Mexico, Texas and Arizona."

After his return from Europe, President Wilson, who had been severely criticized because he would not send troops into Mexico in 1913–14 upon the appeal of investors and others, withheld recognition from Obregon in the absence of assurance that the honestly acquired rights of Americans would be protected in Mexico. The Mexicans later giving the guarantees demanded, Obregon was recognized by the new administration. President Coolidge issued orders late in 1923 permitting arms to go to Mexico to the Obregon Government, but not permitting insurgents to transport arms from this country when there was an insurgent force seeking to overthrow Obregon. Mexico's pathway to prosperity and quiet still has obstacles. But its prospects are immeasurably better because of the policy pursued by Woodrow Wilson. His attitude as to Mexico was thus stated by him at the service in honor of the dead at Vera Cruz: "We have gone down to Mexico to serve mankind if we can find the way. We do not want to fight the Mexicans. We want to serve the Mexicans if we can, because we know how we would like to be free, and how we would like to be served if there were friends standing by in such case ready to serve us. A war of aggression is not a war in which it is a proud thing to die, but a war of service is a thing in which it is a proud thing to die."

"I am willing," said Wilson, "no matter what my personal fortunes may be, to play for the verdict of mankind."

The verdict on his Mexican policy, even by many who doubted and dissented and criticized, in the calm light of history is "well done."

He was vindicated.

## Chapter XVII

# ISLAND TERRITORIES

DEWEY'S THEORY OF CAPACITY OF FILIPINOS FOR SELF-GOVERNMENT PUT IN PRACTICE—WHY VIRGIN ISLANDS WERE ACQUIRED—PORTO RICO AND HAWAII HELPED—HAITI AND SAN DOMINGO SAVED FROM EUROPEAN CONTROL—DOLLAR DIPLOMACY ENDED—CLOSER RELATIONS WITH LATIN AMERICA

*"Here we are trustees."*—Wilson

ONE of the first acts of keeping faith, after President Wilson had safely launched the tariff and currency reform measures, was to take steps to give the Filipinos what the Americans had solemnly promised that people. Admiral Dewey, who combined statesmanship with naval greatness, was no party to the war that followed in the Philippines. He had, as a true disciple of his naval hero, sailed into Manila Bay, acting in the spirit of Farragut's "damn the torpedoes, go ahead." When war with Spain began, few people foresaw that Manila Bay would bring glory to a naval hero. The naval commanders were eager for a command near the waters of Cuba. Dewey alone of the officers of rank applied for Asiatic duty. He was regarded as "out of the war" as he sailed away. On the morning of May 2, 1898, the world woke up to find Dewey the one hero of the Spanish-American War. He was more than that: he performed no act in the Philippines while in direction there, that committed his country to any course of action. Without any commitment he had dealings with Aguinaldo and other leaders. He reported that the Filipinos were "far superior in intelligence to the Cubans and more capable of self-government." Instead of following Dewey's lead, the administration at Washington proceeded to buy the islands from Spain and to send troops to coerce the people to accept American rule. When the Filipinos objected to being transferred, they were shot down. Without adopting either the Jeffersonian principle of "consent of the governed" or Wilson's "self-determination," this country asserted title to the islands and to the sovereignty of the people by purchase from Spain. Many brave American soldiers gave their lives in the conquest of the islands. In vain did Senator Hoar invoke the fundamentals of American ideals. In vain did the cry of the Filipinos resound in the hearing of all who had ears, pleading for the right to govern themselves. The policy of "benevolent assimilation" at the point of the bayonet went forward, though good President McKinley at heart wished to help those peoples.

Under the Governorship of Mr. Taft, many ameliorating influences contributed to friendship. Schools were organized, roads built, and internal improvements undertaken. Mr. Taft, speaking of the McKinley policy of "benevolent assimilation," asserted that it "must logically reduce and finally end the sovereignty of the United States." Later he declared that "when the Filipino people, as a whole, show themselves reasonably fit to conduct a popular self-government, maintaining law and order and offering equal protection of the laws and civil rights to rich and poor, and desire complete independence, they shall be given it." But up to 1913, while Mr. Taft gave kindly and paternal regard to the Filipinos, they had been given little chance to show whether, as Dewey had said, they were "more capable of self-government than the Cubans," whose right to independence Congress declared April 19, 1898, their independent government following the war.

That was the situation in the Philippines when the Democratic Convention nominated Mr. Wilson for the Presidency. That body made this declaration:

"We affirm the position thrice announced by the Democratic National Convention assembled against a policy of imperialism and colonial exploitation in the Philippines or elsewhere. We condemn the experiment in imperialism as an inexcusable blunder which has involved us in enormous expense, brought us weakness instead of strength, and laid our nation open to the charge of abandonment of the fundamental doctrine of self-government.

"We favor an immediate declaration of the nation's purpose to recognize the independence of the Philippine Islands as soon as a stable government can be established, such independence to be guaranteed by us until the neutralization of the Islands can be secured by treaty with other powers. In recognizing this independence of the Philippines, our government should retain such land as may be necessary for coaling stations and naval bases."

In his address to Congress, December 2, 1913, Wilson said: "We must hold steadily in view their ultimate independence, and we must move toward the time of that independence as steadily as the way can be cleared and the foundations thoughtfully and permanently laid."

President Wilson's practical mind took practical direction. Legislation was enacted giving to the Filipinos a larger measure of freedom than they had been enjoying.

Mr. Wilson coupled with announcement of the passage of the act with the definite assurance that this step had been taken "with a view to the ultimate independence of the island and as preparation for that independence." He declared: "By their counsel and experience, rather than by our own, we shall learn how best to serve them and how soon it will be possible to withdraw our supervision." The Jones Law, passed in response to the President's recommendation, in its preamble, declared that "it is, as it has always been, the purpose of the people of the United States, to withdraw their sovereignty over the Philippine Islands and to recognize their independence as soon as a stable government can be established therein." For the first time the Filipinos had cause to rejoice at the policy of the American government, and for the first time the principle of self-determination had a chance in those islands. Under the governorship of Mr. Wilson's appointee, Francis Burton Harrison, the provisions of the Jones Act were carried out in friendly spirit and with the best results. The Governor gave it as his opinion that "by temperament, by experience, by financial ability, in every way, the ten million Filipinos are entitled to be free from every government except of their own choice. They are intelligent enough to decide for themselves."

The Danish Islands of the West Indies came under the American flag during the Wilson administration. The paramount advantage to be gained by the United States from its acquisition of these islands was the large measure of safety they confer upon the Panama Canal. The strategic wisdom of gaining control of the islands lay not so much in the need of the United States of a naval base located in one of the harbors. It was the danger to the safety and amicable relations of the United

States which would result from the acquirement of the islands by some other power.

Toward Porto Rico and Hawaii and all territories separated from the continent, Wilson's attitude was expressed when he said, "We are trustees." They "are ours, indeed, but not ours to do what we please with." His whole attitude as to them and the Philippines was thus stated: "Such territories, once regarded as mere possessions, are no longer to be selfishly exploited; they are part of the domain of public conscience and of serviceable and enlightened statesmanship. We must administer them for the people who live in them and with the same sense of responsibility to them as toward our own people in domestic affairs."

"Dollar Diplomacy" as practiced on this continent, which had been assailed in 1912, found no support from President Wilson. Consular officers, indeed, were alert and were encouraged to advance America's good offices to promote trade in Latin-America, but no diplomacy directed to secure purely commercial advantages to favored Americans was even winked at. In the presence of the diplomats from Latin-American countries, President Wilson, in his famous Mobile speech October 27, 1913, opened the way for the better understanding with those neighbor nations. He was speaking at the time of the opening of the Panama Canal, and predicted an "emancipation" of those states from "subordination to foreign enterprise." He pointed out that they had "harder bargains driven with them in the matter of loans than any other peoples in the world," and he declared, "we ought to be the first to take part in assisting in that emancipation."

The Pan-American Conference and the tender and

acceptance of the mediation of Argentina, Brazil, and Chile in the Mexican controversy were but two of the outstanding practical evidences of the growth of lasting understanding and friendship with Latin-American nations, which in the World War blessed mankind.

The spirit of the Monroe Doctrine that no European country may add territory on this continent caused the President in 1914 to direct the Navy Department to bring about tranquillity in the neighbor island of Haiti and San Domingo. It was necessary for this government to take action in those lands to prevent European countries landing to prevent what they regarded as jeopardy of their interests by repeated revolutions. As to Haiti the aim of the United States in connection with the landing of Marines by the United States and the seizure of customs houses and their administration by American officials was well set forth in a statement issued by Secretary Lansing August 25, 1915, in which he said: "We have only one purpose—that is, to help the Haitian people and prevent them from being exploited by irresponsible revolutionists. . . . The United States Government has no purpose of aggression and is entirely disinterested in promoting this protectorate." Similar purposes animated the Government in its establishment of a temporary protectorate in San Domingo.

No selfish aggression.

**AT WORK IN THE WHITE HOUSE** *© U. & U.*

President Wilson wrote at this desk those great State Papers whose eloquence thrilled the whole world

*Photo. International Newsreel*

**ALUMNI DAY AT PRINCETON**

Woodrow Wilson marching at the head of the class of '79 in the annual parade of classes at Princeton

## CHAPTER XVIII

# REDEEMING THE PLEDGES

LEGISLATION FULFILLING PROMISES—REPEAL OF THE PANAMA CANAL TOLLS AN EARLY TEST OF POWER—CLASH BETWEEN RAILROADS AND THE BROTHERHOODS—ANTITRUST LEGISLATION—"CRIME IS PERSONAL"—"THE MOST ADEQUATE NAVY IN THE WORLD"

*"It is a record of extraordinary length and variety, rich in elements of many kinds, but consistent in principle throughout."*—WILSON

THE story of 1913–1921 is a story of redeemed pledges. Woodrow Wilson was chary with promises. His word, once given, was better than a bond.

Perhaps the best test of Wilson's leadership in obtaining legislation was in securing the repeal of the law giving American ships freedom from Panama Canal tolls. The act exempting vessels engaged in the coastwise trade of the United States had passed Congress August 24, 1912. It had been received with apparent general approval as encouragement to the American Merchant Marine and had passed Congress in the face of contention that it violated the Hay-Pauncefote Treaty. Its repeal was stubbornly fought. In his shortest message to Congress, Mr. Wilson urged repeal "with the utmost earnestness of which I am capable," and closed by saying: "I ask this of you in support of the foreign policy of the administration. I shall not know how to deal with other matters of greater delicacy and nearer consequence if you do not grant it to me in ungrudging measure." He did not enter into legal and technical questions that had been raised or into the effect upon American shipping. "Whatever may be our own differences of opinion concerning this much debated measure," he said, "its meaning is not debated outside the United States. Everywhere else the language of the treaty is given but one interpretation, and that interpretation precludes the exemption I am asking you to repeal."

His appeal was to "deserve our reputation for generosity and for the redemption of every obligation without quibble or hesitation." It was not, however, "granted" without bitter opposition and the charge that it was "a surrender to Britain" and the "encouragement of British shipping at the expense of America's merchant marine." How often opponents charged Wilson with favoring the British and how often he was assailed for being so hard upon them! Conscious that he was neither "pro" nor "anti" but wholly for what he regarded the right thing, no matter what nation was helped or injured, he heard such charges unmoved.

In the Panama tolls contest a favorite argument by the strong opponents to repeal was: "The Panama Canal was built upon territory secured by Americans; it was built by American money and American ships are entitled to an advantage." The answer was that in the Hay-Pauncefote Treaty we had pledged there should be no discrimination. President Wilson urged that our word was plighted and, therefore, there could be no debate as to our keeping faith. "We consented to the treaty," he said. "Its language we accepted, if we did not originate it; and we are too big, too powerful, too self-respecting a nation to interpret with a too strained or refined reading the words of our own promises just because we have power enough to give us leave to read them as we please. The large thing to do is the only thing we can afford to do—a voluntary withdrawal from a position everywhere questioned and misunderstood."

The repeal carried in the House by a vote of 247 to 162, and in the Senate by a vote of 50 to 35.

From the day of his inauguration President Wilson regarded himself as industrial as well as political leader of the nation. If there were threatening clouds he did not wait for the storm to break. He moved to avert disturbance to business and the distress from unemployment. The severest challenge to this wise leadership came in August, 1916, in the midst of his campaign for re-election, when a clash between railroad brotherhoods and the roads over hours and wages became acute. He was counselled that the poker was hot at both ends and that he should let the railroad companies and their employees "fight it out." No timid course or shifting of responsibility appealed to him. Four hundred thousand trainmen had demanded an eight-hour day with no reduction in the pay they were receiving for the ten-hour day. Conferences with the railroad managers and employees failed to result in an agreement. In a referendum, 90 per cent of the trainmen voted to strike. The United States Board of Mediation and Counsel failed in efforts to avert the strike. President Wilson called a conference of the disputants at the White House on August 13. He proposed as a basis of settlement: That the eight-hour day be conceded, that the overtime demand of the trainmen and certain demands of the railroads be postponed awaiting inquiry, and that in the meantime Congress authorize him to appoint a commission to observe and report on the results.

The trainmen accepted this proposition, but it was rejected by the railroad managers. President Wilson then called the railroad presidents to Washington. They declined to adopt his suggestion and made counter-proposals. In the meantime the labor leaders, distrusting any other remedy, issued a strike order to take effect September 4. The President requested the withdrawal of the order, but was informed that the committee of brotherhood chairmen, which had already dispersed, was the only body empowered to withdraw it. After several conferences with leaders in Congress—always "common counsel" in big matters—President Wilson recommended immediate legislative action. He suggested the legal recognition of the eight-hour day, the creation of a commission to study the effects of the change and related legislation. But as the immediate task was to avert the strike, Mr. Adamson, of Georgia, chairman of the House Interstate Commerce Committee, brought in a bill covering only the two points mentioned and providing for the wage to remain in effect until thirty days after the report of the commission of inquiry.

While there was sharp criticism of Wilson's course, the legislation he approved passed the House September 1 by a vote of 239 to 56, showing that most of the members of both parties approved the necessity and wisdom of prompt and effective action. Such Old Guard leaders in the House as ex-Speaker Cannon gave it their support, though Leader Mann opposed it. By the time it had reached the Senate the Republican leaders thought they saw in it a winning campaign issue. Of the Republican Senators only La Follette voted for it. The Republican campaign speakers denounced it in the closing days of the campaign and most Democrats defended it, but not all. There was no unanimity. The country as a whole believed that Wilson had found a way to prevent the prostration of business. They were more influenced by desire for industrial peace than by any hostility to the method employed. What effect did it have on the election? Wilson lost all the big industrial states where it was predicted his action would aid him, but the labor vote in the West undoubtedly swelled his majority in the states that determined the result. He permitted no political considerations, however, to affect his action.

Preparedness legislation before this country entered the war received its stimulus from President Wilson. Writing from Cornish in the summer of 1915, he requested the Secretaries of War and Navy to give study to the methods to strengthen both branches of the service, and have a program ready for his consideration so it could be presented to the coming session of Congress. When Congress assembled in December of that year, he gave chief place in his message to urging the passage of the measures to put the Army and Navy in shape for national defense. In his tour of the West, in the early part of 1916, he declared "The United States should have the most adequate Navy in the world," and the measures adopted by Congress, if they had been carried out, would today give this country primacy in capital ships. Like insistence upon proper coast defense and increase of the army had brought increased appropriations.

"Crime is personal."

That sentence challenged attention more than a decade ago. Woodrow Wilson, college president, was speaking about the wrongs of combinations in restraint of trade. There had been suits or prosecutions brought against corporations charged with violating the anti-trust laws. He was the first man in America to fix attention to the fact that you can never reach the root of the disease until the guilty man, not the corporation, is brought to account. He made it clear that the crime complained of must have been committed by some man. "Get the man," was the substance of his speech, for he went on to say the laws will be violated as long as the individual can hide behind the corporation.

When he came to the Presidency, he felt the need of additional legislation to prevent restraint of trade. He secured the co-operation of Congress in the enactment of the Clayton anti-trust law. For the first time there was secured the legal recognition of the fact that "labor" is not a commodity.

It would convey a wrong impression to let it be inferred that Mr. Wilson would stand for any injustice to business because it was big. On the contrary, he believed all protection should be thrown around large independent enterprises. "It is a mistake," he once said, "to suppose the great captains of industry are engrossed in a vulgar pursuit of wealth." He said: "These men are not fascinated by the glitter of gold. The appetite for power has not got hold of them. They are in line with the exercise of their faculties upon a great scale. They are organizing and overseeing a great part of the life of the world." He would end all monopoly based upon privilege.

Among the outstanding achievements of his first term, in addition to tariff and currency reform, was legislation for the construction of the Alaskan railroad, authorized by act of Congress, March 12, 1914, which was the initial great step taken to make possible the development of that Territory since its purchase by Andrew Johnson, and the Merchant Marine act which passed May 20, 1916.

The Alaskan railroad measure had support from all parties, but the attempt to give the United States a place in the ocean-carrying commerce, after fifty years of stagnation, was fought at every step by the almost solid Republican vote in Congress. Aided by a handful of Democrats, by a filibuster they postponed the passage many months. That delay in construction of ships proved most injurious when the first and insistent demand was for ships. Because this country had few ships, the owners charged "all the traffic would bear" and three hundred million dollars represented the annual ocean freight bill paid to the foreign owners of ships by American commerce. If there had been no filibuster, the United States would have found itself better equipped with ships when war came. In addition to this wise foresight, Wilson secured provision for greater safety of life at sea by an international conference, the Seamen's Act, designed to end high sea slavery; the Ship Registry Act; and the war risk insurance for merchant ships. As a result, in 1916, for the first time in history, the United States became the foremost ship-building country in the world. All this in pursuance to Wilson's declaration after he had secured tariff and currency reform: "We can develop no true or effective American policy without ships of our own—not ships of war, but ships of peace, carrying goods and carrying much more; creating friendships and rendering indispensable services to all interests on this side of the water. They must move constantly back and forth between the Americas." He had declared when he was a candidate for the Presidency in 1912:

"Without a great merchant marine we cannot take our rightful place in the commerce of the world. Our industries have expanded to such a point that they will burst their jackets, if they cannot find a free outlet to the markets of the world; and they cannot find such an outlet unless they be given ships of their own to carry their goods—ships that will go the routes they want them to go—and prefer the interests of America in their sailing orders and their equipment. Our domestic markets no longer suffice. We need foreign markets. That is another force that is going to break the tariff down. The tariff was once a bulwark; now it is a dam. For trade is reciprocal; we cannot sell unless we also buy."

To these outstanding measures of progress must be added the legislation for the improvement and extension and protection of agriculture, the safety of railway employees, the anti-injunction measure, creating the Federal Trade Commission and Tariff Commission, the ratification of the amendment to elect Senators by the people, the act that began the great program of building hard surface roads on a large scale, and other progressive measures to promote the welfare and prosperity of the people. This unprecedented success in reform measures in so brief a period implied hearty co-operation and teamwork by the executive and the legislators.

The legislation necessary for the carrying on of the war, the mobilization of resources, the conservation of food and the regulation of the price of essential products, the taking over and operation of the railroads because private operation had broken down, the large powers of the Overman act, the creation and administration of agencies for all needed purposes—all these reveal the grasp and wisdom of the man at the helm.

*Photo. International Newsreel*

**AN ANTIDOTE FOR DIPLOMATIC WORRIES**

President and Mrs. Wilson, shortly after their marriage, opening the baseball season at the American League Park in Washington. The President is tossing out the first ball to Walter Johnson. Mrs. Wilson is at the left of the picture beside the President

**PRESIDENT WILSON AND HIS WAR ADVISERS** © *U. & U.*

*Standing*, from left to right: Herbert Hoover, Food Commissioner; Edward N. Hurley, Chairman Shipping Board; Vance McCormick, Chairman War Trade Board; Harry A. Garfield, Fuel Commissioner. *Sitting on second row*, left to right: Benedict Crowell, Assistant Secretary of War, representing Secretary Baker in his absence at the war front; William G. McAdoo, Secretary of the Treasury; President Woodrow Wilson; Josephus Daniels, Secretary of the Navy; Bernard M. Baruch, Chairman of the War Industries Board.

The record of victories in Congress is unparalleled. Every measure which President Wilson urged upon the legislative branch was enacted into law until he was stricken on his Western trip in September, 1919. The White House was the centre of initiative and leadership. Mr. Wilson had cordial relations with Congress. He sought and secured co-operation by the only methods he knew of conducting public business—direction, frankness and persuasion. If members of his own party were not disposed to carry out pledges, he was not averse to persuasion. But he respected the rights and powers of Congress as he was tenacious of the rights of the executive. If he had marked success in his recommendations to Congress, it was because what he urged appealed to its judgment and because he consulted freely with chairmen of all committees dealing with legislation he favored.

Woman suffragists found Mr. Wilson their best champion. "A few Presidents like Lincoln, Garfield and Roosevelt expressed their belief in woman suffrage," declares Mrs. Carrie Chapman Catt, President of the American Woman Suffrage Association, "but Mr. Wilson was the only President who, while in power, worked for it." And Mrs. Catt enumerates instances from 1915 to the completion of ratification in 1920 showing Mr. Wilson's unflagging interest in the cause, adding: "His active aid was freely given and was invaluable."

Every promise kept.

## Chapter XIX

# PATRONAGE AND MERIT SYSTEM

**BEGAN BY DECLINING TO SEE ANY APPLICANT FOR OFFICE —ALWAYS ASKED: "IS HE THE BEST MAN FOR THE PLACE?"—FIRM IN SUPPORT OF CIVIL SERVICE REFORM —WOULD HAVE NO COALITION CABINET—CALLED PROMINENT REPUBLICANS TO IMPORTANT SERVICE**

*"If our predecessors have played politics with the diplomatic service, is that any reason why we should do likewise?"*—Wilson

ON March 5, the day after his inauguration, with many "deserving Democrats" in Washington wishing to see the new President and present their claims for appointment to office, Mr. Wilson almost took away their breath by this statement:

> The President regrets that he is obliged to announce that he deems it his duty to decline to see applicants for office in person, except when he himself invites the interview. It is his purpose and desire to devote his attention very earnestly and very constantly to the business of the Government and the large questions of policy affecting the whole nation, and he knows from his experience as Governor of New Jersey—where it fell to him to make innumerable appointments—that the greater part both of his time and of his energy will be spent in personal interviews with candidates unless he sets an invariable rule in the matter. It is his intention to deal with appointments through the heads of the several executive departments.

To that policy Wilson adhered throughout his two terms. Patronage did not interest him. He needed his time for policies. He trusted the members of his Cabinet to make appointments and recommendations. The course he had pursued in the selection of his Cabinet indicated his policy of selecting officials of the United States Government. Perhaps for the first time in the history of the country the Cabinet contained no member from New England, an omission which later cost Mr. Wilson support he might otherwise have received. The great pivotal Middle West was not represented. He paid no heed to the criticism that "the South was over-favored," made by those fond of seeing sectionalism where none exists. McReynolds, Burleson, Daniels and Houston were from the South. McAdoo was born in Georgia, but had long lived in New York. President Wilson was little influenced by place of residence. He would have named all his Cabinet from one state if he had found what he regarded as the fittest and most suitable men in one commonwealth. He had no bias in favor of or against any man because of race, place of residence or creed. "There is neither Jew nor Catholic in the cabinet," was a criticism. He had wished to invite Brandeis, a Jew, but yielded his wishes to Massachusetts opposition. Later he made him Supreme Court Justice, and named such Jews as Baruch, Morgenthau and Elkus to high position. As Private Secretary he chose Joseph Tumulty; Frederic C. Penfield, Ambassador to Austria-Hungary; John Burke, Treasurer of the United States, and assigned hundreds of other Catholics to places of trust. But he never named any one for office, or refrained from naming any one, because he was or was not Protestant, Jew, Catholic, native or foreign-born. He was wholly free from race or religious prejudice. He held that the right to the freedom he claimed for himself must be enjoyed equally by every other American, and that it was impaired if any were either denied or given preference because of their convictions. It did not matter to him where a man lived or what was his religion. The question he made paramount was: "Is he the best man for the place?" It was upon that principle that he acted.

President Wilson's mistakes in appointments to office—and he was not free from them—were mainly due to his absorption in "the large questions of policy." He had no interest in finding "places" for men desirous of public service. In most cases, except as to Ambassadors, Judges, and like positions, he left the selection of appointees to the head of each department. But he was quick to make an exception if there seemed a principle involved. He removed all diplomatic officials, except Ambassadors and Ministers, from appointment otherwise than by certification through the Civil Service Commission. Even as to those, distinguished service led to preferment. He stood firmly for promotion on merit. When he came to the Presidency most places in the diplomatic service were filled by Republicans appointed by previous administrations upon recommendations by Congressmen or politicians. Urged to make enough changes to give Democrats equal representation, he declined: "If our predecessors have played politics with the diplomatic service, is that any reason why we should do likewise? Moreover, unless somebody ends making such service a matter of party reward how will the merit system ever be secured?" This was not popular with many men "on the Hill," who had constituents they wished to see appointed, particularly in the early days of his administration. He believed in the long run that his policy would demonstrate its wisdom. He was not even deterred from it when Ambassadors reported that some of the under officials in the embassies were disloyal and were fond of criticizing Wilson's policies. It is to their discredit that men he retained in positions of trust, particularly abroad, abused his confidence, and were disloyal to the policy of their country.

The most signal proof Wilson gave of his devotion to the merit system and the exclusion of political consideration in making appointments was with reference to naming postmasters. Postmasters had almost always been appointed, since Jackson's day, on the principle "to the victors belong the spoils." There had been, of course, many exceptions and in parts of the country Roosevelt had put into effect the civil service method in selecting postmasters in small places. Wilson introduced the plan of selecting all by civil service examinations. The practice in 1913 was for the Civil Service Commission to send the three highest names to the Postmaster General, who would confer often with the Democratic Congressman for that district and usually recommend for appointment the one the Congressman favored. That method required the appointee to pass an approved examination, but still left the selection to political considerations. Mr. Wilson sent consternation into the ranks of those who believed political service should have controlling weight in naming postmasters when he directed the Postmaster General to send to him the name only of the applicant who had passed the best examination. "But," said Congressmen, "this will in many cases give Republicans postmasterships under a Democratic administration." Wilson's reply was that if the Republican applicant showed most proficiency the merit system required that he be given the appointment.

President Wilson stood like a stone wall against the attempt to force a Coalition Cabinet when war came. This was not because he was unwilling to call Republicans to places of trust. It was because he was convinced that unity in the inner council was as essential as unity on the field. He resented the spirit in Washington behind the Coalition advocacy, as expressed by Senator New, appointed Postmaster General by President Harding after his defeat for re-election to the Senate. "This is the war of no political party. This is the country's war," said New, "and we charge and deplore that the party in power is guilty of practicing petty partisan politics." The selection of Republicans to high station disproved New's calumny. Pershing was given supreme command. If he had any politics, it was believed Republican, but considerations of that kind had no weight with Wilson in his vigorous prosecution of the war. Among the many (Democratic leaders thought too many) Republicans in high place were Herbert Hoover, Charles Schwab, Charles B. Warren, Harry A. Garfield, Frank A. Vanderlip, Benedict Crowell, E. R. Stettinius, Julius Rosenwald, Howard E. Coffin, Edward A. Deeds, to mention only a few of many. In the diplomatic service like recognition was given, and at the Peace Conference on the various important boards many Republicans were chosen.

Grover Cleveland won fame by the utterance "public office is a public trust."

Woodrow Wilson practiced that doctrine and elevated the merit system to a place higher than it had been given by any of his predecessors.

Fitness the test.

## Chapter XX

# WILSON AS A POLITICAL LEADER

**MOST SUCCESSFUL POLITICIAN OF GENERATION—REGARDED HIMSELF AS THE CHOSEN LEADER OF THE PARTY—JACKSON DAY SPEECH—APPEAL FOR DEMOCRATIC CONGRESS—HAD NO MACHINE AND USED NO PATRONAGE—HUMOR IN SPEECHES**

*"My ambition is to add something to the statesmanship of the country, if that something be only thought and not the old achievement of which I used to dream when I hoped that I might enter practical politics."*—Wilson

"WOODROW WILSON is the most successful politician of his generation," was the dictum of a trained journalist of Washington who had known all the political leaders from the seventies. If this journalist is correct, to what is to be attributed his success in politics? He never attended a party convention, and never served on a political committee. His part began and ended with what the average voter would call "high-brow" discussion of government as a science, exposure of governmental errors, fight on unworthy political machines, and life-long zeal for bettering government processes and administration. These are not usually the steps that lead to undisputed leadership of a great political party, the governorship and the Presidency, and a career of triumphs which terminated only when he was stricken with illness.

What is the explanation? It was not due to the creation of a machine, to the activity of political friends, to wide acquaintance, to having anything to give in the way of patronage. Even when Governor and President, he would not employ patronage to advance measures he had deeply at heart.

During his campaign for Governor of New Jersey, a brilliant succession of victories on the platform, Judge Hudspeth said to him: "Dr. Wilson, you need not be surprised that some time during your trip about the state, some exuberant voter will slap you on the back and say, 'Come, Woody, old man, let's have a drink.'" He laughed heartily. "The intimate introduction is all right, but I could draw the line on liquoring up," Wilson said. "You know, I have the reputation of making or having few intimate friends. I suppose it is because of the atmosphere I have passed the greater part of my life in. It is unfortunate for a man to have such a reputation, particularly in politics." Hudspeth subsequently said: "That was not true, so far as there was an implication that he held himself aloof from his fellow-man or was unapproachable. He loved companionship and eagerly coveted the friendship of men whom he admired and had confidence in."

The advertisement of a whiskey, "Wilson—That's All", in days before prohibition sent it into what Mr. Cleveland called "innocuous desuetude," was greatly overworked by presiding officers when Wilson was a candidate for Governor of New Jersey. It became a habit, with a wink and a shrug of the shoulder, for the introducer to say, waving toward the nominee, "Wilson —That's All." On the eve of the election Mr. Wilson was scheduled to address a meeting in Hudson County. The chairman was a German-American citizen. As he walked through the wings to the stage with the President he said to him:

"You know, Mr. Veelson, that vee never say anything in Hudson County now but 'Veelson, that's all.'"

"My!" answered Mr. Wilson, "that has a dissipated sound."

"Only a person who was actually but a little lower than the angels," said a bystander, "could reply so composedly after hearing that ancient wheeze so often."

In an address in Washington, upon the unveiling of the equestrian statue of Phil Sheridan, of New Jersey, Wilson said: "His soldiers always showed fondness by referring to him as 'Phil.' I have always wished I had a name people might shorten without making me 'wood.'"

On one occasion, claiming great things for the Democratic party, Mr. Wilson told a story showing his sense of humor. It was of the condition of a negro who fell sound asleep on a train, his head back, his tongue out. A man near by shook some powdered quinine on his tongue. The negro presently closed his mouth, woke up with a start and called to the conductor in great excitement: "Is dere a doctor on dis train, boss? I done busted my gall."

"I haven't quite busted my gall," remarked Mr. Wilson, "but I haven't the audacity to go too far in claiming any particular virtue for any party."

Upon becoming Governor of New Jersey, Mr. Wilson stated he had been chosen "the leader of the Democratic party in this State." When he became President he made the same statement as to the leadership of the national party. He assumed that leadership as Governor, but found it was questioned seriously when he got to Washington. This was no assertion of personal desire to lead. It was born of a conviction that a party must have a leader. If not the man who is chosen executive, where would he be found? That principle he had expounded long years before the politicians had even heard of the schoolmaster. "The President," he had said, "may be both the leader of his party and the leader of the nation, or he may be one or the other. If he lead the nation, his party can hardly resist him." That was the opinion of Wilson, the student of government. What of it when he became President? In his message to Congress, June 23, 1913, shortly after his inauguration, he asserted for himself what he had long before declared was the function of a President in a government by parties. "I come to you," he said, "as the head of the Government and the responsible head of the party in power."

Many who approved of his exercise of power as national leader in upholding principles, balked when he went so far as to call upon the people of States to defeat Senators who had not supported the policies he had championed. There was resentment in many quarters, when he told the people of Mississippi, for example, as a conspicuous instance, that if they re-elected Senator Vardaman, "I should be obliged to accept their action as a condemnation of my administration." The mass of the people of all parties, seeing that Vardaman had opposed the war and been antagonistic to Wilson's plans, were glad to see the President throw his mighty influence in the scale and retire the Mississippian, even if the exercise of that power in ordinary cases would have been criticized.

In the late spring of 1911, Governor Wilson's friends persuaded him that he ought to accept the many invitations to speak in the West and to make "a swing around the circle" preliminary to his candidacy for the Presidency. He was not pleased with the suggestion. He did not like the idea of being a candidate. He would not solicit support for the great office. Wisconsin Progressives and Texas Democrats and Oregon Forward-Looking men deluged him with invitations. Princeton alumni all over the country added pressure. He accepted an invitation to speak in Pennsylvania, then to Wisconsin and could not resist the appeals to the Pacific slope, traveling 8,000 miles before he got back to New Jersey. The welcome was cheering. The people wanted to hear what "the scholar in politics" would say. They had followed his course in New Jersey and it gave them hope that like reforms and revolutions might be wrought elsewhere. Neither on that trip nor ever after did he "speak down" to the people. He believed too much in them to patronize them and would have lost his respect for himself if he had failed to give the best that was in him to any audience. The high plane upon which he had pitched his campaign for Governor of New Jersey was not changed. His natural fund of humor and his candor and plainness of speech attracted. Moreover, he had the refreshing quality of willingness to admit that he could learn. When he reached Oregon, he was frankly interested in the system of initiative and referendum and recall in operation in that commonwealth. He said afterwards that his visit to Oregon had been a liberal education, to him. "For fifteen years I taught that the initiative and referendum would not work. But they do work," he said.

In New Jersey he had often said: "Back of all reform lies the means of getting it." He was willing to try new ways, all the more ready because in the

Eastern states, as he had put it, "we have been living under the delusion that it is a representative government. That is the *theory*. But the *fact* is that we are not living under a representative government; we are living under a government of party bosses who in secret conferences and for their private ends determine what we shall and shall not have. The first immediate thing that we have got to do is to *restore* representative government." He declared that the people are waiting "to have their politics utterly simplified. They are realizing that our politics are full of secret conferences, that there are private arrangements, and they do not understand it." Then he asked: "Who are the captains? Where are the orders?"

Wilson was a stout partisan when the battle-lines were drawn. Until the issue was made up and the call to battle sounded, there was nothing in him of the hard-and-fast partisan for a cause. He kept his mind "in debate" and was singularly open to reason from any source. Tolerant of difference of opinion, he accorded to men of opposite faith the same sincerity he claimed for himself. He believed men of all parties were equally patriotic and honorable. Mr. Wilson, after his New Jersey campaign, was recognized as an effective political speaker. The two occasions when he revealed himself the party leader most tellingly and in a way to "draw blood," so to speak, were his Jackson Day speech at Indianapolis, January 8, 1915, and his appeal to the voters on October 24, 1918, for a Democratic Congress.

In the first he was in his happiest mood. Like a boy let loose from school, he was speaking in the spirit of the day to members of his own party in a state where politics is a 365-days-a-year profession. He had gone there to cheer the faithful. He spoke without notes and with the utmost freedom, often in a light vein. In a sense it is the best disclosure made of himself as a party leader and speaker, and of his readiness to "poke fun" at the opposition party. He had on his fighting clothes. He began by speaking of the "compelling influences" of Jackson Day. Jackson was a "forthright man," who believed in "fighting in earnest," and he said, "that is the only sort of man worth thinking about." Then he declared: "You will notice that whenever the United States forgets its ardor for mankind, it is necessary that a Democrat be elected President."

"The trouble with the Republican party is that it has not had a new idea for thirty years," he asserted. Then he paused while the Jacksonians applauded, and commented: "I am not speaking as a politician; I am speaking as an historian. I have looked for new ideas in the records and I have not found any proceeding from Republican ranks." That declaration raised a controversy which lasted a year. The Republican speakers and editors disputed the statement. The Democrats replied with a challenge to name the "new ideas." But Wilson did not stop there in his indictment. "The Republican party," he went on, "is still a covert and refuge for those who are afraid, for those who want to consult their grandfathers about everything. They will not trust the youngsters. They are afraid the youngsters may have something up their sleeves."

He told his hearers "the country is guided and its policy is determined by the independent voter." As to his own position he said: "I am not an independent voter, but I am an independent person. I want to say this distinctly: I do not love any party longer than it continues to serve the immediate and pressing needs of America. I have been bred in the Democratic party; I love the Democratic party; but I love America a great deal more than I love the Democratic party, and when the Democratic party thinks that it is an end in itself, then I rise up and dissent." Which party should the independent voter use? He said only one-third of the Republican party is progressive and two-thirds of the Democratic party is progressive. "Therefore the independent voter finds a great deal more company in the Democratic party than in the Republican ranks." He suggested that he would like to see every independent voter become a Democrat. "It is a little cold and lonely out where he is. . . . I want him to come in where it is warm." He called attention to the fact that it had been reported that Republican senators "mean to talk enough" to prevent the passage of the shipping bill. He challenged their right to "stand in the way of the release of American products to the rest of the world!" And he declared with vigor: "The reason I say the Republicans have not had a new idea in thirty years is that they have not known how to do anything except sit on the lid."

Thereafter he entered upon a serious and illuminating discussion of the situation of the Mexican problem and other lesser issues, with a strong plea to help Mexico and not covet her resources.

The other significant utterance in a political campaign was Wilson's appeal to the country in 1918 to elect a Democratic Congress. It was nothing exceptional for Presidents to appeal for support for the party in power in the crucial days of war. Lincoln had urged the people in 1864 not to "swap horses in midstream." Lincoln wrote to General Sherman asking him to arrange for the soldiers in Indiana to vote. In 1898 McKinley pleaded for victory for an administration in "critical times." Roosevelt said, "A refusal to sustain the President this year, will in their eyes (Europeans) be read as a refusal to sustain the efforts of the peace commission." Benjamin Harrison to the same effect had made a like plea, saying, "If the Democrats score a telling victory, Spain will see in it a gleam of hope."

The same reasoning, if sound, called for the election of a Democratic Congress in November, 1918. Mr. Wilson, therefore, in that spirit made an appeal to the voters "in the most critical period our country has ever faced or is likely to face in our time," to elect "a Democratic majority in the United States Senate and House." He prefaced this by saying, "If you have offered me your leadership and wish me to continue to be your unembarrassed spokesman in affairs at home or abroad." He said he had no thought of "suggesting that any party is paramount in matters of patriotism," and he "felt too keenly the sacrifices which have been made in this war by all our citizens, irrespective of party affiliations," to "harbor such an idea." The "difficulties and delicacies of our present task" called for "undivided support under a unified leadership." He went on to say that the Republicans in Congress had "unquestionably been pro-war, but they have been anti-Administration." He added, "Unity of command is as necessary now in civil action as it is upon the field of battle."

The publication of that letter was the signal for the pouring out of the vials of wrath upon the head of Mr. Wilson. Many were made to believe he had reflected upon the patriotism of the Republicans, and their resentment knew no bounds. Democrats believed—or many did—that this resentment cost them the control of Congress. Looking back in the light of history, whatever may be said of the wisdom of Lincoln, McKinley, and Wilson, appealing for a party victory in crucial days of war, the letter of Mr. Wilson contains only one direct appeal: the need of unity of command. It had only one criticism of Republicans in Congress: that they had "sought to take the choice of policy of conduct of the war out of the hands" of the President and "put it under the control of instrumentalities of their own choosing." That was as true as that Republicans had been patriotic in war matters. Let it be conceded the Republicans were wholly sincere in seeking to take control from Wilson, the fact still remains, that unity of command was essential in "crucial days." Wilson was in office for two years more. Nothing could change that fact. If unity was desirable, he ought to have a Congress controlled by men of his party. He asked for that. It was denied him, the Republican leaders declaring that they would co-operate with Wilson in carrying on the war and in reconstruction without party bias. They carried Congress. What happened? From the day they organized Congress, there was a stalemate for two years. In "crucial" years, when there was need for united action after war, nothing was done. Appraising what followed, the verdict of history will be that the prompt adjustment needed after war was prevented by divided counsel. Lincoln was right. McKinley was right. Wilson was right. In days of war and reconstruction it is wisest, no matter whether the President is a Democrat or a Republican, for the

Congress to be controlled by legislators of the same party.

The criticism of Mr. Wilson that had weight was that in the emergency he should have urged the voters to defeat all candidates, Democrats and Republicans, who were not willing to put country above party. If he had done that, say those critics, the result would have been different. Who can say? A short time after the election, speaking to members of the Democratic National Committee, Mr. Wilson said he was not discouraged by the result of the election, and added: "Some of them (defeated Congressmen) got exactly what was coming to them and I haven't any bowels of compassion for them. They did not support the things they pretended to support. And the country knew they didn't."

Party man, yes, but when party associate did not put country above party, he had no comradeship with Woodrow Wilson.

Patriotism above Party!

## CHAPTER XXI

# A BREAKER OF PRECEDENTS

APPEARING IN PERSON TO READ MESSAGES TO CONGRESS—HARDING AND COOLIDGE FOLLOWED WILSON'S PLAN—FIRST PRESIDENT TO GO OVERSEAS—NO SECRET AT CABINET MEETINGS—"A GENTLEMAN AT HIS OWN FIRESIDE."

"*The harness of precedent is sometimes a very sad and harassing trammel.*"—WILSON

IN December, 1912, shortly after Governor Wilson had been elected President, a friend visited him at the executive offices, in Trenton. This gentleman, who afterwards became a member of his Cabinet, had called to secure the influence of the President-elect to adjust differences in Delaware which threatened to defeat the election of a Democratic Senator in that State. A Senate in sympathy was important to the working together to carry out party pledges. Governor Wilson was keen to do anything proper in the matter, but the threatened division was adjusted without the necessity of his intervention.

"Did you ever hear the reading of a President's message at the joint session of Congress?" he asked the visitor, apropos of nothing. His friend had.

"Did anybody pay attention to the reading?" he asked, and his visitor told him that usually the members chatted or read papers while the clerks read the message. Many of them went out, and it was out of the ordinary for anybody to listen to it, the Congressmen preferring to read it for themselves later. That was all, but later when President Wilson stood in Congress to deliver his message in person, the conversation was recalled.

Jefferson had discontinued delivering the messages in person because he thought it savored too much of an "address from the throne." When Wilson announced his intention to return to the practice begun by Washington, old-timers thought it looked too much like possible executive dictation. But after his first appearance, when not only Congress but the diplomats and all who could gain admittance to the House of Representatives listened intently, applauding what they approved, there was none to doubt the wisdom of restoring the Washington practice. This breaking of a precedent an hundred years old was an innovation which demonstrated its wisdom. He prefaced the message by saying: "I am very glad indeed to have this opportunity to address the two Houses directly and to verify for myself the impression that the President of the United States is a person, not a mere department of Government hailing Congress from some isolated island of jealous power, sending messages, not speaking naturally and with his own voice—that he is a human being trying to co-operate with other human beings in a common service." He added: "After this pleasant experience, I shall feel quite normal, in all our dealings with one another." Both President Harding and President Coolidge followed the example of their precedent-breaking and precedent-making predecessor. Wilson ended the spectacle of apparent disrespect shown executive recommendations to Congress. The delivering of the message is now an impressive occasion and the views of the executives receive greater consideration than when the clerks hurried or droned through their messages.

Readers of "The State," written many years before he broke the precedent of a century by delivering his message in person, might have known he would do that very thing. He had said in his book, "Washington and John Adams addressed Congress in person on public affairs, but Jefferson, the third President, was not an easy speaker and preferred to send a written message." Here is his scorn of the way precedents control: "Subsequent Presidents followed his example, of course. Hence, a sacred rule of constitutional action."

"You do not mean to tell me that Wilson is thinking of doing so revolutionary a thing as that?" exclaimed an old-time Senator to a friend of Wilson's shortly before the inauguration in 1913. "The Senators would resent it. It would be a fatal mistake. I hope you will dissuade him if he has such a thing in mind."

The friend of Wilson had just returned from Princeton and was talking to the Senator about his visit. The President-elect had asked him: "Is there not a room in the Capitol set apart for the President?" "Yes." "Does the President ever occupy it?" The answer was that it was occupied by the chief executive only at the close of Congress when he signed measures passed in the rush hours. At other times, it was explained, it was used by the Senators to see favored visitors.

"What would you think," asked Wilson of his visitor, "if I should make use of it now and then when it was desirable to hold conferences with Senators?" The friend, himself lacking reverence for outworn precedents, said that the builders of the Capitol having constructed a room called "The President's Room," he could see no reason why it should not be used by the officer for whom it was set apart, but he added, "If you use it, there will be the cry that you are trying to control legislative action. It has not been used since the time whereof the memory of man runneth not to the contrary."

Later, when President Wilson for the first time occupied the President's room and held conferences there with a number of Senators on important policies, this happened: The old-time Senator, who had been shocked at the very thought of the innovation, in an interview published next morning, expressed his gratification that, instead of sending for Senators to make a trip to the White House, the new President had done them the courtesy to call at the Capitol for conferences. Nevertheless, though this Senator was converted, President Wilson never occupied his room at the Capitol that there was not talk of "executive dictation" and of the attempt "to relegate the Senate to a subordinate position." Most Senators, however, did not indulge in such criticism, for while they found Mr. Wilson earnestly advocating his measures, they found he was seeking a common ground of agreement. Adamant for the principle at stake he was, but reasonable and ready for every helpful concession. Often his open-minded conferences with Senators and Representatives caused him to adopt gladly the methods their experience showed were an improvement on his own. But once the line of battle had been drawn, once the opponents of the principle involved were seeking compromise that would impair the idea aimed at, in the Federal Reserve contest and others, he adopted the motto of Grant: "I purpose to fight it out on this line if it takes all summer."

It has been a precedent time out of mind in the White House that no one must sit down while the President is standing. There is a story that years and years ago, a lady of fifty took a seat while waiting for her husband at the close of a brilliant reception. A White House visitor reminded her of the rule and told her it was regarded as lese majeste. President Wilson upon all formal occasions made no change in rules. One evening when the receiving party were gathered in the library upstairs awaiting the signal to descend the stairs in the "grand march" as it is called, a member of the Cabinet and a lady house guest drew up their chairs by the fireplace for a cozy chat, all unmindful that the President was standing. The wife of the Cabinet officer, who was standing and engaged in conversation with the President, gave the wifely command by her eyes to her husband. He obeyed it and came to his feet immediately. Seeing this pantomime, the President walked over to the Cabinet member, placed a hand on each shoulder, pressed him back into the chair, saying with a smile, "Sit down and behave yourself," and, turning to the wife, added that no matter what the policy at formal occasions, no office could make him forget his right to be a gentleman at his own fireside.

"Mr. Bryan was saying to me," said President Wilson at an early meeting of the Cabinet—he repeated the remark that the Secretary of State had made, in a low tone of voice, before the Cabinet session had actually begun. Other members were talking and Mr. Bryan had chosen the moment when the others were so engaged to speak of a state department matter which was not important enough for discussion. "I am repeating this whispered message," President Wilson went on to say, "solely because when I read the 'Diary of Gideon Welles' I was impressed by the resentment felt by the other members of the Cabinet when Seward would take the President aside and talk with him alone, while the other members sat by wondering why they could not be let in on the conversation between the President and the Secretary of State." That precedent of private conferences obtaining in Lincoln days was not followed.

One precedent which had been established from the beginning was that the President of the United States should not go beyond the borders of his country. Some indeed had an idea that it was prohibited by the Constitution or the laws. Therefore, when Wilson decided to go himself to Paris to take part in framing the peace treaty, there was a great outcry that he was not only smashing tradition and breaking precedent, but he was also violating the proprieties. So fierce was the criticism that an outsider would have supposed that Wilson was breaking all the Ten Commandments at once. Mr. Lansing, Secretary of State, whose mind was not open to departures from custom, says in his book, "I felt it to be my duty, as his official adviser in foreign affairs, and as one desirous to have him adopt a wise course, to tell him frankly that I thought the plan for him to attend was unwise and would be a mistake." The assumption that it was Lansing's duty "as official adviser in foreign affairs" to protest against Wilson's going received no rebuke from the President, showing he was often a patient and long-suffering man. "The President, listened to my remarks without comment and turned the conversation into other channels" was the entry Lansing made in his diary after the interview, and again in his diary Lansing says he wrote at the time: "I prophesy trouble in Paris and worse than trouble here."

On the other hand, the New York *Times* succinctly

said Wilson's going to Paris was "one of four times when Wilson fell up stairs." At the Conference of Governors held in Annapolis, December 18, 1918, Secretary Lane gave this effective answer to the criticisms of Wilson's going to Paris:

"I have seen criticisms of the President and so have you for going across the water at this time. The spirit which animates him in going is the spirit of the new day. It is the spirit of giving your hand to your neighbor. It is the spirit that would make this war the end of wars.

"The man who stands as the representative of the foremost democracy of the world goes to Europe, not that he may march down the Champs Elysees, not that he may receive the plaudits of the French multitudes. But he goes to Europe as the champion of American ideals because he wants to see that out of the war comes something worth while. He would have been derelict, he would have been negligent, he would have been false to our ideas of him, if he had not stood in Paris in person as the champion of that principle which we love and those institutions which we hope to see spread around the world.

"To me, Woodrow Wilson in Paris represents not the ambitions of Napoleon, striving to master the world by force, but of the greater Pasteur, the healer of the nation who comes to bring peace, happiness, and to secure gratitude from those whose lives and homes he makes secure."

Every reader of Wilson's "Congressional Government" should have known he would go to Paris to the Peace Conference. "When foreign affairs play a prominent part in the politics and policies of a nation, its executive must of necessity be its guide; must utter every initial judgment, take every first step of action, supply the information upon which it is to act, suggest and, in a large measure, control its conduct," and he added: "He must always stand at the front of our affairs, and the office will be as big and as influential as the man who occupies it."

"After all," he said to the Englishmen in the Mansion House at London, when he visited there in December, 1918—"after all, the breaking of precedents, though this may sound strange doctrine in England, is the most sensible thing to do. The harness of precedent is sometimes a very sad and harassing trammel. In this case the breaking of precedent is sensible for a reason that is very prettily illustrated in a remark attributed to Charles Lamb.

"One evening, in a company of his friends, they were discussing a person who was not present and Lamb said, in his hesitating manner,

"'I h-hate that fellow.'

"'Why, Charles,' one of his friends said, 'I did not know that you knew him.'

"'Oh,' he said, 'I-I-I d-don't. I can't h-hate a man I know.'

"And perhaps that simple and attractive remark may furnish a secret for cordial international relationship. When we know one another we cannot hate one another."

He walked the groove of change.

## Chapter XXII

# THE HUMAN SIDE OF WILSON

"HE IS RESPECTED, BUT HE WALKS ALONE"—"MY CONSTANT EMBARRASSMENT IS TO RESTRAIN THE EMOTIONS INSIDE OF ME"—HAD A PASSION FOR THE MASS OF MANKIND—THIRTEEN WAS HIS LUCKY NUMBER—WHEN HE GOT BEST OF PERSHING—ENJOYED STORY AT OWN EXPENSE

*"Let us remind ourselves that to be human is, for one thing, to speak and act with a certain note of genuineness, a quality mixed of spontaneity of intelligence."*—Wilson

"HE is respected, but I observe he walks alone." That was the answer a Trenton hack driver made to a visitor in the early part of 1913 when Governor Wilson was closing his term as chief executive of New Jersey preparatory to his inauguration as President of the United States. Those nine words describe the man. He once said: "The leaders of mankind are those who lift their feet from the dusty road, and lift their eyes to the illumined future." Mr. Wilson was not a "good fellow" in what is meant by that term in popular parlance. He was reserved by nature and by his studious habits. From youth he set himself tasks that necessitated husbanding his time and practiced self-reliance that called for little aid.

"Does Wilson really love anybody outside his family?" a gentleman once asked a member of his Cabinet.

"Yes," was the reply. "To his chosen friends he

gives his affection, and it is deep and genuine. Even as to them he would, except under some peculiar circumstance, regard display of his love as something wanting in taste. But," added the Cabinet member whose affection for the President was deep and who knew it was reciprocated, "while Wilson gives his love to few, he has a passion for the mass of mankind and is wholly devoted to their welfare." He loved to walk the streets, to see people enjoying themselves, and to feel a comradeship of interest and feeling if there was little comradeship of association. If he felt lack of association, he was buoyed up by the feeling that in spirit he was mingling with his countrymen. "I count it a fortunate circumstance," he once said, "that almost all the windows of the White House and its offices open upon unoccupied spaces that stretch to the banks of the Potomac and then out into Virginia and on to the heavens themselves, and that as I sit there I can constantly forget Washington and remember the United States."

Again, here is proof of the passion for the people when he said, "Down in Washington sometimes when the days are hot and business presses intolerably and there are so many things to do that it does not seem possible to do anything in the way it ought to be done, it is always possible to lift one's thought above the task of the moment, and, as it were, to realize that great thing of which we are all parts, the great body of American feeling and American principle. No man could do the work that has to be done in Washington if he allowed himself to be separated from that body of principle. He must make himself feel that he is a part of the people of the United States, that he is trying to think not only for them, but with them, and then he cannot feel lonely. He not only cannot feel lonely but he cannot feel afraid of anything."

No one can study his career without being struck by his tenderness of heart and his eagerness to be of service when there was a service needed. In his State papers and addresses there are repeated evidences of his lively solicitude for the weak and the unfortunate. In speaking in his inaugural address of the industrial achievements of the nation, he remarked: "We have not heretofore stopped thoughtfully enough to count the human cost, the cost of lives snuffed out, of energies overtaxed and broken." He emphasized the duty of "humanizing" every process of life. In the same address he advocated beneficent laws determining conditions of labor. And all through his speeches and writings on national affairs there was the thought of the duty of government to see that justice was done the weak. "This is no sentimental duty," he said. "The first basis of government is justice, not pity." But then he added: "These are matters of justice. There can be no equality of opportunity—the first essential of justice in the body politic—if men and women and children be not shielded in their lives, their very vitality, from the consequences of great industrial and social processes which they cannot alter, control or singly cope with."

Rev. James H. Taylor, D.D., pastor of Central Presbyterian Church, Washington, where President Wilson worshipped, in an article for the *Sunday School Times*, writes of Mr. Wilson: "He was very human in his relationships and had that wonderful gift of great men, in that he was able to make you feel at home in his presence. He would often talk about many matters of great interest and concern with perfect freedom. You felt as if you had been suddenly lifted to a position of importance by being treated with such unusual confidence.

"An example of his human feeling is illustrated in his deep concern for the soldier boys. When warned about undertaking the tour on behalf of the League of Nations, he replied in effect that if the boys could risk their lives in the trenches or go over the top, so he too should not hesitate to risk anything for the great cause. One soldier boy sent him a khaki-bound copy of the New Testament, such as the dough-boys carried into the trenches with them, asking him to read it every day. He kept this agreement, never failing to read this khaki-bound Testament, and no matter how hard he had worked during the day, or how late the hour at night, he read that Testament and kept faith with the boys."

"Tenderness, I think, was easily his outstanding characteristic," said Doctor Stockton Axson, brother-in-law of President Wilson. Dr. Axson met Mr. Wilson for the first time when he had been engaged to his first wife for about a year. "My earliest recollections of him," he says, "are of his great kindliness of manner, his unfailing courtesy and consideration for others."

Macaulay's description of the great man fitted Wilson. He is the man, said the great Englishman, who is not influenced by those who are near to him and can do him some favor in return. Rather the truly great man is he whose heart and service go out to those who do not know him, may never see him, will never thank him and can never do anything for him.

In his address on Lincoln at the log cabin, where he was born—believed by many to be his best—Mr. Wilson is thought to have revealed his own feelings in difficult days. "There is a very holy and very terrible isolation," he said, "for the conscience of every man who seeks to read the destiny in affairs for others as well as for himself, for a nation as well as for individuals. That privacy no man can intrude upon. That lonely search of the spirit for the right perhaps no man can assist."

Restraint of feeling and the reticence of expression and apparent aloofness are not incompatible with Wilson's own interpretation of himself: "I sometimes feel like a fire from an extinct volcano," and he added, "If the lava does not seem to spill over, it is because you are not high enough to see into the basin and see the cauldron boil." Again: "My constant embarrassment is to restrain emotions that are inside me." While there are few who ever saw "the cauldron boil" in the self-restrained Wilson, there are not a few who rested in the assurance of his affection, who received proofs of it in ways that were precious, and who cherish his words of affection. They kept these confidences in their hearts, but were ever troubled that his reserve and devotion to duty denied others the nearness which warmed their hearts. The truth is that Mr. Wilson had to conserve his strength. When urged to see more people, he would say: "I have just so much vitality. I see everyone who has a matter of importance to discuss. If I expend all my energy upon receiving people who call to pay their respects, there is too little energy left for the big task." Moreover, he never could understand why visitors to Washington wished to "see the President." Never in his life had he turned aside to shake hands with a President. He had never had a wish to see any man in high station except to discuss a policy. Why should they wish to see him? Why should he expend his nervous energy in receptions to folks who came to Washington when it was needed to keep him fit to serve the hundred million who never came to the National Capital? Moreover, he was never very robust. He always had to conserve his strength. He had come to the White House after two years of heavy strain in New Jersey. It was necessary to go South the first winter to gain strength.

Perhaps one reason President Wilson was called cold was the fact that he was utterly sincere. He did not know how to pretend to be what he was not. He did not flatter, he slapped nobody on the back to win favor by a familiarity not felt. He would not waste time in adulation or idle talk, but he always had time to show appreciation of real merit—plenty of time if the occasion required it.

The New York *World* tells a story which shows how far from the truth was the assertion that Wilson was selfish and lacking in human sympathy. In 1911, William Teal McIntyre, newspaper and magazine writer, lay dying of cancer in St. Vincent's Hospital in New York. He had been at Princeton when Wilson was President. In September, 1911, Mr. Wilson, then Governor of New Jersey, spoke in Jersey City. A friend of both men told him of McIntyre's condition and suggested that a letter would cheer the sick man. "I'll go see him," said Governor Wilson. The *World* then continues the story:

"Cancelling his plan to return to Trenton, the then Governor took a room in a hotel here and next morning called at the hospital. Mrs. Bessie T. McIntyre, her spirit saddened by months of hopeless watching at her son's bedside, greeted Mr. Wilson, already mentioned as candidate for President in the following fall's election.

"She led the Governor into the sick room, but the

nurse held up a warning finger and whispered that McIntyre had just fallen asleep after a night of restlessness. The mother would have awakened him, but Governor Wilson held her back and said:

" 'I can wait. I'll come back in a couple of hours.'

"Bill was awake then—staring at the monotony of the ceiling. He turned his head to see who his visitor was, and beheld his former chief. What strength was in him was electrified into action and for the first time in weeks he sat bolt upright in bed.

" 'Hello, Prexy!' he said, and stretched out his hand.

"Two weeks later Bill McIntyre died. He never knew the heights to which 'Prexy' rose. He never heard his idol assailed as cold of heart."

No greater mistake was ever made than to say Woodrow Wilson was all mind and no heart. Was not the warmth of his heart one of the incentives to his marvelous achievement? He wrought tremendously for his fellow human beings because he loved them with a great love.

Sailors on the *George Washington*, on which the President journeyed to and from Europe, became his staunchest friends. They regarded him as their "shipmate" and one of the many newspaper accounts of his voyages speaks of "his many acts of kindness and attention in which he displayed a complete humanness."

MacQueen S. Wightman, secretary to Mr. Wilson from 1902 to 1904, had excellent opportunity to observe and in the intimate relations which reveal the real man. He writes:

"They say that Woodrow Wilson lacked human interest and understanding.

"Saturday is the big day during commencement at

Princeton. The crowds are densest, the President entertains at luncheon and the alumni parade in the afternoon to the game. It is the day in the year on which the President most needs his secretary.

"I was filling that office at the close of my senior year and, as usual, I reported at Prospect, the President's house, at 9.30 o'clock, knowing that there were several important letters which had gone over from the day before, when Mr. Wilson had been in New York.

"But Friday night the seniors hold their farewell dinner, and in those pre-Volsteadian days senior dinners and the parties which followed them were not conspicuous for their sobriety.

"I don't know how I looked as I dropped into a chair in the big, high-ceiled library that June morning, but if it was half as awful as I felt I might readily have served as the horrible example. Mr. Wilson came in a moment later, fresh, clear-eyed and serene, as one always found him in the morning.

"He chatted for an instant about the prospects for the day, seated himself at the table, and then for the first time really looked at me. His expression did not change, but a glint of comprehension came into his eyes. With a glance at the unanswered pile of letters, he pushed his chair back from the table.

" 'We are both going to be busy today, Wightman,' he said, 'suppose we let this correspondence go over until Monday.' "

"He was always serene and he seemed to me to get an immense amount of enjoyment out of life," his former secretary writes.

"Certainly three times a week, if not oftener, he had a new story before we began our day's work. I never learned where he found them, but he never repeated one, and they all seemed vastly interesting and amusing, except when I tried to tell them myself."

To his secretary he used to divulge some of his theories on education, remarking once: "You can't educate a man; he must educate himself, and the way he must do it is by reading. The most we can do is to direct that reading."

"And that is the reason," Wightman added, "why the students' rooms which had heretofore been full of pipes and steins, became suddenly full of books."

"He was a man full of deep and warm feeling, in whom the heart often found it hard to yield to the demands of the intellect," declared Prof. Frank Thilly, of Ithaca, N. Y., who was a member of the Princeton faculty during Mr. Wilson's term as president. "And he was one of the most lovable men with whom I have ever come into contact, the kind of human being for whom one has genuine affection from the very beginning of one's acquaintance with him. There was a manly gentleness about him, a quiet, unaffected charm, an unobtrusive cordiality, a trustfulness and sincerity that marked him as an unusual personality."

Born in the South, Mr. Wilson never lost his touch with his colored friends or failed to understand them and to seek to help them. One of his last visitors was David Bryant, of Wilmington, N. C. Bryant nursed President Wilson's father in his last illness. Paul D. Satchwell, now living in Washington, D. C., sent a clipping to Bryant from a Washington paper and making reference to Bryant's attachment to President Wilson's father. In his answer, Bryant wrote that he had promised Wilson's father that if the son ever ran for President he would vote for him. Writing to Satchwell and repeating the promise, Bryant went on to say: "I did promise Dr. Wilson to cast my vote for his son if he was not living. So I did and am proud of it. He always allowed me $50 every month just to help me, I suppose, just because he knew I was the family servant when they lived here (Wilmington) and even in his father's last days I was his nurse." "Although I had known Bryant intimately for a long time," says Satchwell, "this was the first intimation that his loyalty and devotion to the late President was being so handsomely rewarded. Bryant typifies the noblest and loftiest virtues of his race in the South."

It was rare that Wilson did not have a story for Cabinet meetings, even in the stress of war. He was not a story-teller in the ordinary meaning. He did not save up stories to drag in. Rather they came spontaneously. They were apropos of the subject matter in hand, and they illustrated the point. Ludicrous situations appealed to him, and limericks stuck in his memory. Learning that he had a penchant for limericks, people sent them to him from even across the sea. He always had one for every occasion. They seemed to stick in his mind and come forth without effort. His associates were wont to vie with him and often half a dozen choice ones regaled the members of the Cabinet before weighty business was introduced.

Was he superstitious? Not in the least. His favorite number was thirteen. He had a penchant for remembering the number of good things that had happened to him on the thirteenth. "It is my lucky day," he was wont to say. There are thirteen letters in his name. It was the thirteen electoral votes of California that made his reelection possible. He was inaugurated in 1913. He landed in Brest on December thirteenth.

The saving grace of humor was pronounced in Mr. Wilson. He could enjoy jokes at his own expense. He greatly enjoyed this one and often told it:

Some years ago a magazine sent a correspondent to Hannibal, Mo., to try to obtain some stories of Mark Twain when he was a boy. He was referred to a half-witted man, the only one living there when Samuel Clemens was growing up. In order to lead up to his questions, the writer asked the ignorant old man:

"Did you ever know or hear of Tom Sawyer?"

The old man scratched his head and after a pause, said "No."

"Did you ever hear of Huckleberry Finn?"

The pause was longer. The man searched his shallow mind, but could not remember.

"Did you ever hear of Pudd'n' Head Wilson?" was asked as a last shot. This was in 1913.

The dull man looked up. A ray of intelligence flashed and he answered confidently:

"Oh, yes, I voted for him last year."

It is doubtful if any man charged with grave responsibilities can stand great strain unless he can see the humorous side even in serious situations. Lincoln was saved by his love of fun, even when the unimaginative Stanton thought fun evidence of lack of greatness.

This incident explains one side of the man: One day President Wilson was accompanying General Pershing on a tour of inspection in France. Commenting on the efficiency of the soldiers' equipment, General Pershing picked up from one soldier's outfit a folding tent pole, and explained how it worked. When he had done with it he threw it across the laid out equipment, where everything was in its proper place.

"Are those boys not likely to be inspected further after we have passed?" Mr. Wilson asked the General.

"Yes, sir, they may be."

"One other thing, General. I am the commander-in-chief of the army and authorized to give you orders, am I not?" queried the President.

"Certainly, sir."

"Then, General, you will replace that tent pole as you found it."

And the general, smiling, knelt, folded the tent pole and put it in its proper position. Some of the soldiers in the outfit said the President winked at them.

The author of "The Stroller," a department in the Portland (Maine) *Express and Advertiser*, thinks that if Wilson had been able to put through all of the reforms he desired at Princeton he might never have entered politics. The writer was influenced to that belief by something Mr. Wilson said to him once. He writes:

"I happened to meet him in the book department of the Wanamaker store in New York City shortly after he was chosen president of Princeton. I had been one of his students and he greeted me cordially. I asked him what he was doing in the big city, thinking, perhaps, that he had run over to make an address at some gathering of Princeton men.

" 'Oh, I've just come to New York for a few days' rest,' he replied, 'but, as you see, I'm still browsing among books, as I suppose I shall always do, reading a lot and writing a little. New York is all right for a visit now and then, but I confess I prefer the quiet of Princeton to the bustle and hurry of this great city.' "

The same writer tells of a visit to Professor Wilson at the Nassau Hotel at Princeton, where he was living temporarily, his family being away. The visit was concerning the making up of some back work. Mr. Wilson cordially asked the student how he was getting on with his work. The reply was, "I think I am holding my own." Mr. Wilson indulged his fondness for illustrating with a joke, saying he hoped the student was "holding his own" better than a farmer of whom he had heard, and adding the story, which ran something like this:

A farmer and his wife, Samantha, were jogging along a country road, when they met a pedestrian going the other way.

"How far is it to Smithville?" asked the farmer.

"About six miles," was the reply.

The farmer whipped up old Dobbin and started on. After going several miles he stopped another farmer, who was plowing in a field by the road. He repeated the question and to his surprise the man in the field said:

"It's about six miles to Smithville."

Again, but somewhat discouraged, the farmer drove on, and again after driving for a half hour or more he stopped another farmer.

"How far is it to Smithville?" he said.

"Well," replied the farmer, "I reckon it's about six miles from here."

The farmer in the buggy then turned to his wife and giving old Dobbin another crack of the whip, said:

"Well, thank goodness, Samantha, we are at least holding our own."

Arguing on his preparedness tour for a stronger navy, Mr. Wilson told one of his best jokes. He said the Navy was rated as fourth in strength, but when he went on board the ships and saw their equipment and talked with their officers he suspected that they could give an account of themselves which would raise them above the fourth class. He said it reminded him of the quaint saying of the old darky preacher, "The Lord said unto Moses, Come forth, and he came fifth and lost the race."

Mr. Wilson said he felt the Navy then would not come fourth in the race, but higher.

When Secretary Tumulty wrote him at Paris that he was likely to wreck his constitution if he went on at the pace he was going, Mr. Wilson replied, "Constitution? Why, man, I am already living on my by-laws."

Wilson was not all tenderness, as his antagonists in the Senate and in other arenas discovered. He knew how to be cutting and severe. Alfred O. Anderson, publisher of the *Dispatch*, Dallas, Texas, and one-time student under Wilson at Princeton, said in a reminiscent article in his paper on the occasion of President Wilson's death:

"One day some of the boys in the back of the hall disturbed Professor Wilson as he was lecturing. He spotted them, but said nothing. The interruption recurred. Looking directly at the group, Professor Wilson quietly said:

" 'Gentlemen, don't be any less gentlemen than you cawn't help.'

"That was all, but it was plenty."

Mr. Wilson had a keen and ready wit and often evinced it in his relations with newspaper correspondents at Washington. On one occasion Andrew Carnegie had visited the President.

"What did Mr. Carnegie want?" a correspondent asked at the weekly meeting with the newspaper men.

"As I understand it," Mr. Wilson replied, "Mr. Carnegie is beyond want."

Wilson's heart warmed to some people, and intuitively became frigid toward others. Speaking before a Sunday School convention at Pittsburgh while he was President of Princeton, he told of how some men attracted him and others repelled him. "I cannot sit in a railroad station comfortably," he said, "because men will come in whom I want to kick out, and persons will come in whom I want to go up to and speak to, and make friends with, and I am restrained because when I was small I was told that it was not good form, and I would not for the world be unlike my fellow men. So I sit still and try to think about something else, and my eye constantly wanders to some person whom it would, I am sure, be such fun to go and talk to."

"Woodrow Wilson was a man neither tall nor short; of medium weight, conveying the impression of leanness; walking with quick, firm strides, indicating health and vigor," said one of the vast number of articles written about him at the time of his death.

"Angular features marked his face, the long jaw showing determination and persistence. He wore eyeglasses over eyes that were thoughtful in expression and illuminated with interest when he spoke in a well modulated voice or when he smiled on friend or visitor and exerted that 'magic of personality' many noticed in him and which attached the personal regard of hundreds.

"Of his personality this was said by a man who passed him one day in the streets in Washington:

" 'As I looked at him he turned his face toward me—and I found my hat in my hand. It was like saluting the flag.'"

"One who loves his fellow men."

## Chapter XXIII

# NEUTRALITY

NEARLY ALL AMERICA FAVORED NEUTRALITY UPON OUTBREAK OF EUROPEAN WAR—ROOSEVELT AT FIRST FAVORED AND LATER VIGOROUSLY OPPOSED POLICY—DIPLOMATIC CORRESPONDENCE—ARMED GUARD ON SHIPS—WILSON CONSISTENT IN DEMAND "WILL OMIT NO WORD OR ACT"—THE McLEMORE RESOLUTION—"LITTLE GROUP OF WILFUL MEN"

*"We are not trying to keep out of trouble; we are trying to preserve the foundation upon which peace can be rebuilt."*—Wilson

THE days of neutrality were 976—from August 4, 1914, to April 6, 1917. They began with the invasion of Belgium. They ended with the studied invasion and disregard of just American rights and the deliberate murder of noncombatants on the high seas. The policy of neutrality was announced in August, 1914, and compressed in these words:

"We are a true friend to all the nations of the world, because we threaten none, covet the possessions of none, desire the overthrow of none. Our friendship can be accepted, and is accepted, without reservation, because it is offered in a spirit and for a purpose which no one need ever question or suspect. Therein lies our greatness. We are the champions of peace and of concord.

"Woodrow Wilson."

The formal declaration of the end of neutrality was contained in these words, in President Wilson's message delivered to Congress, April 2, 1917:

"Neutrality is no longer feasible nor desirable where the peace of the world is involved and the freedom of its peoples, and the menace to that peace and freedom lies in the existence of autocratic governments backed by organized force which is controlled by their will, not by the will of the people. We have seen the last of neutrality in such circumstance. We are at the beginning of an age in which it will be insisted that the same standards of conduct and responsibility for wrong done shall be observed among nations and their governments that are observed among the individual citizens of civilized states."

What should be the policy of the United States with reference to the World War? That was the question debated in the late summer of 1914 when the fires of war blazed overseas. With almost perfect unanimity, the feeling in the first few months was that the United States should preserve a neutral position. Those who believed otherwise in 1914 were negligible in numbers. On August 19, fifteen days after the invasion of Belgium by Germany, Wilson issued an appeal for neutrality. "Every man who really loves America will act and speak in the true spirit of neutrality, which is the spirit of impartiality and fairness and friendliness to all concerned." He called attention to the character of the population of America "drawn from many nations," said it was "natural and inevitable that there should be the utmost variety of sympathy" and that it "will be easy to excite passion and difficult to allay it."

On September 16, a Belgian Commission visited President Wilson, asking American help to redress the wrongs visited upon them. He gave them cordial welcome, told them the American people "love justice, seek the true path of progress, and have a passionate regard for the rights of humanity." He told them "it would be inconsistent with the neutral position of any nation, which like this, has no part in the contest, to form a final judgment." He was moved by the outrages in Belgium and said to the members of the mission, "Presently, I pray God very soon, this war will be over. The day of reckoning will come when, I take it for granted, the nations of Europe will assemble to determine a settlement. Where wrongs have been committed, their consequences and the relative responsibility involved will be assessed."

Mr. Wilson shared the feeling of indignation at the wrongs to Belgians and did everything possible to relieve their sufferings, that did not demand taking part in the war. His position, criticized in some quarters, was approved by most of his countrymen. Undoubtedly, criticism of his course was lessened by its approval by Mr. Roosevelt, who later became his severest critic. In an article in the *Outlook* of September 23, 1914, Mr. Roosevelt declared: "It is certainly eminently desirable that we should remain entirely neutral and nothing but urgent need would warrant breaking our neutrality and taking sides one way or the other." This was said apropos of a visit of the Belgian Mission. "What action we can take I know not," he said as a preface to his saying only "urgent need would warrant breaking our neutrality." He added: "Of course, it would be folly to jump into the gulf ourselves to no good purpose; and very probably nothing that we could have done would have helped Belgium. We have not the smallest responsibility for what has befallen her, and I am sure the sympathy of this country for the suffering of men, women and children in Belgium is very real. Nevertheless, the sympathy is compatible with full acknowledgment of the unwisdom of our uttering a single word of official protest unless we are prepared to make that protest effective; and only the clearest and most urgent national duty would ever justify us in deviating from our rule of neutrality and noninterference." Not only did Mr. Roosevelt take the same position Mr. Wilson felt constrained to take at that time, but in the same article he wrote what was regarded as at least an extenuation of Germany's action in Belgium. "Of course," he said, "if there is any meaning in the words 'right' and 'wrong' in international matters, the act was wrong. The men who shape German policy take the ground that in matters of vital moment there are no such things as abstract right and wrong, and that when a great nation is struggling for its existence, it can no more consider the rights of neutral powers than it can consider the rights of its own citizens as these rights are considered in times of peace, and that everything must bend before the supreme law of national preservation. Whatever we may think of the morality of this plea, it is certain that almost all great nations have in times past again and again acted in accordance with it."

As an example, Mr. Roosevelt cited "England's conduct toward Denmark in the Napoleonic wars, and the conduct of both England and France toward us during the same wars," and "our conduct toward Spain and Florida nearly a century ago." He said he wished it "explicitly understood that I am not at this time passing judgment one way or the other upon Germany for what she did to Belgium." He went on to say: "They (the Belgians) are suffering somewhat as my own German ancestors suffered when Turenne ravaged the

Palatinate, somewhat as my Irish ancestors suffered in the struggles that attended the conquests and reconquests of Ireland in the days of Cromwell and William." He wished it to be understood that at that time he was not condemning the Germans, for he added: "I think, at any rate, I hope, I have rendered it plain that I am not now criticizing, that I am not passing judgment one way or the other, upon Germany's action. I admire and respect the German people. I am proud of the German blood in my veins. When a nation feels that the issue of a contest in which, for whatever reason, it finds itself engaged will be national life or death, it is inevitable that it should act so as to save itself from death and to perpetuate its life." His conclusion was, "The rights and wrongs of those cases where nations violate the rules of abstract morality in order to meet their own vital needs can be precisely determined only when all the facts are known and when men's blood is cool."

It is necessary, in order to convey an understanding of the atmosphere of 1914, which was almost wholly in approval of a course of neutrality, to read the point of view expressed by Wilson and Roosevelt, the two leaders of the great parties in America. In the light of later events, and America's whole-hearted and patriotic championship of the principles at stake, it is not easy to understand the temper of the country in the summer and fall of 1914.

Shortly after the appearance of his article in the *Outlook*, Mr. Roosevelt in a vigorous and earnest way denounced the German invasion of Belgium, and with great zeal made himself leader of the forces which were urging earlier participation in the war than Mr. Wilson favored. The time was to come when both these leaders, in spite of the difference in temperament and politics, and the antagonism of 1915–17, were to lead in protest against hyphenated Americanism and for the vigorous prosecution of the war. But before that time Roosevelt was the voice of hostility to the Wilson program of continued neutrality.

No selfish belief in isolation influenced Wilson's policy of neutrality. In the weary months of correspondence, with promises extorted from Germany one day to be broken the next, President Wilson kept ever before him the hope that the hour of "mediation" would come when this country could help to bring peace to the warring nations. It was in that spirit that Wilson carried on the negotiations, secured the promises from Germany which were kept for a time, and stood firm for American rights and the rights of humanity. From the note of February 15, 1915, to April 6, 1917, when war was declared by the United States, there runs through every word and action devotion to neutrality so long as it could be pursued without sacrifice of the things America held dear. But no longer.

President Wilson always felt the difficulties and delicacy of the position. He would often say in that perplexing period, as he said at Cleveland, Ohio, on January 29, 1916, in his campaign for effective national preparedness:

"I want to remind you, and remind you solemnly, of the double obligation you have laid upon me. I am constantly reminded of it by conversation, by letter, by editorial, by means of every voice that comes to me out of the body of the nation: 'We are relying upon you, Mr. President, to keep us out of this war, but we are relying upon you, Mr. President, to keep the honor of the nation unstained.'" This dual, perhaps impossible duty, gave him pause and anxiety. "Do you not see," he asked, "that there may come a time when it is impossible to do both of these things?" In public and private utterances he reverted to the double, perhaps conflicting expectations, again and again. "We are in the midst of a world that we did not make and we cannot alter and I must tell you that the dangers are infinite and constant." He was always saying that while a "partisan of peace" he yet realized that "peace is not always within the choice of the nation," and he pointed out on many occasions that one reckless commander of a submarine might "set the world on fire." Again at Pittsburgh he emphasized the fact that war was possible by the act of others. "You have bidden me," he said, "to see to it that nothing stains or impairs the honor of the United States and that is not a matter within my control; that depends upon what others do, not upon what the Government of the United States does. Therefore there may come a time at any moment when I cannot preserve both the honor and the peace of the United States." However, for two and a half years he piloted the ship of neutrality between Scylla and Charybdis with infinite patience and infinite concern. "We are not going to invade any nation's rights," he said in 1916, and asked, "but suppose some nation should invade our rights? What then?" The only answer in his mind was the course he took in 1917.

The diplomatic correspondence of those days was voluminous, beginning on August 6, 1914, when Ambassador Page was directed "to inquire whether the British Government is willing to agree that the laws of naval warfare as laid down by the Declaration of London of 1909 shall be applicable to naval warfare during the present conflict," expressing the view that "an acceptance of these laws by the belligerents would prevent grave misunderstandings that may arise as to the relations between neutral forces and the belligerents." Britain's reply was not compliance with, but that she would adopt "generally the rules of the Declaration subject to certain modifications." France and Britain adopted steadily increasing definitions and lists of contrabands and made such other radical modifications of the Declaration that our State Department withdrew its proposal. In its note of October 22, 1914, Britain and France were notified of such withdrawal and the note said, "Therefore this Government will insist that the rights and duties of the United States and its citizens in the present war be defined by the existing rules of international law and the treaties of the United States irrespective of the Declaration of London." On November 3, 1914, Britain declared the entire North Sea a war-zone. On February 4, 1915, Germany declared the waters surrounding the British Isles and the whole English Channel a war-zone. It also announced that, in retaliation for Britain's violations of the maritime rules of war, all enemy merchant vessels found in the zone would be destroyed after February 18. Navigation in the waters north of the Shetland Islands, and in the eastern part of the North Sea, and a zone thirty miles wide along the Dutch coast was expressly declared as being outside the danger zone.

On February 10 a note was dispatched to Germany calling attention to the critical situation in respect to relations between this country and Germany which might arise were the German naval forces, in carrying out the policy foreshadowed in the Admiralty's proclamation, to "destroy any merchant vessels of the United States or cause the death of American citizens." In clear and unmistakable language, if an American vessel or the lives of American citizens should be destroyed, the note signed "Bryan" declared, "The Government of the United States would be constrained to hold the Imperial German Government to a strict accountability for such acts of their naval authorities and to take any steps it might be necessary to take to safeguard American lives and property and to secure to American citizens the full enjoyment of their acknowledged rights on the high seas." It closed with "the hope and expectation that the Imperial German Government can and will give such assurance that American citizens and vessels will not be molested by the naval forces of Germany, otherwise than by visit and search, though their vessels may be traversing the sea area delimited in the proclamation of the German Admiralty."

On the same date a note was addressed to the British Government pointing out "the serious consequences" which might result to American vessels by the practice of the deceptive use of a flag of a neutral power, and requested it to restrain vessels of the British nationality from the deceptive use of the flag of the United States in the sea area defined in the German declaration. On February 20 an identical note was sent to Britain and Germany with the request that "through reciprocal concessions" both countries "find a basis for agreement which will relieve neutral ships engaged in peaceful commerce from the great dangers which they will incur in the high seas adjacent to the coasts of the belligerents." It outlined in detail what it wished each country to do for the "common interests of humanity." Germany's reply was a practical agreement in terms, but Britain's reply recited Germany's offenses against humanity and declared it did not understand from Germany's reply that it would abandon submarine warfare. It upheld the necessity of carrying on its blockade. The next note of March 5 to the French and British Governments protested against their policy of "taking into custody all ships, both outgoing and incoming, trading with Germany." This, it was pointed out, "presents a proposed course of action previously unknown to international law; the consequences of which would be that neutrals have no standard by which to measure their rights or to avoid danger to their ships and cargoes." October 21, a note was sent to Britain reciting the grievances of American merchants. It declared that "the United States is reluctantly forced to the conclusion that the present policy of His Majesty's Government toward neutral ships and cargoes exceeds the manifest necessity of a belligerent and constitutes restrictions upon the rights of American citizens on the high seas which are not justified by the rules of international law or required under the principle of self-preservation." The British answer to several notes having the same object in view were lengthy, and correspondence was carried on throughout the entire year.

The country as a whole approved the demands by the State Department for the protection of American citizens and American shipping made in the numerous notes from time to time, but indignation was stirred to white heat by the sinking of the *Lusitania*, which was torpedoed on May 7, 1915, off Kinsale Head, Ireland. It sank almost immediately, causing the loss of more than

1,200 lives. There was demand in some quarters that war be declared at once on Germany, but the preponderating American sentiment was with President Wilson in the course he pursued. There was no suggestion of war in Congress. On May 13, a note was dispatched to the Imperial German Government recounting the sinking of the *Lusitania* by which 114 American citizens lost their lives, and the sinking of other ships resulting in the death of American citizens. The note reminded the German Government that the United States had understood its instructions to its naval commanders to be "on a plane of humane action" and it could not bring itself to believe "that these acts, so absolutely contrary to the rules, the practices, and the spirit of modern warfare, could have the countenance of the German Government." It was pointed out at length in the note that "submarines cannot be used against merchantmen without an inevitable violation of many sacred principles of justice and humanity." A demand was made for "just, prompt and enlightened action," and the note, which was signed "Bryan," closed with this significant declaration:

"The Imperial German Government will not expect the Government of the United States to omit any word or any act necessary to the performance of its sacred duty of maintaining the rights of the United States and its citizens and safeguarding their free exercise and enjoyment."

Germany's reply, dated May 28, while evidently intended to be conciliatory, was wholly unsatisfactory to Wilson. It sought to mitigate its offense by the claim that the *Lusitania* was armed and that the rapid sinking was due not to the torpedo, but to the explosion of ammunition the ship was carrying to England. It requested permission to defer its final reply until it received an answer to its plea of confession and avoidance. On June 4 it sent a more satisfactory explanation of the attacks on the American cargo steamships *Gulflight* and *Cushing*, in which it recognized "the principle of the freedom of all parts of the open sea to neutral ships and the frank willingness of the Imperial German Government to acknowledge and meet its liability where the fact of attack upon neutral ships 'which have not been guilty of any hostile act' by German aircraft or vessels of war is satisfactorily established." On June 9, the United States Government, in a note signed "Lansing" (Mr. Bryan having resigned), replied at length to the German note. It was plain that Wilson was resolved to admit of no temporizing, for it "very earnestly and very solemnly reviews" the demand in the note of May 13, "The Government of the United States is contending for something much greater than mere rights of property or privileges of commerce. It is contending for nothing less high and sacred than the rights of humanity, which every government honors itself in respecting and which no government is justified in resigning on behalf of those under its care and authority." It closed with a demand for "assurances" that Germany would carry out what our Government had all along insisted upon. Still Germany sought to palliate its action and, instead of giving the "assurances," it stressed Great Britain's "illegal blockade" and offered to grant complete immunity to "passenger ships under the control of the American Government and distinguished by special marks." The answer to Germany went into the questions at issue at great length, closing with these words of portent: "Friendship itself prompts us to say to the

Imperial Government that repetition by the commanders of the German naval vessels of acts in contravention of those rights must be regarded by the Government of the United States, when they affect American citizens, as deliberately unfriendly." Then after vigorous and unmistakable assertion of the position of the United States, Germany made the promises Wilson had demanded. When the *Arabic* was torpedoed and sunk on August 19, 1915, the German Ambassador promised "full satisfaction" and the German submarine commanders were instructed to attack no liners without warning.

For some weeks after this promise, it looked as if it was made to be kept, but on November 7 a submarine in the Mediterranean carrying the Austria-Hungary flag, sunk the *Ancona*, and a large number of passengers, including citizens of the United States, lost their lives. In a letter of December 6 to the Austrian Government the facts were detailed and the Government was called upon to denounce the act as "inhumane and barbarous" and make reparation. The Austrian reply was entirely satisfactory. On December 29 the British ship *Persia*, carrying a gun, was sunk in the Mediterranean. Among those who lost their lives was Dr. Robert McNeely, the American consul at Aden. Germany, Austria-Hungary, and Turkey denied that the ship had been sunk by any of their submarines.

On the twenty-fifth day of February Senator Gore, of Oklahoma, introduced a resolution to the effect that American citizens should "forbear to exercise the right to travel as passengers upon any armed vessel of any belligerent power" and that no passport should be issued to any American citizen for the purpose of such travel. In the House, Mr. McLemore, of Texas, introduced a resolution which requested the President to warn American citizens that they should refrain from traveling on armed belligerent ships and that any such travel in neglect of this warning would be at their own risk.

The feeling was intense in Congress and in the country. Senator Stone, Chairman of the Foreign Relations Committee, had written the President on February 24, that the situation was such as to "excite a sense of deep concern in the minds of careful and thoughtful men," and he added, "As much and as deeply as I would hate to radically disagree with you, I find it difficult from my sense of duty and responsibility to consent to plunge this nation into the vortex of this World War." Senator Stone was of Wilson's political party and up to that time had supported and championed Wilson's policies. He and those with him believed this country would soon be in the war if Wilson's declared purpose was carried out. As subsequent events proved, the Senator was resolved to do everything possible to keep the United States out of "the vortex of war." Wilson replied, calling attention to the fact that the Central Powers had in the past kept the promises he had obtained, and he hoped existing difficulties could be peacefully adjusted. Otherwise, he declared with the spirit that left no room to doubt his determination:

"We should, it seems to me, have in honor no choice as to what our course should be. For my own part, I cannot consent to any abridgment of the rights of our citizens in this respect. The honor and self-respect of the nation are involved. We court peace and shall preserve it at any cost but the loss of honor. . . . If, in this instance, we allowed expediency to take the place of principle, the door would inevitably be opened to still further concessions. Once accept a single abatement of right and many other humiliations would certainly follow."

The next day, pursuing the fixed habit of conferring with responsible leaders of Congress upon important policies, President Wilson had a conference with the leaders of the House. Speaker Clark, after the conference, said: "We told the President that the warning resolution (McLemore) would carry two to one if we ever got a chance to vote."

It was evident that there were those who wished to avoid direct action. Wilson felt the supreme necessity of a clear and vigorous policy. If there was a two-to-one majority in favor of surrendering the right of Americans to travel on the seas in pursuit of legitimate business, he wished to know it. If, as he believed, the country and the Congress would not surrender that inherent right for fear of the consequences, he wished it to be affirmatively declared. He thought the country shared his point of view. He, therefore, with what opponents of his policy called "a dramatic suddenness" requested Mr. Pou, Chairman of the House Committee on Rules, to secure an "immediate opportunity for full public discussion and action" upon the McLemore resolution.

Pending action by the House, the Senate took up the Gore resolution, its author substituting a new one, declaring that "the sinking by any submarine without notice or warning of an armed merchant vessel of her public enemy resulting in the death of a citizen of the United States would constitute a just and sufficient cause for war between the United States and the German Empire."

There was no debate, the Senate by a vote of 68 to 14

tabling the resolution, Gore voting to table his own resolution. The result was, of course, virtual defeat of Gore's original proposal that American citizens should "forbear to exercise the right to travel as passengers upon any armed vessel of any belligerent nation." Its author admitted defeat when he amended it beyond recognition and then joined in tabling it without debate. The Senate, by its lack of action, gave the President a free hand. There were not a few Senators who preferred not to go on record and were agreeable to the dog-fall. In the House, however, Wilson had his way in everything except securing "full public discussion." On March 7, the McLemore resolution came up for consideration. That body adopted the previous question, shutting off debate by a vote of 256 to 160; approved the rule itself by a vote of 272 to 137; and tabled the motion by a vote of 276 to 133. The majority included 182 Democrats, 93 Republicans, 1 Progressive. The minority embraced 33 Democrats, 102 Republicans, and 5 Progressives. This was equivalent to an approval of the policy of President Wilson and a rejection of any surrender of the right of Americans on the sea.

This victory, won only by supreme resolution and courage on Wilson's part, over the opposition of men, supposed up to that time to have controlling influence in Congress, presaged the succession of victories that followed and insured the co-operation of Congress in the subsequent measures leading up to war and in the vigorous prosecution of war.

The unrestrained submarine warfare abated, but on April 18, 1916, it became necessary to send a note on the explosion which wrecked the *Sussex* and also on the general submarine warfare against merchant ships. The note named instances of "the deliberate method and spirit of indiscriminate destruction of merchant vessels of all sorts and nationalities." This ultimatum was given: "Unless the Imperial German Government should now immediately declare and effect an abandonment of its present methods of submarine warfare against passenger and freight-carrying vessels, the Government of the United States can have no choice but to sever diplomatic relations with the German Empire altogether." This ultimatum was made not only to protect American rights, but, as Wilson declared, "in behalf of humanity and the rights of neutral nations."

On April 19, 1916, President Wilson, in pursuance of his fixed policy of keeping in touch with the legislators and keeping them informed of every important step, in a special message delivered to Congress, gave a full résumé of the correspondence with the German Government with reference to submarine destruction. "Again and again," he said, "the Imperial German Government has given this Government its solemn assurances" and "again and again permitted its undersea commanders to disregard these assurances with entire impunity." He told Congress our Government "has been very patient"; it had "accepted the successive explanations and assurances of the Imperial Government as given in entire sincerity and good faith, and had hoped, even against hope," that these promises would be kept. He said the German Government had "been unable to put any limits or restraints upon its warfare," and it had become "painfully evident that the use of submarines for the destruction of an enemy's commerce is incompatible with the principles of humanity, the long established and incontrovertible rights of neutrals, and the sacred immunities of non-combatants." He therefore stated he had said to the Imperial German Government that "if it is still its purpose to prosecute relentless and indiscriminate warfare" there would be no choice but to sever diplomatic relations with the Government of the German Empire altogether. He added as the reason that had impelled him "with keenest regret to this course," this statement: "We cannot forget that we are in some sort and by the force of circumstances the responsible spokesman of the rights of humanity, and that we cannot remain silent while those rights seem in process of being utterly swept away in the maelstrom of this terrible war." The result of this note and message was that the German Government in a long reply gave the promises and assurances demanded. In its note Germany expressed the confidence that the United States would demand that the British Government should observe the rules of international law. To this on May 8, the United States Government answered, accepting Germany's "declaration of its abandonment of the policy which seriously menaced the good relations" and announcing that it would "rely upon a scrupulous execution of the new and altered policy." It added that it could not "for a moment entertain, much less discuss, a suggestion that respect by German naval authorities for the rights of citizens of the United States upon the high seas should in any way, or in the slightest degree, be made contingent upon the conduct of any other government affecting the rights of neutrals and non-combatants" and concluded with the pregnant sentence: "Responsibility in such matters is single, not joint; absolute, not relative."

Wilson had won the victory. Germany had surrendered. The pledge that merchant vessels would not be sunk without warning and without saving human lives was observed from May 4, 1916, to January 31, 1917. Wilson had indeed been "very patient," but he had never altered his ultimatum made on May 13 that the American Government "would not omit any word or act" to secure what Germany at last pledged its honor to do. For nine months the promise was kept and the summer and fall of 1916 gave hope that the submarine menace was a thing of the past. Wilson was so encouraged that on December 18 he sent a note to the belligerent governments, suggesting to each that they state the terms on which peace would be acceptable. The responses were somewhat encouraging, and on January 22, 1917, he addressed Congress on the essential terms of peace in Europe. That olive branch, which at first seemed to be well received, was followed shortly by Germany's breaking its word and its renewal of the unrestricted submarine warfare. In that situation, as in every crisis, Wilson conferred with congressional leaders. Senator Robinson thus relates what happened:

"When the German Government announced its purpose to resume submarine warfare, the President went to his room in the Capitol, summoned a number of Senators and said:

"'You know the situation in all its details. I wonder what you are thinking I should do?'

"One Senator replied: 'Give the German Ambassador his passports and order him forthwith to leave the country.'

"Another declared: 'I heartily approve of that suggestion.'

"A third Senator, however, suggested that perhaps

it might be well to dispatch a communication remonstrating against the avowed purpose of Germany. President Wilson's jaws snapped. His features became pale and rigid. Drawing himself erect and casting a stern glance upon the crowd which had gathered while the consultation was in progress, he said, in substance:

" 'Let us be done with diplomatic notes. The hour to act has come. We scarcely can hope that Germany will recede. The German Ambassador will be advised that unless immediate abandonment of the submarine policy is announced, his further presence in the United States is not desired.' "

President Wilson in a message delivered to Congress on February 3, 1917, reviewed the circumstances and stated that he had taken steps to sever all relations with the German Empire. He added that the American Ambassador at Berlin would be withdrawn, and the German Ambassador at Washington would be handed his passports. He still hoped the "overt act" would not occur. If, however, "American ships and American lives should be sacrificed," Wilson added, he would come to Congress again "to ask that authority be given me to use any means that may be necessary for the protection of our seamen and our people in the prosecution of their peaceful and legitimate errands on the high seas." He closed with the declaration that he proposed to "vindicate our right to liberty and justice and unmolested life," and made this prayer: "God grant we may not be challenged to defend them by acts of wilful injustice on the part of the government of Germany!"

"Has the Navy the guns and gunners to arm and man merchant ships?"

"How soon can you put guns and gunners on merchant ships?"

President Wilson asked these questions of the Secretary of the Navy at a Cabinet meeting early in the year 1917. He was told the Navy could arm them as fast as the ships were ready.

The Central Powers had announced that after March 1, they would treat armed enemy merchantmen as ships of war. Prior to that, on February 15, a statement was given out to the press by the administration that merchantmen had a legal right to carry armament for the purpose, the sole purpose, of defense and that the right of American citizens to travel on such vessels should not be impaired. Wilson believed he had the right to arm merchantmen, but on February 26, in an address to both houses, he requested Congress to "supply our merchant ships with defensive arms, should that become necessary, and with the means of using them, and to employ any other instrumentalities or methods that may be necessary and adequate to protect our ships and our people in their legitimate and peaceful pursuits on the seas." A bill to that effect, introduced at once, promptly passed the House by a large majority, but failed in the Senate by reason of a filibuster conducted by a handful of Senators whose continual debate prevented the bill from coming to a vote before the end of the session of Congress, March 4. It was that filibuster which called forth the President's denunciation of the "little group of wilful men" who had, with utter disregard of the necessity of action, prevented the legislation. He also suggested a change in the rules of the Senate so as to make it impossible for a small group to defeat the will of the overwhelming majority of

Senators. The need for such protection of American merchant ships called for no delay. Before adjournment, a large majority of the Senators signed a document, stating that they favored the bill to arm American merchantmen, and would have voted for it, if they had been given the opportunity. Confident that he had the power under the Constitution, and a large majority of both Houses of Congress having expressed willingness to grant him specific authority, President Wilson, on March 12, directed the Secretary of the Navy to furnish guns and naval gunmen to American ships. In two days guns were installed in the *Manchuria*, *St. Louis* and *Aztec;* four days later the *New York* and *St. Paul* were equipped. The *Manchuria* sailed for England March 15, and thereafter a constant succession of merchant ships, carrying armed guards, left our ports for Europe.

Up to this time the majority sentiment of the country had seemed to be averse to America's participation in the European war. In November Mr. Wilson had been re-elected by a popular majority of 590,785. A militant and growing minority had been critical of Wilson's policy. But sentiment for action was crystallizing, and when Wilson brought the matter to a head by asking Congress to "supply our merchant ships with arms" that naval gunners might give protection to them, there was such response as to show the country was behind its President in his resolve at any cost to give protection to American lives on the high seas. His measure had passed the House by a vote of 403 to 13 and only the "little group of wilful men" in the Senate stood against the course he had marked out.

Solemnly as he had called the nation to war, after exercising every possible means to avert its entrance, consistent with devotion to humanity and duty to America, President Wilson welcomed release from the longer impossible attempt to preserve neutrality. From the sinking of the *Lusitania*, there had been a growing feeling in the country that the United States could not avoid participation. Wilson, when urged to keep the nation "out of war," in his earnest desire to do so consistent with duty, had reminded the people that conditions might at any time arise when it would not be possible to do so. On April 2, all efforts for peace having proved unavailing, Wilson delivered his famous war message to Congress, advising that Germany's course be declared war against the United States.

Neutrality was ended. War was on.

## Chapter XXIV

# RE-ELECTED TO THE PRESIDENCY

**PAULINE REVERE RODE OUT OF THE WEST, BRINGING VICTORY—THE HYPHEN ISSUE LOOMED LARGE—WILSON SCORNED DISLOYAL VOTE—"HE KEPT US OUT OF WAR"—HUGHES INDULGED IN PETTY CRITICISMS—THREATENED RAILROAD STRIKE AVERTED**

*"If you think too much about being re-elected, it is very difficult to be worth re-electing."*—WILSON

THE year 1916 was critical in the political life of Woodrow Wilson. In the election of 1914, the bulk of the voters, who had joined the Progressive party in 1912, gave their suffrage to Republican nominees. This was in the face of the fact that their representatives in Congress had supported most of the measures of reform and progress initiated by Wilson and approved by the platforms of both the Democratic and Progressive parties. The big Democratic majority of 1912 had shrunk to a bare majority after the 1914 election. Wilson found 290 Democrats and 127 Republicans in the House, and 51 Democrats and 45 Republicans in the Senate when he stood up to deliver his first oral message in 1913. When he came to the same duty in 1915, there was a Democratic majority of only 33 in the House, though the majority in the Senate remained the same as in 1913. This presaged what followed, a close election in 1916. The result showed that the Progressive party had lost its representation in Congress. Would it be a factor at all in 1916? That question was debated, but when the Republican and Progressive National Conventions were announced to be held in Chicago at the same time, it was accepted that there was to be a merger. Still there were many Progressives who had no mind to return to the Republican party. This element demanded that Roosevelt accept a re-nomination and carry on the fight. In an enthusiastic, but not otherwise impressive, convention, the Progressives nominated Roosevelt, with John M. Parker of Louisiana as his running mate. Roosevelt declined the nomination to the undoing of the Progressive party, and Parker later took the stump for Wilson. The remarkable organization which, in 1912, had polled 4,119,538 votes, dissolved. The bulk of its Republican membership, who had joined it as a revolt against what they regarded as reactionary policies, elected to return to their old party allegiance along with their brilliant leader. The Democrats who had supported Roosevelt likewise returned to their old party. The election of 1916 hung largely upon how the minority, or as they called themselves, "conscience Progressives," would vote in November.

The Republicans nominated Charles Evans Hughes, who had won high place in popular regard as Governor of New York, and who was then serving as Associate Justice of the Supreme Court. The average prognosticator east of the Mississippi River looked for an easy victory for Hughes. If he could hold the Taft vote, which seemed certain, and if Roosevelt, who gave him support, could bring him the Progressive vote, the election was already won. And he would have been elected but for one thing:

> "Oh, East is East, and West is West,
> And never the twain shall meet."

For the first time in a presidential contest the parties felt called upon to stress the doctrine of Americanism. The outstanding slogan had relation to the newly emphasized word "hyphen." Mr. Roosevelt and Mr. Wilson joined in their demand that the hyphenated citizenship should end. The Republican platform appealed to "all Americans, whether naturalized or not, to prove to the world that we are Americans in thought and in deed, with one loyalty, one hope, one aspiration." It was in these words:

"In 1861 the Republican party stood for the Union. As it stood for the Union of States, it now stands for a united people, true to American ideals, loyal to American tradition, knowing no allegiance except to the Constitution, to the Government and to the flag of the United States. We believe in American policies at home and abroad. Such are our principles, such are our purposes and policies. We close as we began. The times are dangerous and the future is fraught with perils. The great issues of the day have been confused by words and phrases. The American spirit which made the country and saved the Union, has been forgotten by those charged with the responsibility of power. We appeal to all Americans, whether naturalized or native born, to prove to the world that we are Americans in thought and in deed, with one loyalty, one hope, one aspiration. We call on all Americans to be true to the spirit of America, to the great traditions of their common country, and, above all things, to keep the faith."

The Democratic platform rang out clear and strong, without possibility of being open to any doubtful meaning or any appeal to the un-American policy of "looking two ways" as was possible in the Republican declaration:

"In this day of test, America must show itself not a nation of partisans but a nation of patriots." It made vigorous denunciation of the activities of any agencies that owed first allegiance to any other country. That declaration, in the spirit if not the actual words of Woodrow Wilson, read thus:

"Whoever, actuated by the purpose to promote the interest of a foreign power, in disregard of our own country's welfare or to injure this Government in its foreign relations or cripple or destroy its industries at home, and whoever by arousing prejudices of a racial, religious or other nature creates discord and strife among our people so as to obstruct the wholesome process of unification, is faithless to the trust which the privileges of citizenship repose in him and is disloyal to his country. We, therefore, condemn as subversive of this Nation's unity and integrity, and as destructive of its welfare, the activities and designs of every group or organization, political or otherwise, that has for its object the advancement of the interest of a foreign power, whether such object is promoted by intimidating the Government, a political party, or representatives of the people, or which is calculated and tends to divide our people into antagonistic groups and thus to destroy that complete agreement and solidarity of the people and that unity of sentiment and purpose so essential to the perpetuity of the Nation and its free institutions. We condemn all alliances and combinations of individuals in this country, of whatever nationality or descent, who agree and conspire together for the purpose of embarrassing or weakening our Government or of improperly influencing or coercing our public representatives in dealing or negotiating with any foreign power. We charge that such conspiracies among a limited number exist and have been instigated for the purpose of advancing the interests of foreign countries to the prejudice and detriment of our own country. We condemn any political party which, in view of the activity of such conspirators, surrenders its integrity or modifies its policy."

This was interpreted and intended as a rebuke of the propaganda by German organizations which approved the sinking of the Lusitania and which, backed by the Gore and McLemore resolutions, were in sympathy with the Von Papen and Boy-Ed plots, or ready for the sabotage which, when it appeared, was suppressed only by Wilson's strong measures. It was also aimed at Republicans who were flirting with the leaders of the hyphenated voters. Always Wilson separated the loyal Americans born in other countries from those who loved some other nation and served it more faithfully than the nation that gave them home and sustenance. "We do not wish," he said at Arlington on May 30, "men to forget their mothers and fathers, their forbears, running back through long, laborious generations," and he added the criticism of "men who have allowed their old ardor for another nationality to overthrow their ardor for the nationality to which they have given their new and voluntary allegiance." Emphasizing the same truth in his Flag Day speech (June 14), he uttered this indictment and condemnation: "There is disloyalty active in the United States, and it must be absolutely crushed."

He arraigned the disloyal who poured the poison of disloyalty into the very arteries of our national life; who have "sought to bring the authority and good name of our Government into contempt, to destroy our industries wherever they thought it effective for their vindictive purposes," and to "debase our politics to the uses of foreign intrigue."

In his speech of acceptance Wilson had said: "I neither seek the favor nor fear the displeasure of the small alien element amongst us which put loyalty to any foreign power before loyalty to the United States." Later as the campaign progressed, Wilson stressed that position. A few weeks before the election, after Maine had gone Republican and the New Jersey primaries presaged a Republican victory in November, Jeremiah O'Leary, who had been vicious in his denunciation of Wilson, wrote the President an offensive letter. As soon as he saw the letter, Mr. Wilson made this answer:

"I would feel deeply mortified to have you or anybody like you vote for me. Since you have access to many disloyal Americans and I have not, I will ask you to convey this message to them."

Never had more scorn been compressed in so few words. That bold rebuke was warmly approved. It was what hunters call "a gut shot." It electrified the country and emphasized the issue Wilson kept to the front, to the confusion of those who were trying to carry water on both shoulders. It was one more evidence that Wilson never trimmed, never evaded, never permitted his position to be clouded. He hit from the shoulder!

The Democrats in the beginning placed their claim for Wilson's re-election mainly upon the record of achievement in domestic policies and upon their Big Brother attitude toward Mexico. The latter probably had been assailed with the harshest condemnation by the Republicans in their platform, but without presenting any concrete Mexican plan of their own. The Democrats also asked for the support of the country upon Wilson's policy of neutrality with insistence upon the protection of American rights on land and sea which the Germans had promised to respect. The war in Europe and the threat of hyphenism at home swallowed up all other issues. As the campaign progressed, the hyphen issue and the question of America's future duty toward the World War became paramount. People paid no heed to the criticisms leveled by Mr. Hughes at the men and measures of the Wilson administration. They paid little, if any, more to the Democratic story of the reform measures Wilson had put in operation. It is safe to say that by October these matters, which seemed so important when letters and speeches of acceptance were being framed, were forgotten by the voters. In the East the feeling that America must enter the World War had been strong from the day of the sinking of the *Lusitania*. Many had been held back from advocacy of declaring war by the promises Wilson extorted that the men guilty should be punished and acts of destruction on the sea should end. But the feeling that America should enter the war against Germany was strong and growing. However, it was far from compelling and no considerable number of Congressmen had sought to commit the country to war. In the main, the sentiment on the Atlantic seaboard was critical of Wilson. Hughes made no promise to go in, so that no direct issue was made there. Roosevelt, who was opposing Wilson more than he was supporting Hughes, wished America to join forces with the Allies. Candidate Hughes contented himself with criticism of Wilson without a clear-cut policy of either going in or staying out. The Republican platform had declared: "We desire peace, the peace of justice and right, and believe in maintaining a strict and honest neutrality between the belligerents in the great war in Europe." It aimed this dart at Wilson: "We believe that the peace and neutrality, as well as the dignity and influence of the United States, cannot be preserved by shifty expedients, by phrase-making, by performances in language, or by attitudes ever changing in an effort to secure groups of voters." What would the Republican party do if given power? It promised "a firm, consistent and courageous policy" of—what? It did not say, except such as had "always been maintained by Republican Presidents." Nothing more, except "we believe in the pacific settlement of international disputes, and favor the establishment of a world court for the purpose."

In the West, where the sentiment to enter the European war was much less than on the Atlantic seaboard, Wilson's policy was more generally approved. In fact, the prevailing sentiment was strongly against entrance into the World War. Indeed, it was so strong that "he kept us out of war" became a slogan, obtaining its inspiration in the keynote address of Governor Martin H. Glynn, temporary chairman of the Convention that renominated Wilson and Marshall. In that address, referring to the policy of neutrality and insistence upon American rights, Governor Glynn was given long applause when he said:

"This policy may not satisfy those who revel in destruction and find pleasure in despair. It may not satisfy the fire-eater or the swashbuckler, but it does satisfy the mothers of the land at whose hearth and fireside no jingoistic war has placed an empty chair. It does satisfy the daughters of this land from whom bluster and brag has sent no loving brother to the dissolution of the grave. It does satisfy the fathers of this land and the sons of this land who will fight for our flag and die for our flag when reason primes the rifle, when honor draws the sword, when justice breathes a blessing on the standard they uphold."

The slogan, "He kept us out of war," so generally used in the 1916 campaign, was not of Wilson's making. He wished peace, but in every discussion of what the future held in store, he made it clear that the issue of peace or war was not in his keeping.

During the campaign, except for a few short trips to the West and his final speech at Long Branch, Mr. Wilson remained at Shadow Lawn, N. J., while Mr. Hughes spoke in all parts of the country. Every Saturday afternoon Wilson delivered an address from his porch, dealing in his own telling way with every issue that arose. The country was surprised at the rather petty criticisms with which Mr. Hughes started his campaign. Mr. Wilson's only comment on the criticisms were: "If you will give that gentleman rope enough he will hang himself. He has forgotten many things since he closeted himself on the bench and he will soon find himself out of touch with the spirit of the nation. His speeches are nothing more or less than blank cartridges and the country, unless I mistake the people very much, will place a true assessment upon them." That expressed his real sentiment and when he was in a fight Wilson had a way of saying what he thought, even if it had a sting. The vicious and petty pin-pricks of Hughes justified an answer in kind. As the campaign progressed, however, Mr. Hughes discarded the advice of small partisans and discussed larger issues and more ably and pitched appeals upon the questions presented in his platform. But he was hazy at what he would do if elected. Mr. Wilson's campaign speeches were among his best,

**COLUMBUS DAY IN NEW YORK** 

President Wilson leading a parade of thousands of marchers down Fifth Avenue to help boom the Fourth Liberty Loan. In the front, from left to right, are: Secretary Tumulty, Real-Admiral Grayson, President Wilson, and Brigadier-General Geo. R. Dyer, the Grand Marshal

U. S. Official Photograph

**THE BIG FOUR**

Premier Lloyd George, Premier Orlando, Premier Clemenceau and President Wilson

always bold and on the offensive. He charged and never was on the defensive. In September the threatened railroad strike called for action. Wilson met it with customary directness, secured the passage of the Adamson law, prevented a break-down of transportation, and confounded those who thought his courageous course would defeat him.

If, however, the two distinguished candidates in the main observed the amenities, so much cannot be said for many of their partisans. It is perhaps true that no campaign in the history of the country has been quite so marked by viciousness, bitterness and invective. All the elements of hate and misrepresentation were brought into play. While most leading Democrats in the East looked toward November with apprehension, Wilson looked toward it with both confidence and philosophy. He never doubted the verdict of the people. If it was not right today, it would be right tomorrow. So he slept soundly the night before the election. He always declared he played for the verdict of history.

The election of 1916 was one in which both parties celebrated victory. By nine o'clock on the night of election day it was apparent that the normally pivotal states—New York, Indiana, Connecticut and New Jersey—had gone for Hughes. The great newspapers supporting Wilson conceded the election of Hughes, who was congratulated. He went to sleep believing he was the President-elect. Wilson went to sleep believing he had been defeated. The morrow was to tell another story. Westward the course of pivotal states had taken flight. Ohio had gone for Wilson and so had Kansas. It looked as if Minnesota and California and practically every state west of the Mississippi had voted the same way. The next few days were hectic. Minnesota swung to Hughes by a few hundred. The West had elected Wilson if he had won the California electoral vote. It hung in the balance. The count in Los Angeles was provokingly slow. Suspicious Democratic watchers in that city kept vigil over every uncounted box. Armed and vigilant they feared they might be tampered with. They remembered 1876 and feared they might again lose the Presidency by a narrow margin. The country watched and waited. The final count gave California to Wilson by a majority of 3,777. The story of the victory was epitomized in Rollin Kirby's cartoon in the *World*,—a young woman on horseback called Pauline Revere riding from the sunset to the national Capital. The result was accepted and Wilson was happy that his countrymen had understood and trusted him. His electoral vote was 277 to 254 for Hughes and his popular majority over Hughes was 568,822. With the impressive vote of 9,116,296, the largest vote ever given to a President up to that election, he faced the future with full knowledge of the responsibilities, imposed upon him. His first act was to keep his organization intact by writing to the members of his Cabinet appreciation of their co-operation and asking them to go with him into the larger duties of the new term.

What did it hold in store—Peace or War?

"I pray God I may be given the wisdom and the prudence to do my duty in the true spirit of this great people" was the prayer in his second inaugural as he plead for American solidarity in these words: "United alike in the conception of our duty and in the high resolve to perform it in the face of all men, let us dedicate ourselves to the great task to which we must now set our hand."

Dedication was renewed.

## Chapter XXV

# ACCEPTING THE GAGE OF BATTLE

PRESIDENT WILSON, IN PRESENCE OF DISTINGUISHED GATHERING, ASKS CONGRESS TO DECLARE WAR—PRESENTED BY SPEAKER CLARK—A FIGHTER WITHOUT HATE—"THE WORLD MUST BE MADE SAFE FOR DEMOCRACY"—"THE RIGHT MORE PRECIOUS THAN PEACE"—"GOD HELPING HER, SHE CAN DO NO OTHER"

"*It is not an army that we must shape and train for war; it is a nation.*"—Wilson

"IT is a fearful thing to lead this great peaceful people into war, into the most terrible and disastrous of all wars, civilization itself seeming in the balance," declared Woodrow Wilson toward the close of his war message of April 2, 1917. These words correctly described his feelings. It was "a fearful thing," but he was upheld by the thought next presented: "But the right is more precious than peace, and we shall fight for the things which we have always carried nearest our hearts."

The setting was fitting. The most distinguished gathering in the life of America looked down upon him, as President Wilson entered the House of Representatives that evening. Every member of both houses of Congress was in his seat. The Supreme Court, headed by the venerable and patriotic Chief Justice, occupied seats near the Speaker's desk. Diplomats from every nation, in official robes, looked down from their positions of vantage. The press gallery was crowded, great editors present with the regular correspondents. Army and navy officers in their uniforms suggested the coming of war. Mrs. Wilson and wives of Cabinet officers, flanked by hundreds of wives of legislators and diplomats, lent distinction and color to the scene.

There was an air of expectancy and consecration. The tense feeling left no place for trivialities. The applause that greeted President Wilson as he entered the chamber was rather giving vent to suppressed emotion than to personal compliment. It was an occasion too sacred for plaudits to any man. There were mothers there with blanched cheeks, already feeling the pangs of the supreme sacrifice their sons must make. Light and color and glory shone on the surface. Consecration, sacrifice, grim duty reigned in their hearts.

"The President of the United States," said Speaker Clark as the echo of the gavel died away. The grim Speaker had contested with the President for the high honor. Both were walking through Gethsemane. The high call made them comrades.

Any stranger would have chosen Wilson as the Leader if he had looked down upon that gathering of the great. Erect, with a sense of stern responsibility, face drawn with determination, eyes giving cheer and confidence, there was a gravity and distinction about his bearing that marked him for what the world soon hailed him: The Voice and Inspiration of the Crusade for Righteousness and Peace. But before the goal of victory was the conflict of battle.

He stood there every inch the fighter. The days of debate and forbearance were adjourned. It was to be war "without rancor and without selfish object," and without revenge. The spirit of the Covenanter was upon him as with firm and solemn voice he made clear "there is one choice we are incapable of making: we will not choose the path of submission and suffer the most sacred rights of our nation and our people to be ignored or violated."

The chamber breathed its approval and dedication. In clear tones rang out the shibboleth and aim: "The world must be made safe for democracy." This challenge lifted the Cause to the heights. The "force to the utmost" must not be for conquest. Why must we fight? "For democracy, for the right of those who submit to authority to have a voice in their own governments, for the rights and liberties of small nations, for a universal dominion of right by such concert of free peoples as shall bring peace and safety to all nations and make the world itself at last free."

As this noble conception was unfolded, the hearts of men and women went out to the leader who had phrased for them the high purposes of their own souls. There was the hush of accord and gratitude that no hint of hate marred the solemn declaration. It seemed that the benediction of the God of Right and Justice rested on that assemblage where no small or unholy thoughts could live. It was as if there had been a rush of wings and the voice of the angels stilling and strengthening for the days ahead.

Would Americans be equal to the challenge for such a blessing for mankind? The Leader lifted his voice. It was the voice of faith and devotion—his own and that of all the people. Every ear was strained to catch the closing words and their significance.

"To such a task," rang out the final note that

summoned to whole-hearted espousal, "we can dedicate our lives and our fortunes, everything that we are and everything that we have, with the pride of those who know that the day has come when America is privileged to spend her blood and her might for the principles that gave her birth and happiness and the peace which she has treasured."

And then came the prayer that was upon every tongue in the crucial days:

"God helping her, she can do no other."

The die had been cast. The echo of the cavalry on Pennsylvania Avenue, as the Commander-in-chief was escorted to the White House, broke the silence. It was the reverberation of what was to become a familiar sound in the months ahead.

War was on.

## CHAPTER XXVI

# THE WORLD WAR

**THE DRIVING POWER OF THE COMMANDER-IN-CHIEF OF THE ARMY AND NAVY—"FORCE TO THE UTMOST" —"DO THE THING MOST AUDACIOUS TO THE UTMOST POINT OF RISK AND DARING"—REAL COMRADE AND SHIPMATE TO FIGHTING MEN—WINNING THE WAR—VICTORY MESSAGE TO CONGRESS**

"*The supreme test of the nation has come. We must all speak, act, and serve together.*"—WILSON

WAR was declared by Congress April 6, 1917. A resolution carrying the President's recommendation that Congress declare the recent course of the Imperial German Government to be, in fact, nothing less than "war against the Government and people of the United States" was adopted in the Senate April 4, by a vote of 82 to 6. The House completed action at 3 o'clock on the morning of April 6 by a vote of 373 to 50 and President Wilson promptly affixed his signature. It was at the Cabinet meeting on March 20 —it might be called the Day of Decision—that every member of the Cabinet counselled President Wilson that war was inevitable and the call was made for a special session of Congress "to receive a communication by the Executive on grave questions of national policy which should be taken into consideration."

The business of carrying on war became the only business in America. The War and Navy Departments, anticipating the event, had made every preparation consistent with the national policy. From the moment the United States entered the war, Wilson's resolute policy carried on under high pressure was, as he stated: "Force! Force to the utmost! Force without stint or limit! The righteous and triumphant Force which shall make Right the law of the world, and cast every selfish dominion down in the dust."

Two decisions of Wilson indicate his militant leadership. Hardly had our soldiers begun to land in France before there came urgent insistence from Allies that they be used as "replacement troops." Some short-sighted Americans abroad joined in the unwise suggestion. Pershing had been sent across by Wilson and Baker to command an "American Army." He had no patience with the replacement propaganda. When Baker brought the matter up in the Cabinet, Wilson declared with great emphasis: "No, we will leave to General Pershing the disposition of our troops, but it must be an American Army, officered and directed by Americans, ready to throw their strength where it will tell most." And he added in substance: "It may not be impossible before the war is over that we shall have to bear the brunt. We must be prepared for any demand with all the agencies necessary to supply our army and secure victory." The replacement dispersion was nipped in the bud.

It was largely due to Wilson that the weakness of divided command was ended and Foch became the Commander-in-chief of all the forces engaged in the war. Even before the United States entered the war, he criticized the lack of unified command. Immediately upon our entry, in concert with Lloyd George, he threw his powerful influence for the new organization that gave coherence and new power to the allied forces.

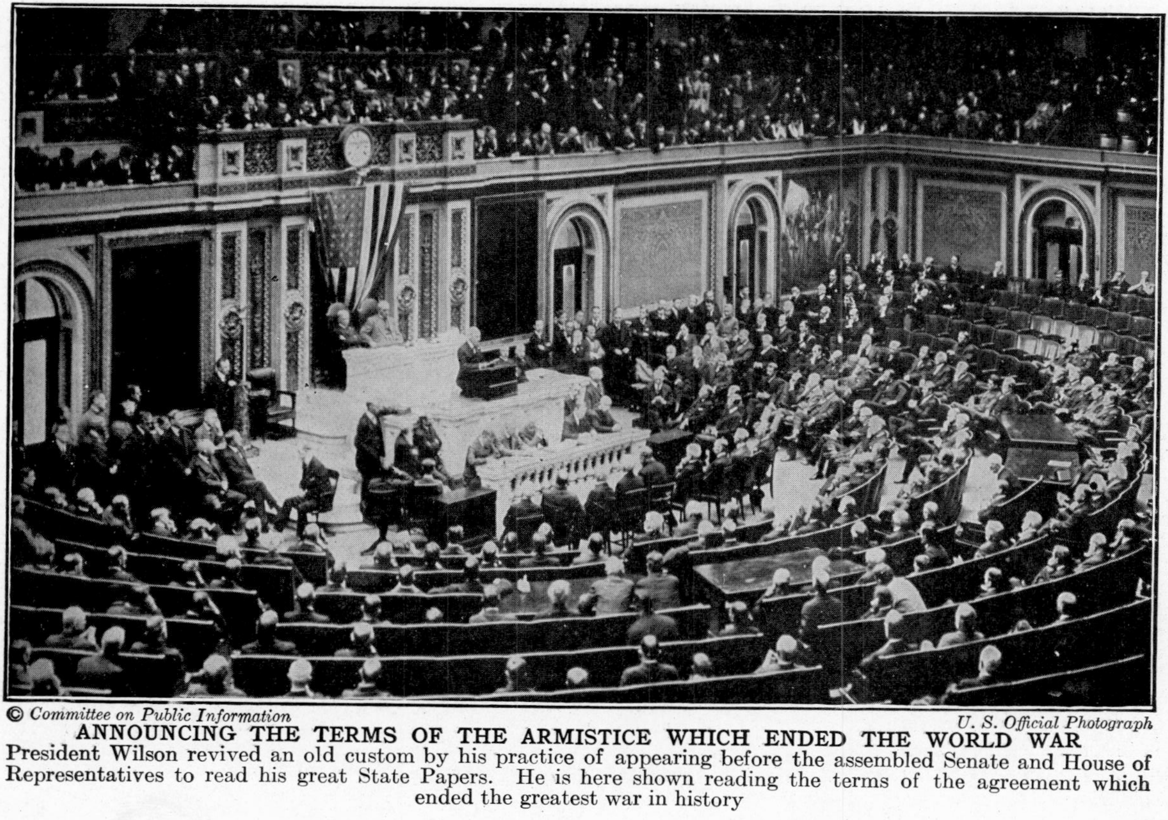

 *U. S. Official Photograph*

**ANNOUNCING THE TERMS OF THE ARMISTICE WHICH ENDED THE WORLD WAR**

President Wilson revived an old custom by his practice of appearing before the assembled Senate and House of Representatives to read his great State Papers. He is here shown reading the terms of the agreement which ended the greatest war in history

**THE CORNER-STONE OF THE AMPHITHEATRE AT ARLINGTON** *Photo. Int'l. Newsreel*

This beautiful memorial amphitheatre at Arlington Cemetery was built as the final resting place of America's Unknown Soldier from France, who here holds his faithful watch forever.

In the field of preparation and conduct of the war, and in strategy too, he demonstrated ability. Military men came to lean on his judgment, and in strategy he showed that a military chieftain was lost when he gave himself to letters, to study of government, and to statesmanship. He was not only the commander-in-chief in name, but in deed also. He early saw the necessity of war mobilization of every industry and activity. He welcomed the organization of the Naval Consulting Board in 1915 which made the first survey of industry for war. Before war began he created the Council of National Defense. He brought into being the War Industries Board, the War Trade, Food, Fuel, Labor, Shipping, Welfare, Publicity, and other agencies, without which the mobilization of all American power for the successful prosecution of the war would have been impossible. He not only called them into being. He kept in close touch with their work, and gave prompt and effective co-operation. Once every week at the White House he held conferences with what came to be called—it had no official name—"the Super War Cabinet or Council," composed of the Secretary of the Treasury, Secretary of War, Secretary of the Navy, Bernard M. Baruch, Harry A. Garfield, Herbert Hoover, Edward N. Hurley and Vance McCormick. This body was the clearing house. To it he brought grave questions for consideration and all the members brought their perplexities for his clear counsel and direction.

Concurrent with the practical direction and inspection of his captains in these practical fields, he was in close touch with the allied powers, receiving and conferring with delegations from all the Allied and Associated nations, and keeping in close touch with every movement in the Cabinet or on the field. He read practically all the cablegrams that came to the Army and Navy Departments and followed the active operations of both arms of the service in France and afloat, giving suggestion and direction, with commendation to wisdom and courage. He was in closest touch with the State Department directing the weighty foreign policies and problems, all of which went to him for determination. Neglecting no agency, his chief interest was international. In the midst of the prosecution of war he kept his mind on the time he felt sure would come when the United States might couple world deliverance from war with the conclusion of peace terms.

By messages to Congress, by letters, by addresses to fighting men, to organizations and political bodies he stimulated deeper patriotism and greater consecration. He marched down Pennsylvania Avenue, scorning to ride, and down Fifth Avenue in great parades planned to give enthusiasm to the Liberty Loan and other drives. All the time he must be in touch with the leaders of Congress, give impulse to their fine desire to afford all means and assistance to win victory, and pilot emergency legislation.

The legislation providing for the Selective Draft was the outstanding constructive new method of securing recruits to carry on the war. This made it democratic to the core, calling upon all men to render the service most needed. It could not have been put through Congress except by the driving force of Wilson and his irresistible arguments. It was the first time in history that a plan of obtaining soldiers through the good offices of civilian boards had been undertaken. It was so justly administered by patriotic citizens, selected with great care, as to convince even those who had been hostile to departing from the voluntary system. Under it every man was commandeered to the khaki, to the factory, to the farm—wherever he could render best service in winning the war.

A departure that was distinctive was the greater care for the health and morale of the soldiers and sailors. Safety zones were created wherever men were in training and immoral houses were banned. Cities were called upon to repeal segregation district laws. Welfare agencies contributed to the comfort, health and clean living of the fighting forces. The medical care was unequalled and the self-mobilization of surgeons and physicians and nurses reduced sickness and the death rate. In all these agencies President Wilson took the deepest interest and gave the most cordial support. War-time prohibition demonstrated the wisdom of its adoption.

President Wilson was the inspiration of naval achievement. Early in his administration he had said: "We shall take leave to be strong upon the seas," and early in 1916 he declared for "the most adequate navy in the world." Before this country entered the war he thought the British ought to convoy their merchant ships and "shut the hornets up in their nest." He took that position in advance of naval officers in Britain or America. He gave support when our Navy adopted his suggestions, and was impatient because the British Navy delayed its approval of the barrage across the North Sea.

The total number of men who served in the Army was 4,272,521. The story of its distinguished service is the glory of America. Under the direction of the able Secretary of War, Newton D. Baker, supported at every turn by President Wilson, the American Expeditionary Force made possible the victory in France. The selection of General Pershing, who had proved his fitness in Mexico, by the Secretary of War and approved by the President, guaranteed efficient leadership. The application of Theodore Roosevelt to go overseas in high command, declined by the President, caused much criticism, which Mr. Wilson's letter somewhat mitigated. Roosevelt's subsequent death proved he was not physically up to the task, though in heart and spirit and patriotism he had the courage of youth. It was necessary also to run counter to the request of General Leonard Wood for a command in France. In war there must be a supreme commander. General Pershing did not ask for Wood. He did ask for Liggett and others. In that, as in all else for the successful prosecution of war, the President and Secretary of War gave to Pershing full support.

"No such movement of troops ever took place before across 3,000 miles of sea, followed by adequate equipment, and carried safely through extraordinary dangers of attack," said President Wilson in his Victory Message to Congress December 2, 1918. He pointed out that in twelve months the Army had enlisted, equipped and trained and sent overseas 1,950,513 men, an average of 162,542 each month, rising to 307,182 in the month of July. "Of all this movement," he said, "only 758 men were lost by enemy attacks—630 of whom were upon a single British transport which was sunk near the Orkney Islands."

Five minutes after the President signed the war resolution, orders were given for the mobilization of the fleet. So completely was it prepared that Admiral

Henry T. Mayo, Commander-in-Chief of the Naval forces then and throughout the entire war, said he "did not have to give a single order to pass the fleet from a peace to a war basis and that it was in a better state of preparedness than it had ever been and there was a feeling of confidence in the personnel of being able to cope with any emergency." The Navy made ready in every possible way. Before the declaration of war it had increased its enlistment to 87,000, which it increased to 533,000 officers and men during the war. Never at any time from April 6, 1917, till the Armistice was a ship ready (and the number was increased to 2,000) when officers and men were not promptly furnished to man it.

The first military order of the war was made by the Secretary of the Navy April 14. It was, "Fit out for long and distant service" sent to the Commander of the Eighth Destroyers Division. This had been done immediately after a conference in Washington with the naval representatives of the British and French Governments which agreed upon the plan of co-operation. Upon the arrival of the first division of destroyers in Europe, the British Admiral asked the Commanding Officer:

"When will you be ready to go to sea?"

"We are ready now," was the answer.

That was the record of the American Navy throughout the war. Its record was such as to justify Senator Lodge in saying on the floor of the Senate in June, 1918, when U-boats appeared on the Atlantic seaboard: "The Navy has been doing the greatest possible work everywhere. It has not failed in convoying the troops. It has not failed in its work in the Baltic and in the Channel and the Coast of France and the Mediterranean, and it will not fail here. It will do everything that courage and intelligence and bravery can possibly do."

The outstanding achievement of the Navy was that it kept the road open to France so that of the 2,079,880 men in the Army sent overseas, not one soldier on an American troopship lost his life on the way to France. "We fully realize," said Pershing, "that had it not been for the Navy, which kept watch and guard night and day over our transport fleet, the American effort in France would never have been successful." Of its collateral work, of assistance in relief, Hoover said: "I do not see how we could have carried on the work without the wonderful help of the Navy."

The second outstanding achievement of the Navy was the laying of the barrage across the North Sea. Only nine days after war was declared the Bureau of Ordnance outlined the plan which had to its credit when the war ended 8½ per cent of the total number of enemy submarines put out of business. The barrage was in operation only in the last few weeks of the war.

The most remarkable address of the war, certainly as it related to the Navy, was made to the assembled officers of the fleet from the quarterdeck of the *Pennsylvania*, August 11, 1917. President Wilson told the officers to "leave out of your vocabulary altogether the word 'prudent'," and counselled them, "Do not stop to think about what is prudent"; and "Do the thing that is audacious to the utmost point of risk and daring."

In his Victory Message to Congress, December 2, 1918, President Wilson made this appraisement and paid this tribute to the spirit and achievement of the Americans in the World War:

"I am proud to be the fellow-countryman of men of

such stuff and valor. Those of us who stayed at home did our duty: the war could not have been won or the gallant men who fought it given their opportunity to win it otherwise; but for many a long day we shall think ourselves 'accurs'd we were not there, and hold our manhood cheap while any speaks that fought' with those at St. Mihiel or Thierry. The memory of those days of triumphant battle will go with those fortunate men to their graves; and each will have his favorite memory. 'Old men forget; yet all shall be forgot, but he'll remember with advantages what feats he did that day.'

"What we all thank God for with deepest gratitude is that our men went in force into the line of battle just at the critical moment when the whole fate of the world seemed to hang in the balance and threw their fresh strength into the ranks of freedom in time to turn the whole tide and sweep the fateful struggle—turn it once for all, so that henceforth it was back, back, back, for their enemies, always back, never again forward! After that it was only a scant four months before the commanders of the Central Empires knew themselves beaten: and now their very armies are in liquidation.

"And throughout it all how fine the spirit of the nation was! What unity of purpose! What untiring zeal! What elevation of purpose ran through all the splendid display of strength, its untiring accomplishment!"

"Thus the war came to an end."

## CHAPTER XXVII

# PEACEFUL PENETRATION

MORAL OFFENSIVES UNDERTAKEN—THE FOURTEEN POINTS ACCEPTED—THE ARMISTICE SIGNED—RACE BETWEEN WILSON AND HINDENBURG—GERMAN OPINION AS TO WILSON'S DEMAND—IT MEANT UNCONDITIONAL SURRENDER—FOCH SAID THE ARMISTICE OBTAINED THE REMEDY FOR WHICH THE WAR WAS WAGED

"*We cannot be separated in interest or divided in purpose.*"—WILSON

WILSON had other weapons which he brought into play to win the war. While never letting up in the least upon the use of "force without stint or limit" he forged effective weapons in the form of moral offensives. He always separated the people of Germany from the Imperial German Government. There was criticism at home for this differentiation. In the Central Empire it was recognized as an effort to show the rank and file that America had no hate and no desire to crush the German people. Wilson believed that if the mass of fighters and civilian population could be made to see that we were not waging war for their destruction, but truly to relieve them from autocratic sway while securing the rights of all nations, they would demand a cessation of war. He, therefore, undertook a series of moral offensives.

Our "war aims," stated in terms so plain and so just that they were approved by the people of all nations, were the weapons of peaceful penetration. The neutral countries were won to friendship by Wilson's broad and humane declarations; the allied forces saw in them a new era. Sent by cable and wireless and translated into every tongue, they became hope to those who sat in darkness. More than that: translated into the German language, they were broadcasted all over the German empire. As the people read Wilson's program of peace, his freedom from passion, his pleas for world fellowship, many hearts turned toward his ideals. His "Fourteen Points" set forth in his message to Congress, January 8, 1918, was like a ray of light in a world of gloom. Followed by his Mount Vernon Fourth of July speech and his New York address of September 27—these all together made Wilson's Magna Charta of World Peace. Read in great and humble homes of Europe, they heartened despairing peoples.

The "Fourteen Points" were as follows:

I.—Open covenants of peace, openly arrived at, after which there shall be no private international understandings of any kind, but diplomacy shall proceed always frankly and in the public view.

II.—Absolute freedom of navigation upon the seas, outside territorial waters, alike in peace and in war, except as the seas may be closed in whole or in part by international action for the enforcement of international covenants.

III.—The removal, so far as possible, of all economic barriers and the establishment of an equality of trade conditions among all the nations consenting to the peace and associating themselves for its maintenance.

IV.—Adequate guarantees given and taken that national armaments will be reduced to the lowest points consistent with domestic safety.

V.—Free, open-minded, and absolutely impartial adjustment of all colonial claims, based upon a strict observance of the principle that in determining all such questions of sovereignty the interests of the population concerned must have equal weight with the equitable claims of the Government whose title is to be determined.

VI.—The evacuation of all Russian territory and such a settlement of all questions affecting Russia as will secure the best and freest co-operation of the other nations of the world in obtaining for her an unhampered and unembarrassed opportunity for the independent determination of her own political development and national policy, and assure her of a sincere welcome into the society of free nations under institutions of her own choosing; and, more than a welcome, assistance also of every kind that she may need and may herself desire. The treatment accorded Russia by her sister nations in the months to come will be the acid test of their good-will, of their comprehension of her needs as distinguished from their own interests, and of their intelligent and unselfish sympathy.

VII.—Belgium, the whole world will agree, must be evacuated and restored, without any attempt to limit the sovereignty which she enjoys in common with all other free nations. No other single act will serve as this will serve to restore confidence among the nations in the laws which they have themselves set and determined for the government of their relations with one another. Without this healing act the whole structure and validity of international law is forever impaired.

VIII.—All French territory should be freed and the invaded portions restored, and the wrong done to France by Prussia in 1871 in the matter of Alsace-Lorraine, which has unsettled the peace of the world for nearly fifty years, should be righted, in order that peace may once more be made secure in the interest of all.

IX.—A readjustment of the frontiers of Italy should be effected along clearly recognizable lines of nationality.

X.—The peoples of Austria-Hungary, whose place among the nations we wish to see safeguarded and assured, should be accorded the freest opportunity of autonomous development.

XI.—Rumania, Serbia, and Montenegro should be evacuated; occupied territories restored; Serbia accorded free and secure access to the sea; and the relations of the several Balkan States to one another determined by friendly counsel along historically established lines of allegiance and nationality; and international guarantees of the political and economic independence and territorial integrity of the several Balkan States should be entered into.

XII.—The Turkish portions of the present Ottoman Empire should be assured a secure sovereignty, but the other nationalities which are now under Turkish rule should be assured an undoubted security of life and an absolutely unmolested opportunity of autonomous development, and the Dardanelles should be permanently opened as a free passage to the ships and commerce of all nations under international guarantees.

XIII.—An independent Polish State should be erected which should include the territories inhabited by indisputably Polish populations, which should be assured a free and secure access to the sea, and whose political and economic independence and territorial integrity should be guaranteed by international covenant.

XIV.—A general association of nations must be formed under specific covenants for the purpose of affording mutual guarantees of political independence and territorial integrity to great and small States alike.

Within a week after his New York address, in which he had outlined the principles of what he specifically called a "League of Nations," the Germans made overtures for an armistice. The peaceful penetration of Wilson's idealism and the vigorous penetration of the allied armies were doing their perfect work. The Austro-Hungarian Government a week later made the same request. Answering the German note, the President asked if he was to understand that the German Government accepted the terms laid down in the "Fourteen Points" and his later addresses, and "if its object in entering into discussion would be only to agree upon practical details of their application." He added that he could consider nothing that did not carry with it "immediate evacuation" of invaded territory. October 12 the German Government gave an affirmative answer. October 14 Wilson wrote that the conditions of an armistice must be arranged by the military advisers of the Allied Nations, and added that no arrangement could be accepted that did not provide "absolutely satisfactory safeguards and guarantees of the maintenance of the present military supremacy of the armies of the United States and the Allies in the field"; that no armistice could be considered until all U-boat warfare ceased; and that guarantees of a new and representative character of the German Government must be given. There must be no misunderstanding, no easy peace. Germany on October 20 accepted in toto all the requirements laid down by Mr. Wilson. On October 23 the President replied that he had communicated the correspondence to the Allied Powers, with the suggestion that, if they were disposed to effect the peace upon the terms and principles indicated, they would ask their military advisers to draw up armistice terms of such a character as to "insure to the associated governments the unrestricted power to safeguard and enforce the details of the peace to which the German Government has agreed." The Allied Governments agreed with certain qualifications. The German Government accepted the Wilson plan with a few additions suggested by the Allies on October 27.

The terms of the Armistice were drawn up by the military advisers, submitted to Germany November 8, and signed by the German Government to become effective 11 A. M., November 11, 1918. The war was therefore concluded upon the terms Wilson had presented time and again during the conflict and had formally made in specific points in his addresses on January 8 and subsequently. It was the first time in history when what had been derided as the ideals of a civilian ruler had been accepted as the terms of surrender by the military chieftains. Wilson had made no easy peace and the Allies had not subscribed to a program that was less than a complete victory. But Wilson's terms carried no revenge or woe to the vanquished. They pointed the road to honorable rehabilitation, and, later, association with all the countries of the world in a League of Nations for peace, justice, equality, and an end of wars. They had much to do with the German collapse.

Was the Armistice a virtual surrender?

The refusal of the Senate of the United States to approve the Covenant and enter the League of Nations was followed in Europe by drift and debacle. That condition has caused critics to cry out that Wilson's policy was wrong and that the Army should have gone on to Berlin and made Germany taste something of the destruction it had carried into France. That is not an indictment of Wilson any more than of Lloyd George, Clemenceau, Orlando, the King of Belgium and all the Allied leaders, civil and military. As complete answer to such criticism, let the statement of Foch, the commander-in-chief of the Allied forces, be quoted. Asked, after the terms of peace had been drawn up, whether he would rather the Germans would reject or accept it, the great French General said: "The only aim of war is to obtain results. If the Germans sign an armistice on the general lines we have just determined, we shall have obtained the result we seek. Our aims being accomplished, no one has the right to shed another drop of blood."

What was the German opinion? Ludendorff writes in his memoirs: "On October 22 or 23 Wilson's answer arrived. It was a strong answer to our cowardly note. His terms he made quite clear that the armistice conditions must be such as to make it impossible for Germany to resume hostilities," and he added: "In my view, there could no longer be doubt in my mind that we must continue the fight." Hindenburg signed an order October 24, "for the information of all troops," containing these words: "Wilson will negotiate with Germany for peace only if she concedes all the demands of America's allies as to the internal constitutional arrangements of Germany. . . . Wilson's answer is a demand for unconditional surrender. It is unacceptable to our soldiers. Continue resistance with all our strength." But the German civilian population had read and approved Wilson's just program of peace. The war lords were overruled. Peaceful penetration in Wilson's "offensive by reason," had broken the civilian resistance and the Allied and Pershing's armies had won successes, presaging complete victory.

In the spring of 1918, when the issue hung in the balances, Lloyd George had said:

"It is a race between Wilson and Hindenburg."

Wilson had won.

November 11, 1918, took its place in the American calendar alongside of Independence Day and Thanksgiving. In the ecstasy of joy with which it was hailed both seemed rolled into one.

"And thus the war comes to an end," said the master leader, who had lifted it out of a combat for power or defense into a struggle for world deliverance from imperialism and greed and war.

Could "the world be made safe for democracy"?

The words of Wilson's first inaugural come back: "Men's hearts wait upon us; men's lives hang in the balance; men's hopes call upon us to say what we will do.

"Who dares to fail to try? I summon all honest men, all patriotic, all forward-looking men, to my side. God helping me, I will not fail them, if they will but counsel and sustain me."

That was a consecration before the crucial days of war. It seemed to have been uttered for the days that followed the armistice.

He did not "fail them."

## Chapter XXVIII

# THE PRESIDENT IN EUROPE

UNPARALLELED WELCOME EVERYWHERE—PEOPLE'S HOPES HUNG ON WILSON—FROM FIRST TO LAST HIS ONE THOUGHT WAS TO SECURE LEAGUE OF NATIONS—EUROPEAN DIPLOMATS DELAYED CONFERENCE—ACCESSIBLE TO REPRESENTATIVES OF SMALL NATIONS—WELL SUPPLIED WITH ADVICE—THE BATTLE ROYAL AND WILSON'S VICTORY ON THE MAIN ISSUES.

IT was a shell-shocked Europe that awaited Wilson when he was piped down the gangplank of the *George Washington* as his ship landed in Brest on December 13, 1918. But it was an expectant Europe. The coming of Wilson was hailed by the people as they had welcomed no other man in centuries. He set foot on French soil amid a demonstration of popular enthusiasm that was unequalled even from the emotional and patriotic French people. Warships and land batteries roared their salute. The official and popular welcome in Brest gave promise of the historic reception at the French capital on the morrow.

Paris had been in holiday attire to welcome many of the world's heroes, but the reception to Wilson was without parallel. It was a greeting, not alone by Poincaré and Clemenceau and the dignitaries and the victorious men of the army. They gave it official éclat. It was the pouring out of the heart of the French people to the American President, who in the darkest hour of French history had saved France. That feeling was in every heart as Poincaré and Wilson drove down the Champs Elysees. Women in black waved their gratitude and maimed soldiers made him feel their thanks. It was these evidences that touched Wilson more than the pomp and circumstance. It humbled him, too. He had come to Paris with the high emprise to free the Frenchmen and all people from the dread and tragedy of war. Could his desire and their hopes be realized?

Responding to Poincaré's official address, Wilson said: "From the first, the thought of the people of the United States turned toward something more than the mere winning of the war. It turned to the establishment of eternal principles of right and justice."

Replying to the welcome of the Socialist delegation, December 16, he outlined the things to be done, saying: "This has indeed been a peoples' war. It has been waged against absolutism and militarism, and these enemies of liberty must from this time forth be shut out from the possibility of working their cruel will upon mankind. In my judgment, it is not sufficient to establish this principle. It is necessary that it should be supported by a co-operation of the nations which shall be based upon fixed and definite covenants, and which shall be made certain of effective action through the instrumentality of a League of Nations."

Functions and dinners and luncheons and honors followed in quick succession, every courtesy being extended to President and Mrs. Wilson. They were to live while in Paris at the residence of Prince Murat, one of the most magnificent homes in Paris. It was here that Wilson was to receive the delegations from all the little peoples of Europe, as well as the great. Here he was to hear appeals to be given the right of "self-determination" by small nations which had never known that boon. He was inaccessible to many of the mighty, but not to the representatives of peoples yearning for a chance to live their own lives. Here the Big Four were to meet, to debate, to differ, to plan, and finally to agree in its essentials upon the Wilson Peace he had laid down in the terms upon which the German Army ceased fighting.

But that was of the future. For the present—he was to have the disappointment of delay when a suffering world demanded action.

President Wilson had hurried from Washington with the purpose to have the peace treaty and the association of nations agreed upon without delay. The Allies had officially agreed upon the chief terms when they accepted peace on the basis of Wilson's Fourteen Points and stipulated additions. It was a simple matter to put these in shape and let the work of rebuilding the nations go forward. To his regret he found that Lloyd George had "gone to the country" in his khaki election and must await the result and reorganization before Great Britain could be represented at Paris. European statesmen had accepted Wilson's altruistic plans in their eagerness to see the end of fighting. Almost any terms to bring peace would have been accepted. Later study of what they had so hurriedly agreed to disclosed that the peace terms would work revolution in all previous ideas of peace treaties. They would prevent the garnering of any of the spoils of war. Their countries wished colonies and indemnities and territory and sea power and concessions, particularly in oil and other natural resources. Some diplomats, eager to grasp every possible advantage for their respective countries, feared to see Wilson go into the conference with all the prestige which had come to him as the leader of the American people and the fashioner of peace. They played for time. Every pretext for delay was employed. And while the opening of the conference was being delayed, the effort was made to incline Wilson to a severe peace. To this end, he was urged, almost commanded by the intensity of the requests, to visit the devastated sections of France. He knew that France had suffered terribly, and he had come to Paris to alleviate such sufferings and to make their renewal impossible. He never departed from that purpose or lacked sympathy for France's grievous losses. But he did not believe France could be fully compensated without imposing a burden that would be destructive to Europe's recovery. He did then what is now being attempted after four years of travail—called for a determination of Germany's capacity to pay. The experts reported to him that Germany was able to pay and should pay a sum not less than ten billion or more than fifteen billion dollars. He sensed the large gain which would result from a speedy and final appraisement of what would be required of Germany. But he was overruled and the world has paid in innumerable deaths and boundless suffering because his wise counsel was not accepted.

January 18 was finally fixed as the day upon which the Peace Conference was to assemble. Pending that time the following commissions were organized: On the League of Nations, on Responsibility for the War, on Reparation, on International Labor Legislation, and on International Control. There were other commissions, but those named were the more important ones. The necessity for a large body of expert opinion had been foreseen and there went along with the Commission to Negotiate Peace a group of the ablest experts in the United States including financiers, historians, specialists in economics, international law and colonial questions and in other matters that were likely to come up at a congress when a new map of Europe was to be made. The President, always forehanded, called a conference of these experts on board the *George Washington* and reminded them how dependent he was upon them. "You are my advisers," he said. "When I ask you for information I will have no way of checking it up, and must act upon it unquestioningly. We will be deluged with claims plausibly and convincingly presented. It will be your task to establish the truth or falsity of these claims out of your specialized knowledge, so that my position may be taken fairly and intelligently."

It was charged that the President did not sufficiently take counsel with his advisers. "The fault, if any, was really on the other side," says Ray Stannard Baker, who was with Wilson in Paris. "He tried too hard to get every angle, every point of view—he was tempted to wait too long to be absolutely sure of facts upon which he must base his decisions."

After committing to his associates the task of making a study of the questions to be considered by the Conference, so that upon his return to Paris he would be fortified by facts, President Wilson, with Mrs. Wilson, accepted an invitation to visit England. But before that on Christmas Day he reviewed the American troops at Chaumont. A soldier himself, the Commander-in-Chief, he looked upon the victorious army with pride and satisfaction. It was at Chaumont Pershing had maintained headquarters and there plans for America's large part in the war were laid. It interested the President to follow the charts showing how the plans had been worked out, to greet the soldiers, and to give them America's gratitude. He went from Chaumont to Calais, where he took ship for Dover. His arrival at that ancient seaport, on the morning of December 26, was signalized by the firing of a royal salute and the path to the train was strewn with petals of roses. At Charing Cross station Mr. and Mrs. Wilson were greeted by King George, Queen Mary, Princess Mary, Premier Lloyd George and other members of the British Cabinet.

"The great moment of President Wilson's first day in England," says the Associated Press account, "was when he stood with the King and Queen and Mrs. Wilson in the balcony of Buckingham Palace today (December 26) facing a multitude which stretched down the Mall to the Admiralty, half a mile distant, and overflowed St. James Park on one side and Green Park on the other. Only a corporal's guard could hear the President's brief speech, but the people, who had demanded that he show himself, gave him a greeting more clamorous than to any other guest of the nation within the memory of the oldest Londoners."

On the night of December 27 a great banquet was given at Buckingham Palace, where, says the same news association's story, royal formality which had attended epochal occasions at the palace for 200 years was carried out. The President gave utterance to the mission which had brought him to Europe, saying: "There is a great tide running in the hearts of men. The hearts of men have never beaten so singularly in unison before. Men have never been so conscious of their brotherhood. Men have never before realized how little difference there was

20

between right and justice in one latitude and in another, under one sovereignty and under another.

"And it will be our high privilege, I believe, not only to apply the moral judgment of the world to the particular settlements which we shall attempt, but also to organize the moral force of the world to preserve those settlements, to steady the forces of mankind, and to make the right and the justice to which great nations like our own have devoted themselves the predominant and controlling force of the world."

The next day he spoke at historic Guildhall, and added this interpretation of his mission: "The peoples of the world want peace, and they want it now," he said, "not merely by conquest of wars but by agreement of mind. It was this incomparably great object that brought me overseas. It has never before been deemed excusable for a President of the United States to leave the territory of the United States, but I know that I have the support of the judgment of my colleagues in the government of the United States in saying that it was my paramount duty to turn away, even from the imperative task at home, to lend such counsel and aid as I could to this great, may I not say, final enterprise of humanity."

Leaving London, Wilson journeyed to Carlisle, where his grandfather, Dr. Thomas Woodrow, preached for many years and where his mother was born. December 30 he was received with great acclaim at Manchester. Then back to Paris. Two weeks more remained before the slow-working European diplomats would be ready for the Peace Conference. Brief consultations followed with some of the American experts, and then Mr. and Mrs. Wilson departed, January 1, for Rome.

The trip through Italy was a continuous ovation by day, and at night bonfires marked the route of the presidential train. Arriving at the Italian border the Americans were met by aides of King Victor Emmanuel and conducted to a royal train in waiting. At the station in Rome the President and Mrs. Wilson were received by King Victor Emmanuel and Queen Helena, members of the government and representatives of the city authorities. Immense crowds greeted them at every public appearance. They lunched with the Queen Mother, Margherita, and were the guests of honor at a reception given by Parliament. Roman citizenship was conferred upon him and he was elected a member of the Royal Academy of Science. The Pope granted him a long interview, presenting him with a surpassingly beautiful and historical mosaic.

In his speech in Rome, January 3, at the Chamber of Deputies, Mr. Wilson, referring again to his plan for world peace, said: "Our task at Paris is to organize the friendship of the world, to see to it that all the moral forces that make for right and justice and liberty are united and are given a vital organization to which the peoples of the world will readily and gladly respond. . . . We know that there cannot be another balance of power."

As President Wilson visited the Sacred Way in Rome, Boni pointed out the tomb of Romulus and other sacred places, and presenting him with branches of laurel and myrtle, said: "Today I offer these symbols to you, the upholder of the freedom and civilization of peoples." Wilson replied: "These sacred symbols speak a great and profound language." The great archæologist replied: "You Americans have something more sacred still, but you carry it in your heart—love for humanity."

Speaking at Turin, making reply to Baron Sonnino's argument for the extension of the sovereignty of Italy over the Italian population, President Wilson said facetiously: "I am sorry we cannot let you have New York, which I understand is the greatest Italian city in the world," and he added: "I am proud to be President of a nation which contains so large an element of the Italian race, because as a student of literature I know the genius that has originated in this great nation, the genius of thought and of poetry and of philosophy and of music, and I am happy to be a part of a nation which is enriched and made better by the introduction of such elements of genius and inspiration."

When the Peace Conference assembled, Mr. Wilson as the lone exponent of the principle of "self-determination," had war on his hands from the beginning. The great figures at the conference besides himself were, of course, the premiers of the governments actively associated with the United States in the war—Lloyd George, of England; Clemenceau, of France; and Orlando, of Italy. These, with Mr. Wilson, were the Big Four.

Clemenceau was a nationalist, of an extreme type. In the early stages of the conference he was frequently opposed to the altruistic aims for which Wilson contended, induced thereto by his passion for the safety of France. However, when Lloyd George and Wilson agreed to recommend to their governments that both nations should come to the aid of France in case it was invaded, the old Tiger gave adhesion to Wilson's policies which he had first opposed. Upon his recommendation France joined the League of Nations.

Lloyd George, at heart a sincere believer in world peace, was always with Wilson when he followed his

**THE AMERICAN COMMISSION TO NEGOTIATE PEACE** *Photo. U. & U.*

The full personnel of the American Commission taken at their headquarters, Hotel Crillon, Paris, just before the signing of peace. In the front row, from left to right, are: Col. E. M. House, Robert Lansing, President Wilson, Henry White, General Tasker H. Bliss

**ON THE BRIDGE OF THE GEORGE WASHINGTON** © *Western Newspaper Union*

President Wilson's return from Paris after signing the Treaty of Peace with Germany was marked by a tremendous ovation which began as soon as his ship reached Quarantine and continued throughout his progress up New York Bay

liberal instinct. But the head of a coalition cabinet wishing colonies and concessions, he was one day himself and the next day an imperialist. What has been called dexterity in Lloyd George is chiefly to be attributed to the conflicting influences controlling his country. Mr. Baker, who was a close and discriminating observer, says: "Lloyd George was powerfully on one side one day and powerfully on the other the next; but on the whole and in the great main issues he sided with the President." Great Britain's dominant resolve to maintain its supremacy as mistress of the seas and its colonial ambitions and necessities impelled him to demands which in some cases Mr. Wilson could not favor. But his unbounded optimism and his faith were only less valuable in the conference than Wilson's idealism and firmness.

Orlando was a liberal in his own views, but he had to consider the attitude of reactionaries at home. They were near at hand and could make their influence felt in Paris more effectually than like influences in America could bring pressure to bear on Wilson. The demand for Fiume and for territory, coming up from Rome, made his position very difficult.

Wilson had the task of preventing the untoward influences of the old time European diplomacy from controlling the Conference. He was not fully able to give the transactions of the body the lofty tone which he had hoped to give it. But he influenced it powerfully toward policies that made for enduring peace. Often his liberal ideas came into conflict with the imperialistic aims of the European diplomats. He always championed them with power, and in many of the forensic encounters came off the victor.

One of the clashes in which he showed the stuff of

which he was made was over the disposition of the German colonies. England, France, and Italy saw opportunity to add to their territorial possessions and made ready to grasp it, with plans all worked out and ready for approval by the Conference. Wilson insisted that the first thing to determine was what the people in the colonies wanted and what the peoples of the world favored. He invoked the fifth of his famous "Fourteen Points," which declared that "the interests of the populations concerned must have equal weight with the equitable claims of the government whose title is to be determined." He did not obtain all he fought for—concessions were made to both France and Japan—but, in the main, he did achieve a victory and one of the sections of the peace treaty embodies his proposals for mandatories where peoples were not prepared for self-government.

The main thing that President Wilson went to Paris for was to have a League of Nations written into the Peace Treaty. He saw in such an organization the only sure way for the prevention of another world war which he felt would mean the destruction of civilization. As chairman of the Commission on the League of Nations he framed, with the aid of experts, the Covenant of the League and was instrumental in having a Plenary Session of the Peace Conference adopt a resolution declaring that the League should be treated as an integral part of the general treaty of peace.

Then he sailed for the United States to sign the bills of an expiring Congress, carrying with him the constitution of the League. During his absence in America, the League had been removed from the program of the conference and there was about to be concluded a preliminary peace with the League to come up afterwards.

This disturbing information reached him just before he sailed from New York. When he heard it he made this declaration as he was embarking for Paris: "When that treaty comes back, gentlemen on this side will find the Covenant not only in it, but so many threads of the Treaty tied to the Covenant that you cannot dissect it from the Treaty without destroying the whole vital structure." They were in his mind one and inseparable, and he believed that united they afforded the only assurance of a permanent association for peace.

The day after his arrival in Paris he issued the following statement:

"The President said today that the decision made at the Peace Conference in its plenary session, January 25, 1919, to the effect that the establishment of a League of Nations should be made an integral part of the Treaty of Peace, is of final force and that there is no basis whatever for the reports that a change in this decision was contemplated."

There followed a sharp passage-at-arms with Clemenceau and Lloyd George, who were indignant that their decision had been revoked. Wilson's argument was unanswerable. There could be no real and lasting peace without a means of administering it. The means lay and lay only in a League of Nations. The President won his fight. His declaration that the agreement of January 25 would not be reconsidered was made good. March 26, twelve days after he had returned from the United States, it was announced that the Covenant of the League of Nations would be an integral part of the treaty.

"Contrary to the assertions spread by the German press and taken up by other foreign newspapers, we believe that the French government has no annexationist pretensions, openly or under cover, in regard to any territory inhabited by a German population. This remark applies particularly to the regions comprised between the frontier of 1871 and the frontier of 1914."

That item, headed "France's Claims," appeared in *Le Temps*, April 8, 1919. On April 7 President Wilson had directed the Secretary of the Navy to order the *George Washington* to sail for Brest. The announcement of that order created consternation in Paris. There was an immediate connection between the appearance of the editorial and the Presidential order. Mr. Wilson had become exasperated by the French and British greed for annexations. He resolved not to be a party to plans contrary to his principles. His sending for the *George Washington* was an impressive gesture that brought disavowal of imperialistic plans. He did not sail for America. It wasn't necessary. The article in *Le Temps* was the signal for a general reduction of territorial demands.

Perhaps the most dramatic occurrence of the Peace Conference, certainly the one with the most dramatic dénouement, was Wilson's announcement of his position on the claims of Italy to Fiume. He firmly gave it as his opinion that Italy had no just claim on this port and did not need it while Jugo-Slavia did. A large part of the Italian delegation became incensed and withdrew from the conference. Wilson was not unyielding. He was willing to agree to international control for Fiume. The Italians, however, would not agree to that. This was one decision in which Wilson had the support, though tacit (the hot end of the poker being as usual left for him), of the most of his associates. In fact the pact of London had withheld Fiume from Italy.

Jugo-Slavia had been set up by the Conference as an independent nation. Many of its people had been forced to fight with the Central Empires. The understanding mass of the people had been in sympathy with the Allies' cause. Having decreed that they should have a nation of their own on the principle of self-determination, Wilson felt that it was necessary that they should have a seaport, both for commercial reasons and to maintain the independent existence given them. He had made one of the conditions of peace that *Italia irredenta*, long under foreign rule, should go back to Italy. He wished Italy strengthened but not at the expense of the new nation of Jugo-Slavia.

The President suffered more mental anguish over the Shantung settlement than over any of the other dispositions made by the Peace Conference. The award of the peninsula to Japan was in conformity with the treaty made by England and France with that country when Japan entered the war. Wilson wished Shantung to be restored to China and insisted upon it, but Lloyd George and Clemenceau were in no position to resist Japan's claim to all German territory taken in the Far East, this having been promised in the treaty. Wilson did, however, secure an agreement by Japan that it would later restore Shantung in full sovereignty to China. Japan has kept its promise.

The story of the trials of the five months before the treaty was signed tells of the evolution from ancient diplomacy to a large measure of new and juster ideals of making peace. The clashes of interest and the clashes of inherited national jealousies marked the deliberations and delayed the conclusions. Clemenceau and Lloyd George and Orlando were pressed by nationalist aims and ambitions. In spite of radical differences, in the beginning, however, these four great men emerged from the conference with mutual respect. More than that, they reached, with all its defects, a working agreement where all the controverted issues might be properly adjusted in the League of Nations they were setting up.

It was on June 28 in the same imperial hall where the Germans had humbled the French forty-eight years before, that the Treaty of Versailles was signed. Though some of the American Peace Commissioners had differed with President Wilson during the making of the treaty, the instrument bore the names of all: Woodrow Wilson, Robert Lansing, Edward M. House, Henry White, Tasker H. Bliss.

The setting typified its importance. It lacked the perfection denied to all human productions, but it was shot through with Wilson's idealism.

The League of Nations it set up was the first concrete international plan of permanent peace. With America's participation, it guaranteed peace and justice and stability. The American President had won the great thing for which he went to Paris, and had cause for satisfaction as he signed his name to the Treaty.

Wilson set sail for home.

## Chapter XXIX

# A VISION OF WORLD PEACE

WHEN THE LEAGUE OF NATIONS WAS BORN IN THE MIND OF WILSON—APPROVED THE BRYAN "TALK-IT-OVER" TREATIES WITH THIRTY-ONE NATIONS—SENT HOUSE TO EUROPE BEFORE SERBIAN KILLING TO SOUND OUT HEADS OF GOVERNMENT—A PLEDGE TO AMERICAN SOLDIERS—"WE LIVE IN OUR VISION"

*"The cause of peace and the cause of truth are of one family. Whatever has been accomplished in the past is petty compared to the glory of the promise of the future."*—Wilson

"We live in our vision." These words, uttered by President Wilson at Arlington Cemetery, May 30, 1915, give insight into the spiritual foundation that kept his purpose firm. "Let us go away from this place," he went on to say, "renewed in our devotion to daily duty and to those ideals which keep a nation young, keep it noble, keep it rich in enterprise and achievement; make it lead the nations of the world in those things that make for hope and for the benefit of mankind."

Wilson had approved and sent to the Senate the Bryan treaties, calling for a year to "talk it over" before war was declared, and had urged their ratification. Thirty-one nations gave approval to that excellent step toward the prevention of hasty war, such as came so suddenly in 1914. In his first annual message to Congress, December 2, 1913, the President said: "It has been the privilege of the Department of State to gain the assent, in principle, of no less than thirty-one nations, representing four-fifths of the population of the world, to the negotiation of treaties by which it shall be agreed that whenever differences of interest or of policy arise which can not be resolved by the ordinary processes of diplomacy they shall be publicly analyzed, discussed, and reported upon by a tribunal chosen by the parties before either nation determines its course of action."

In the spring of that year he had given Colonel House a mission to sound out the authorities of Britain, France, and Germany, looking to some agreement with the United States to prevent war. Unfortunately Germany did not ratify the Bryan treaty and the Kaiser gave no welcome to the tentative plan Colonel House presented.

When was the League of Nations born in the resolve of Woodrow Wilson? It may be truly said it was the growth of long study of world conditions and conviction that the old order must give way to a new understanding between nations. From the moment Belgium was invaded a concrete league of nations was developing in his mind and he counselled with friends that it must come with peace.

In an address before the League to Enforce Peace, in Washington, May 27, 1916, President Wilson said: "The nations of the world must in some way band themselves together to see that the right prevails as against any sort of selfish aggression. It should be a universal association of nations to prevent any war begun either contrary to treaty agreements, or without warning and full submission of the causes to the opinion of mankind."

President Wilson rarely made an address which did not in some form present the idea "force will not accomplish anything that is permanent." One reason that

*Photo. Kadell & Herbert, N. Y.*

**PRESIDENT AND MRS. WILSON WITH THE KING AND QUEEN OF BELGIUM**

It would be difficult to imagine a more distinguished group than that composed of the President of the United States at the topmost pinnacle of his power and influence and the heroic soldier king of Belgium with their faithful helpmates

**AT THE ST. GERMAIN CONFERENCE** © *U. & U.*

The Chief Executive arriving at the Castle of St. Germain, where the terms of the Allied Peace Treaty were handed to the Germans. The President is accompanied by his personal medical adviser, Real-Admiral Cary T. Grayson, U. S. N.

early impelled him to neutrality was the belief that there should be one free nation "to assist in an association to prevent war when the fighting is over." Memorial Day, 1916, he reaffirmed his belief that the people of the United States were ready to become partners in any alliance of the nations that would guarantee public right above selfish aggression. From that time on the President lost no opportunity to stress the point that the United States should be a leader in a movement to restore a broken world. In an address delivered to the cadets graduating from West Point June 13, 1916, he said that America carried "the guiding lights of liberty and principle and justice."

In his address September 2, 1916, accepting the nomination for re-election, he pointed out "that the nations of the world must unite in joint guarantees that whatever is done to disturb the whole world's life must first be tested in the court of the whole world's opinion before it is attempted." Throughout the campaign he dwelt upon the duty of the United States to seek to promote in all ways "the interest of justice, righteousness and human government." At Indianapolis October 12, he said: "It will be the duty of America to join with the other nations of the world in some kind of league for the maintenance of peace." On numerous other occasions he repeated and emphasized the same thought.

When the United States entered the war and American youths were going to Europe by the hundreds of thousands to undergo the horrors and hardships of war and many of them to lose their lives, President Wilson's desire for some avenue by which the world might escape another such tragedy became even stronger. In his famous speech asking Congress to declare the existence of a state of war, he said that the object of the United States was "to vindicate the principles of peace and justice in the life of the world as against selfish and autocratic power and to set up amongst the really free and self-governed peoples of the world such a concert of purpose and of action as will henceforth insure the observance of those principles."

He outlined in his address to the Senate, January 22, 1917, the essential terms of peace, giving in the large what he afterwards insisted upon in Paris and "proposing, as it were, that the nations with one accord adopt the doctrine of President Monroe as the doctrine of the world." Again this idea is foreshadowed in his second inaugural when he said "we wished to play the part of those who mean to vindicate and fortify peace."

"What we are striving for," he told Congress February 11, 1918, "is a new international order based upon the broad and universal principles of right and justice—no mere peace of shreds and patches." He warned thus early against "the method of the Congress of Vienna," which some Americans were willing to follow in Paris. He knew that in its sordid decisions lay the seeds of the great struggle that called the world to war in 1914, and that it was the unworthiest assemblage of men who ever undertook a mighty task.

Just two days before setting sail for the Peace Conference, addressing Congress December 2, after reviewing America's glorious part in the war, President Wilson announced that the goal of permanent peace was near. "And now," he said, "we are sure of the great triumph for which every sacrifice was made. It has come, come in its completeness, and with the pride and inspiration of those days of achievement quick within us we turn to the task of peace again—peace secure against the violence of irresponsible monarchs and ambitious military coteries —and make ready for a new order, for new foundations of justice and fair dealing.

"We are about to give order and organization to this peace not only for ourselves but for the other peoples of the world as well, so far as they will suffer us to serve them. It is international justice that we seek, not domestic safety merely."

Wilson went to Paris not to take part in a mere treaty of peace such as followed the Napoleonic and other wars. Any commission could arrange terms. He went on to "make ready for a new order" and to translate the hopes of two thousand years into a working organization. He did not suppose he had originated the noble conception. Undertakings having the same object in view had been seen in almost every century. He said he was only a "servant of humanity" seeking practical ways to end war.

At Mount Vernon on July 4, Mr. Wilson elaborated his theory for the creation of a League of Nations, declaring America was fighting for "the establishment of an organization of peace which shall make it certain that the combined powers of free nations will check every invasion of right and serve to make peace and justice the more secure by affording a definite tribunal of opinion to which all must submit and by which every international readjustment that cannot be amicably agreed upon by the peoples directly concerned shall be sanctioned."

The vision became reality.

## CHAPTER XXX

# THE FIGHT FOR THE COVENANT

FIRST SHOT FIRED AT BOSTON, HEARD AROUND THE WORLD—TREATY AND COVENANT ONE AND INSEPARABLE—THE ROUND ROBIN—SENATE REFUSED TO HELP FIX AMOUNT OF REPARATIONS—THE PROPAGANDA OF THE BITTER-ENDERS—LODGE'S RESERVATIONS MEANT NULLIFICATION OF THE TREATY, NOT AMENDING IT

"*I am a Covenanter.*"—WILSON

THE first shot in the United States for the League was fired February 24, 1919, at Boston. It was truly "heard around the world."

The *George Washington* landed at Boston. The magnificent reception proved the deep interest of the American people. President Wilson's speech made a profound impression. It contained one sentence that was construed to be aimed at the Senators who afterwards came to be known as "Bitter-Enders." He said: "The people are in the saddle, and they are going to see to it that if their present governments do not do their will, some other Governments shall." In Europe the powers-that-be, looking for a return to old alliances, had resented all his references to "the people" and his appeal to the popular conscience. The same feeling existed among Senators, and the opposition press cried out that "he was going over the head" of a co-ordinate branch of government.

The President knew there was a fight by Senators.

But all through the war there had been such sincere and general response to his pledges that the fruits of war should be garnered in an association of nations for permanent peace, that he did not believe the American people could be persuaded to lose that for which their sons had fought and died. That confidence was expressed in his speech in New York, March 4, as he was going back to Paris. "The first thing I am going to tell the people on the other side of the water," he said, "is that an overwhelming majority of the American people is in favor of the League of Nations." Upon the same occasion ex-President Taft spoke and assured the country that the League would not place the Monroe Doctrine in jeopardy. Wilson was supremely confident the people were with him as the *George Washington* set sail. And all surface indications justified his belief. Most of the Republican newspapers and nearly all the independent papers conveyed that impression and most of them favored the principle.

Irreconcilables and Bitter-Enders, in and out of Congress, were to have their innings. They organized a campaign with appeals to the voters of German birth or blood to oppose "Wilson's League" as they called it, because he had "waged war on Germany" as they put it. They never said that always Wilson differentiated between the Imperial German Government and the German people in all his addresses and notes. They also suppressed information as to Wilson's action in Paris for a just peace that would enable Germany again to re-establish itself and meet its obligations. He looked, indeed, to seeing Germany admitted to the League of Nations in the fulness of time. Senatorial appeal by Wilson-hating Senators to the Irish was based upon the charge that Wilson had refused to demand the freedom of Ireland as a condition precedent to co-operation with Lloyd George, never pointing out that his policy led the way to Home Rule for Ireland and made possible Ireland's becoming a member of the League of Nations. Ireland was admitted to membership in the League in 1923, as Wilson foresaw. The Italians in America were urged to vote against "Wilson's League" and Wilson's party because Mr. Wilson had not given Fiume to Italy. The Italian voters were not told that Wilson made possible a return of Italia Irredenta and was the true friend of Italy's best interests. The recent action by Italy and Jugo-Slavia, giving to Jugo-Slavia a port, on which Wilson insisted, has finally brought about the co-operation between these two countries which Wilson sought to accomplish. To this propaganda, addressed to various groups, was added the fear sent into the hearts of mothers that "American boys could be sent to fight again in Europe by a super government." These various unworthy appeals came to a climax in an appeal to Republican voters that a victory for "Wilson's League" would mean another victory for the Democratic party. It was that danger more than all others which actuated the senatorial opposition. It was largely in order to let this poison propaganda get in its work that the Senate dawdled and debated through the summer and fall.

Wilson had such faith in the people's devotion to peace he could not believe the campaign to prejudice popular opinion against the Covenant had possibility of success.

As Wilson was setting sail for Paris, thirty-seven Senators, more than one-third the total number, signed a "round robin" to the effect that the League of Nations

Covenant "in the form now proposed to the Peace Conference should not be accepted by the United States." This was intended to weaken the influence of the President in Paris, but when he accepted certain suggestions by Taft and Root and Hughes, he believed all reasonable objections to the Covenant had been met. Practically the chief fear in America was that unless specifically incorporated in the document, the Monroe Doctrine would be abrogated. The text of Article XXI, secured by Wilson, removed such fear. It was in these words: "Nothing in this Covenant shall be deemed to affect the validity of international engagements, such as treaties of arbitration or regional understandings like the Monroe Doctrine, for securing the maintenance of peace."

Great excitement followed the unauthorized publication of the Treaty early in June, and the campaign against it was in full force when the President arrived in Washington, ready to begin his fight. On July 10 the Treaty was formally laid before the Senate with a full statement of its provisions, its purposes, and the manner in which it had been framed. The interest was so great that the Senate broke a precedent and for the first time in its history decided to receive and debate a treaty in open session. "My services and all the information I possess will be at your disposal," the President told Senators.

Wilson invited the members of the Foreign Relations Committee of the Senate to dinner at the White House. Some of the Senators made it a condition of their acceptance that what was said should not be regarded as private or confidential. That suited Wilson exactly and all that was spoken at that gathering was taken down by a stenographer. The conference, held August 19, lasted three hours. It was opened with a statement by the President and afterwards there were questions and answers and debates touching the principle and every controverted article "in the Covenant." It was a clash at close quarters of conflicting opinions. The President was never quite so much the master of any gathering in logic and brilliancy of advocacy of a cause. But from the beginning it was clear that there were Senators so committed against the treaty as to forbid the idea of agreement.

The fight was on. The Committee on Foreign Relations ordered hearings. While the Senate debated and listened to parties supposed to have information that would throw light upon the Treaty, the President started on September 3 on a speaking tour in behalf of the League, going as far west as the Pacific Coast.

He saw that nothing would influence the majority of the Senate except an overwhelming mandate from the people. This had been impressed upon him particularly by its refusal to act favorably upon his request that an American member of the Reparation Commission be appointed prior to ratification of the Peace Treaty. If the Senate had granted Wilson's request, it is the belief of the best informed men of the world that the long-drawn-out delay in fixing the reparation Germany must pay would have been avoided. If these men are right, the occasion, or necessity, of sending French soldiers into the Ruhr valley would have been obviated and much of the trouble of these four years would not have arisen. Recently, with the approval, or the knowledge, of President Coolidge, this country accepted representation "unofficially" on the Reparation Commission in the person of General Charles G. Dawes. It has required

**THE LAST HOME OF WOODROW WILSON** *Kadell & Herbert, N. Y.*

**Mr.** Wilson speaking to the crowd in front of the house in S Street, Washington, to which he moved on his retirement from the Presidency and which, for four years, was regarded by the nation as the shrine of world idealism

MR. AND MRS. WILSON IN THE FUNERAL PROCESSION OF THE UNKNOWN SOLDIER
The first appearance of the ex-President in public after the inauguration of President Harding

forty-eight months to undertake by indirection the plain duty the Senate thwarted when Wilson proposed it.

The debate in the Senate and the program of poison propaganda in the country went along *pari passu* all the summer. From the beginning of the debate, Senator Lodge having called the League "a deformed experiment," there was a group of Senators who were bent on preventing ratification. What was not in the League they read into it. Early action was what Wilson and the shell-shocked world demanded. The Senate's answer was hearings, debate, haggle, delay, criticism, conferences, resolutions, and hostility. The treaty was laid before the Senate July 10, 1919. It was done to death by the Senate March 19, 1920. It required sixteen weeks in Paris to draft it. The Senate's *mañana* way of deliberation required thirty-six weeks to prevent ratification.

It was not until September 10 that the report of the Foreign Relations Committee was brought formally before the Senate. It recommended ratification if accompanied by forty-six amendments. The formal reading begun September 5 was concluded October 20. All amendments submitted, including those proposed by the Foreign Relations Committee, were defeated. On November 6, Senator Lodge presented a revised list of fourteen reservations recommended by the Foreign Affairs Committee and a reservation to the preamble. The reservation to the preamble declared that "the reservations and understandings adopted by the Senate" were to be made a part of the treaty, the latter not to take effect until the reservations were accepted by at least three of the principal powers. Thirteen of the fourteen reservations received a majority vote of the Senate.

A summary of the reservations follows:

(1) The United States shall be the sole judge of fulfillment of its obligations in notice of withdrawal from the League of Nations, and notice of withdrawal shall be given by concurrent resolution of Congress.

(2) The United States assumes no obligation to protect the territorial integrity or political independence of any country or interfere in controversies between nations unless Congress, by joint resolution, shall so provide.

(3) No mandate shall be accepted by the United States except by the action of Congress.

(4) The United States reserves the right to decide what questions are within its domestic jurisdiction; declares domestic questions to be solely within its own jurisdiction; and specifically prescribes immigration, labor, coastwise traffic, the tariff, and commerce as domestic questions.

(5) Declares the Monroe Doctrine to be wholly without the jurisdiction of the League of Nations and not subject to inquiry or arbitration.

(6) The United States withholds its assent to the Shantung provisions and reserves full liberty of action with respect to any controversy growing out of them.

(7) Congress shall provide for and appoint all representatives of the United States on commissions set up under the Covenant of the League, and none other than persons so appointed shall represent the United States.

(8) Interference with trade between Germany and the United States by the Reparation Commission shall occur only with the sanction of Congress.

(9) Congress shall control all expenses of United States commissions under the League of Nations.

(10) In case of agreement to limit armaments, the United States reserves the right to increase its armament for defense or when engaged in war without consulting the Council of the League.

(11) The United States reserves the right to permit the nationals of the Covenant-breaking state to continue trading with the nationals of this country.

(12) Nothing in the Covenant or Treaty shall be taken to approve any act otherwise illegal or in contravention of the rights of citizens of the United States.

(13) The United States declines to take an interest in or responsibility for disposition of the overseas possessions of Germany relinquished under the Treaty.

(14) The United States reserves the right to decide what questions affect its honor or vital interests and refuses to submit them to arbitration. (Rejected).

Asked for his opinion as to the treaty carrying Lodge's thirteen reservations, President Wilson on November 18 wrote to Senator Hitchcock: "The resolution in that form (including the thirteen reservations) does not provide for ratification, but rather for nullification of the Treaty." He said: "I sincerely hope that the true friends and supporters of the Treaty will refuse to support and will vote against the Lodge resolution." He added: "I understand that the door will probably then be open for a genuine resolution of ratification."

The Senate failed the world.

## Chapter XXXI

# AN APPEAL TO CÆSAR

"THE ONLY PEOPLE I OWE ANY REPORT TO ARE YOU AND OTHER CITIZENS"—GOES JOYFULLY ON SPEAKING TRIP FOR THE COVENANT—IT TAKES HIM TO THE PACIFIC COAST—ARTICLE X—SHANTUNG—ENTANGLING ALLIANCES—PROPHECY OF ENTRY "INTO PASTURES OF QUIETNESS AND PEACE"

*"All the world is looking to us for inspiration and leadership, and we will not deny it to them."*—Wilson

IT was not long before his return to Europe before Mr. Wilson was convinced that he must make an "appeal to Cæsar" to secure ratification of the Treaty. He was confirmed in this opinion after his conference in the White House with members of the Senate Foreign Affairs Committee and the methods of delay and opposition manifested in the Senate.

His duty was plain to him and he set about it with the fixed resolve to undertake it if it killed him. He gave expression to that feeling in Omaha, September 8, saying: "If I felt that I personally in any way stood in the way of this settlement, I would be glad to die that it might be consummated." Death never had terrors for Woodrow Wilson. Failure to do his duty alone troubled his spirit. In the White House his decision was received with anxious acquiescence. His wife and physician knew the peril and feared he was not equal to the tax on his vitality. Members of the Cabinet sought to dissuade him from the strain. "I must go," was his reply to one of them.

"You are much mistaken. It will be no strain on me—on the contrary, it will be a relief to meet the people. No, the speeches will not tax me. The truth is, I am saturated with the subject and am spoiling to tell the people all about the Treaty. I will enjoy it."

In a sense, seeing the mañana and hostile policy of the Senate leaders, it was a relief to get out of Washington into the free air of the open West where the people would wish only to hear the truth, and as the triumph of the trip proved, to hear it gladly. Wilson "set sail" (he was fond of using naval terms) happily on his last trip. If he had any premonitions that he was not robust enough for the trip he kept them to himself. After the decision was made, he was blithe and happy, for he was never quite so rejoiced as when, all preparations made, he was in a fight for a cause that gripped him. The thought of the trip exhilarated him.

Beginning at Columbus, Ohio, September 4, he spoke every day and night until he was stricken on the way to Wichita, Kansas, on the 26th day of September. "I have for a long time chafed at the confinement of Washington," he said in his first public appeal for popular support for the League. "I have for a long time wished to fulfil the purpose with which my heart was full when I returned to our beloved country—to go out and report to my fellow countrymen concerning these affairs of the world which now need to be settled. The only people I owe any report to are you and the other citizens of the United States." The President seemed in fine fettle as he spoke freely what was in his mind and heart. It required a volume of nearly 400 pages to contain the speeches of that last journey, and it may be doubted if so much of philosophy and sincerity and wisdom has before been compressed in speeches in a "swing around the circle," as presidential tours are called. To be sure the theme—World Peace—was the biggest subject Americans had considered.

Washington's admonition against "entangling alliances" had taken deep root. Many did not at first appreciate that what Wilson was trying to do was to rid the world of such "alliances" as Washington wished Americans to avoid. He had to correct that inherited opinion and get men and women to think in world terms. To those quoting Washington's wise course as to the United States becoming involved in European Alliances, Mr. Wilson at Los Angeles, September 20, made this answer:

"You know, you have been told, that Washington advised us against entangling alliances, and gentlemen have used that as an argument against the League of Nations. What Washington had in mind was exactly what these gentlemen want to lead us back to. The day we have left behind was a day of alliances. It was a day of balances of power. It was a day of 'every nation take care of itself, or make a partnership with some other nation or group of nations to hold the peace of the world steady or to dominate the weaker portions of the world.' Those were the days of alliances. This project of the League of Nations is a great process of disentanglement."

What were the arguments Wilson used in his fight as he met the people face to face? What did he think the Covenant contained that made its ratification mean more than anything else or everything else? Here is the basis of the new idea as he unfolded it at Columbus, Ohio:

"If I were to state what seems to me the central idea of this treaty, it would be this: It is almost a discovery in international conventions that nations do not consist of their governments, but consist of their people. That is a rudimentary idea. It seems to us in America to go without saying, but it was never the leading idea in any other international congress that I ever heard of; that is to say, any international congress made up of the representatives of governments. They were always thinking of national policy, of national advantage, of the rivalries of trade, of the advantages of territorial conquest. There is nothing of that in this treaty. You will notice that even the territories which are taken away from Germany, like her colonies, are not given to anybody."

He was returning again and again to an explanation of Article X, against which the most serious objection was made. Indeed, many people were made to believe that Article X, which Mr. Wilson called "the heart of the Covenant," was some Frankenstein that would destroy American independence. Article X is in these words:

"The members of the League undertake to respect and preserve as against external aggression the territorial integrity and existing political independence of all members of the League. In case of any such aggression or in case of any threat or danger of such aggression the Council shall advise upon the means by which this obligation shall be fulfilled."

A book might be made up of Wilson's explanations and arguments in support of that provision. Perhaps nowhere in all his writings and speeches was he happier in presenting it to the clear understanding of the average man than at Indianapolis, September 4, when he said:

"You have heard a great deal about Article X of the Covenant of the League of Nations. Article X speaks the conscience of the world. Article X is the article which goes to the heart of this whole bad business, for that article says, that the members of this league (that is intended to be all the great nations of the world) engage to respect and to preserve against all external aggression the territorial integrity and political independence of the nations concerned. That promise is necessary in order to prevent this sort of war from recurring, and we are absolutely discredited if we fought this war and then neglect the essential safeguard against it. You have heard it said, my fellow citizens, that we are robbed of some degree of our sovereign, independent choice by articles of that sort. Every man who makes a choice to respect the rights of his neighbors deprives himself of absolute sovereignty, but he does it by promising never to do wrong, and I can not for one see anything that robs me of any inherent right that I ought to retain when I promise that I will do right, when I promise that I will respect the thing which, being disregarded and violated, brought on a war in which millions of men lost their lives, in which the civilization of mankind was in the balance, in which there was the most outrageous exhibition ever witnessed in the history of mankind of the rapacity and disregard for right of a great armed people.

"We engage in the first sentence of Article X to respect and preserve from external aggression the territorial integrity and the existing political independence not only of the other member States, but of all States, and if any member of the League of Nations disregards that promise, then what happens? The council of the league advises what should be done to enforce respect for the covenant on the part of the nation

© *Kadell & Herbert N. Y.*

**THE EX-PRESIDENT ON HIS SIXTY-FIFTH BIRTHDAY**

This portrait, taken on December 28, 1920, was the first made after his serious breakdown in September, 1919

**THE LAST RITES** *P. & A. Photos*

The funeral procession of the nation's dead was marked by the utmost simplicity save for the guard of honor from the Army, Navy and Marine Corps and the many thousands who lined the way

**WASHINGTON CATHEDRAL** *© U. & U.*

Where on February 6, 1924, the remains of America's most distinguished citizen were laid to rest

attempting to violate it, and there is no compulsion upon us to take that advice except the compulsion of our good conscience and judgment. It is perfectly evident that if, in the judgment of the people of the United States the council adjudged wrong and that this was not a case for the use of force, there would be no necessity on the part of the Congress of the United States to vote the use of force. But there could be no advice of the council on any such subject without a unanimous vote, and the unanimous vote includes our own, and if we accepted the advice we would be accepting our own advice. For I need not tell you that the representatives of the Government of the United States would not vote without instructions from their Government at home, and that what we united in advising we could be certain that the American people would desire to do. There is in that covenant not only not a surrender of the independent judgment of the Government of the United States, but an expression of it, because that independent judgment would have to join with the judgment of the rest.

"But when is that judgment going to be expressed, my fellow citizens? Only after it is evident that every other resource has failed, and I want to call your attention to the central machinery of the League of Nations. If any member of that League, or any nation not a member, refuses to submit the question at issue either to arbitration or to discussion by the council, there ensues automatically by the engagements of this covenant an absolute economic boycott. There will be no trade with that nation by any member of the League. There will be no interchange of communication by post or telegraph. There will be no travel to or from that nation. Its borders will be closed. No citizen of any other State will be allowed to enter it, and no one of its citizens will be allowed to leave it. It will be hermetically sealed by the united action of the most powerful nations in the world. And if this economic boycott bears with unequal weight, the members of the League agree to support one another and to relieve one another in any exceptional disadvantages that may arise out of it."

To such appeals, said Wilson, "some gentlemen, who are themselves incapable of altruistic purposes, say, 'Ah, but that is altruistic. It is not our business to take care of the world.' No, but it is our business to prevent war, and if we do not take care of the weak nations of the world there will be war."

For decades the United States has declared its friendship for China. And so, the opponents of the Covenant made considerable headway by saying that Wilson had "sacrificed China to the rapacity of Japan in the Shantung matter." It did look that China had lost out. What was Wilson's answer? Speaking at St. Louis, September 5, he said:

"It was very embarrassing, my fellow citizens, when you thought you were approaching an ideal solution of a particular question to find that some of your principal colleagues had given the whole thing away. And that leads me to speak just in passing of what has given a great many people natural distress. I mean the Shantung settlement, the settlement with regard to a portion of the Province of Shantung in China. Great Britain and, subsequently, France, as everybody now knows, in order to make it more certain that Japan would come into the war and so assist to clear the Pacific of the German fleets, had promised that any rights that Germany had in China should, in the case of the victory of the Allies, pass to

Japan. There was no qualification in the promise. She was to get exactly what Germany had, and so the only thing that was possible was to induce Japan to promise—and I want to say in fairness, for it would not be fair if I did not say it, that Japan did very handsomely make the promise which was requested of her—that she would retain in Shantung none of the sovereign rights which Germany had enjoyed there, but would return the sovereignty without qualification to China and retain in Shantung Province only what other nationalities had already had elsewhere, economic rights with regard to the development and administration of the railway and of certain mines which had become attached to the railway. That is her promise, and personally I have not the slightest doubt that she will fulfill that promise. She can not fulfill it right now because the thing does not go into operation until three months after the treaty is ratified, so that we must not be too impatient about it. But she will fulfill that promise. [Japan's promise was kept.]

"Suppose that we said that we would not assent. England and France must assent, and if we are going to get Shantung Province back for China and these gentlemen do not want to engage in foreign wars, how are they going to get it back? Their idea of not getting into trouble seems to be to stand for the largest possible number of unworkable propositions. It is all very well to talk about standing by China, but how are you standing by China when you withdraw from the only arrangement by which China can be assisted? If you are China's friend, then do not go into the council where you can act as China's friend! If you are China's friend, then put her in a position where even the concessions which have been made need not be carried out! If you are China's friend, scuttle and run! That is not the kind of American I am."

With a wealth of illustration, these and like arguments marked his speeches from Columbus, Ohio, September 4, to people in the principal cities to and on the Pacific coast back to Pueblo, Colorado, September 25. His last words on that trip in his last speech at Pueblo were:

"Now that the mists of this great question have cleared away, I believe that men will see the truth, eye to eye and face to face. There is one thing American people always rise to and extend their hand to, and that is the truth of justice and of liberty and of peace. We have accepted the truth and we are going to be led by it, and it is going to lead us, and through us the world, out into pastures of quietness and peace such as the world never dreamed of before."

The eloquent voice was heard no more.

## CHAPTER XXXII

# BROKEN AT THE WHEEL

THE GREAT CASUALTY OF WAR RETURNS TO WASHINGTON, WHICH HE WAS NEVER TO LEAVE AGAIN—HAPPY IN THE AFFECTION AND COMRADESHIP OF HIS DEVOTED WIFE—HIS MARRIAGE TO MRS. EDITH BOLLING GALT, OF VIRGINIA, CROWNED HIS LIFE WITH HAPPINESS—THE BEAUTIFUL FRIENDSHIP BETWEEN WILSON AND DR. GRAYSON—THE PHYSICIAN'S TRIBUTE

*"Shall the great sacrifice that we made in this war be in vain, or shall it not?"*—WILSON

IT was on the twenty-eighth day of September that President Wilson reached Washington. His sudden illness, which compelled an abandonment of his Western crusade for the League of Nations, made him a semi-invalid for life. He walked unassisted to his automobile at the depot where anxious friends awaited his coming. By his side was Mrs. Wilson, who had been with him every day of every month of the great days since they were married—every trip he had taken, every place he had visited, whether in the palaces of Europe or the quiet drives in their beloved Virginia hills. She was to be stay and comfort in the months of nursing and anxiety that the future held for the greatest casualty of the war, as she had been comrade and sharer in all that touched him, in days when he went from triumph to triumph. It was Saturday at 8.30 P. M., eighteenth day of December, 1915, when Mrs. Norman Galt, born Edith Bolling, became the wife of Woodrow Wilson.

Mrs. Wilson was born in Wytheville, Va., and was one of ten children, nine of whom lived to maturity. All except Rolfe, named for her ancestor who married Pocahontas, were born in Wytheville, where her father, the late W. H. Bolling, was Judge of the County Court for many years. As a member of the military company known as "The Wytheville Grays" Judge Bolling was one of the witnesses of the execution of John Brown at Harper's Ferry. It was an ideal marriage. The country had first surmised the new-found happiness in the late summer of 1915 when Mrs. Galt was a visitor at Cornish, where Mr. Wilson and his family found release for a few weeks from the heat of Washington. Even before then, the close friends, personal and official, knowing of the friendship between Mrs. Galt and Miss Helen Bones and the Misses Wilson, had noted the President's interest in the charming occasional visitor to the White House as the guest of his daughters. But the Cornish visit settled the pleasant reports in the mouths of the public, quick to note any event of interest to an occupant of the White House.

Mr. Wilson never seemed to understand why a President's home and family affairs had any more interest to the public than the private life of any other citizen. He declined to lose the home life which was so dear to him and the marriage in Mrs. Galt's modest home in Washington was as quiet and simple as if Mr. Wilson had still been the professor of political science in Bryn Mawr. The ceremony was performed jointly by Rev. Herbert S. Smith, rector of the Episcopal church of which the bride was a member, and by Rev. James H. Taylor, pastor of the Presbyterian church where Mr. Wilson worshipped. Only the nearest relatives were present.

Following the marriage Mr. and Mrs. Wilson spent two weeks at Hot Springs, Va. Messages of good wishes came from rulers of nations in Europe, presidents of South and Central American countries, Governors of States, diplomats, leaders, and friends.

The wedding trip over, they returned to Washington. The people of the whole country realized that the first lady of the land fitted into her place as if she had been born in it. The President's friends and supporters soon learned how much in cheer and counsel she meant to Mr. Wilson, how wise and wholesome she was, with her charm and graciousness. She possessed tact and judgment, with wit and appreciation of the best things in art and letters, which made the marriage an ideal one. Whatever her interest in politics and public questions—and it was deep, revolving around her husband's participation—she was never quoted. She never failed to measure up to the high standards that American people have set for the mistress of the White House. She was called upon to be hostess to those who sat in the seats of the mighty from every land—statesmen, diplomats, warriors. She herself, when she accompanied President Wilson to Paris, was the guest of royalty. She was the same gracious Virginian there as when she grew up in beauty and grace in her Virginia home.

But Mrs. Wilson was even more esteemed by the country when the lights burned low in those anxious days in Washington as her husband's life seemed to hang by a thread, and all the days of her loving ministrations following the breakdown at Wichita. With a wife's intuition she had feared his strength might not be equal to the Western trip. But with a wife's devotion she shared his feeling that with the Cause at stake, he must make his appeal to his countrymen even if at the sacrifice of life. With the care that love knows she shielded him from overexertion in the days of speaking and the nights of travel across the continent. At Seattle he felt return of the hoarseness and weakness that came after his serious illness in Paris. He left that city nervous and tired. She gave him strength and resolution. And he had the courage to go on his nerve. It never weakened until the ties of earth were broken. And she is of like mettle. She kept in touch with all that would interest him and saved his strength. She was concerned for the fitness of the President of the United States, but it was her husband's health that summoned all her fortitude. When the break came, it was the touch and love of the wife that were both solace and recuperation.

Mr. Wilson was covered with perspiration and almost exhausted when he finished speaking at Wichita. Soon after midnight he complained of being ill. Dr. Grayson's examination revealed the right side of his face twitching, as it had often done before. However, he was alarmed to observe a drooling of saliva from the corner of the President's mouth and also a drooping of the facial muscles on the left side. He feared a stroke of paralysis was impending. He advised that future dates be cancelled and the President proceed to Washington. Urged to sleep, Mr. Wilson said, "I won't be able to sleep at all, Doctor, if you say I must cancel the trip. Even if giving my own life would accomplish this object, I gladly would give it."

After his arrival in Washington, he signed bills and resolutions of Congress, drove through Rock Creek Park, and seemed to be getting along well until October 1. He enjoyed a moving picture show that evening, and he played a game of billiards.

At 4 o'clock in the morning, October 4, Mrs. Wilson heard the President in the bathroom calling. Dr. Grayson was summoned. Mr. Wilson was prostrate on the floor in a semi-conscious condition. His left leg, on which he would never bear his weight afterwards, was crumpled under him. He had been paralyzed on his left side. Regaining consciousness, he exacted a promise from his wife and doctor that his condition, if serious, should not be made known. The country knows how true they were to the promises. He was never unconscious after the first night. His mind was always active. He grew a mustache and whiskers, for no one entered the sick chamber except his wife, doctors, and nurses.

Dr. Grayson summoned from Philadelphia Dr. Francis X. Dercum, a specialist, also Rear Admiral E. R. Stitt of the Naval Medical Corps and Dr. Sterling Ruffin of Washington, Mrs. Wilson's family physician.

A two-hour consultation developed the agreement that Mr. Wilson had suffered what is medically known as a cerebral thrombosis—a blood clot in one of the blood vessels in the right side of his brain. Its effect was to impair the motor nerves of the left side as well as the sensatory nerves.

The physicians concluded that there had been no lesion but that there was danger of one. If the clot were a hard one and should be swept along in the blood circulation to the heart and jam a valve the result probably would be death. If it were a soft clot there was hope for absorbing it. On that slender hope the battle for life began.

Mr. Wilson had suffered the retinal hemorrhage in his right eye years ago and Dr. Grayson wanted the oculist, Dr. George de Schweinitz, to examine it.

"I want to look at your pupils," said the oculist.

"You'll have a long job," shot back the sick President, "I've had many thousands of them."

He was thinking of college days, but the remark was an example of how he always joked his doctors, even when he was desperately ill. But sick as he was, he chafed at confinement to bed and wanted to get up.

"Your temperature is exactly normal this morning," said Dr. Grayson on one occasion soon thereafter.

"My temper won't be normal if you keep me in this bed much longer," returned Mr. Wilson, saying he desired to try his legs.

Will-power, skilled treatment, tender nursing and quiet won over the danger of death. When he left the White House Dr. Dercum said he might live five minutes, five months, or five years. He lived nearly three years.

Mrs. Wilson stood between the President and every possible thing that might retard his improvement. In the early days after his return to Washington, as he grew stronger in the fall of 1919, official papers came to him for action through her and her intelligent presentation saved a tax upon his powers. In a few weeks he was able to write the characteristic "Woodrow Wilson" almost as well as ever. He was tenacious in the performance of duty and to the last was the President of the United States. When Senators, hearing that he was suffering from "disability," sent two of their members to "make a survey" they reported that he was fully able to transact the public business. The Congress having been organized by the opposition party, very little legislation was enacted, but, though knowing the most of his recommendations would not be carried out, Mr. Wilson failed in no particular in presenting policies deemed necessary for the reconstruction after war. When Cabinet meetings were resumed, Mrs. Wilson was never far away. Day and night in the four years when he could not walk unaided, it was this good wife who brought sunshine into his life, and whose presence comforted him as he passed into the silence and thence to the reward. The love the American people bore Mr. Wilson they shared with his wife and comrade, and it goes to her, now that he is gone, in full measure.

There are in history few friendships that are as intimate as that which existed so long between President Wilson and Admiral Grayson. Wilson knit his friends to him by hooks of steel. The presence of Princeton schoolmates when he was inaugurated, and his unbroken friendships with the choice spirits of those happy days were grateful to his soul. During the last years of his life, in the White House, in his perplexity in the Mexican and Neutrality periods; in the crucial days when the direction of the World War called for all that was in him; in Europe where, amid shoals and quicksands, he never lost the way to Peace; in the Western trip when the break to physical strength came; and in the long vigils of serious illness in the White House, with conscientious devotion to duty often overtaxing his strength, and during the quiet and often anxious days in the S Street home—always near him was his friend and physician, Dr. Cary Grayson. Their relationship began on the evening of the inauguration. The President's sister, Mrs. Howe, sustained a slight injury. "Where shall I find a doctor?" asked Mr. Wilson of his classmate and close friend, Dr. E. P. Davis, of Philadelphia, who was with him at the White House. Dr. Grayson, a navy surgeon, was on duty at Washington. "Knowing the high reputation of naval surgeons," said Dr. Davis, "I advised him to send for Dr. Grayson."

From that moment until his death Mr. Wilson and Admiral Grayson were closely associated. At first, professional, it ripened into regard. It burgeoned into complete understanding and tender friendship. The older man loved youth, particularly young men of clear thinking and clean living. He had no son—perhaps that was a regret he never uttered. His paternal regard embraced the younger physician. They rode and walked and played and talked together. Dr. Grayson knew his constitution, knew how he must take care of himself and conserve his strength. But he knew his responsibilities and how he would meet them, sick or well. He was the skilled physician who studied to keep the President fit. He was the skilled physician who in Paris brought him through a serious illness. He was the skilled physician who was with him almost daily for more than eleven years. But he was much more than that: he was the true and trusted friend, the agreeable companion who brought him good stories and kept him advised about what went on in the world about him, who shielded him and was toward him all that a son might have been, if God had given the world a second Woodrow Wilson. He knew his moods, his ways, he knew his heart, and he possessed Mr. Wilson's affection without limit and his full confidence. Of the thousands of tributes paid Mr. Wilson the day the wires flashed his death, perhaps none gave truer appraisement than that of Admiral Grayson, who said:

"It was my privilege to be Woodrow Wilson's friend as well as his physician, and it would be difficult for me to put in words the affection for him which grew during nearly twelve years of close personal association and confidence.

"It will not be for me to express my estimate of his ideals and his character and leadership, nor for me to write his epitaph. Time alone will do that. But in sick days and well, I have never known such single-minded devotion to duty as he saw it against all odds, such patience and forbearance with adversity, and finally such resignation to the inevitable.

"I once read an inscription in a southern country church yard. It said: 'He was unseduced by flattery, unawed by opinion, undismayed by disaster. He faced life with antique courage, and death with Christian hope.'

"Those words, better than any words of mine, describe Woodrow Wilson."

Love crowned his life.

## CHAPTER XXXIII

# THE INVALID PRESIDENT

AN INTIMATE PICTURE OF HIS CLOSING YEARS AS TOLD BY OLD SCHOOLMATE—"THE ROAD AWAY FROM REVOLUTION" HIS LAST ARTICLE—HONORING THE UNKNOWN SOLDIER—AT PRESIDENT HARDING'S FUNERAL—MESSAGE ON ARMISTICE DAY BROADCASTED—HIS LAST RECEPTION—THE BETTER WAY

*"That we shall prevail is as sure as that God reigns."*—WILSON

"WHEN Woodrow Wilson entered the White House as President his first anxiety was, lest he should not be physically able to fulfil the duties of president," said Dr. E. P. Davis, physician of Philadelphia, schoolmate at Princeton and intimate friend of Wilson, a few days after his death, to the writer. "He had been a delicate child, had never excelled in muscular strength, but had courage and endurance, and had used his body relentlessly in his studies. During his most active literary work he seriously damaged one of his eyes. He suffered seriously from neuritis in the left arm and leg. During his Princeton days he had an operation for hernia. He was sent abroad by a consultation of physicians with a statement that his health was badly impaired, and consulted a distinguished Scotch authority who said to him: 'President Wilson, if the other University presidents of the United States are no worse off than you, there will be no vacancies in those high offices for an indefinite time.' He had the lack of digestive assimilation which brain workers often show, and came to the White House in good, but not in robust general health.

"Under medical advice he took up a régime which included golf as a medicinal measure, and to this régime he unswervingly adhered until his going abroad. He gained in weight and strength during his first administration. He once remarked that the legitimate duties of the Presidency are not a burden upon a man who works with system, and observation shows that it is politics and politicians, and not the duties of the Presidency which kill Presidents.

"His life as an invalid was characteristic of the man. Each morning, unless feeling unusually depressed, he breakfasted with Mrs. Wilson at nine, in the window of the dining room where the morning sun came in most abundantly; then to the office of his secretary, John Randolph Bolling, where he dictated answers to from twenty-five to forty letters, often walking back and forth, standing, or sitting on the arm of the chair while dictating. Then to his bedroom where he completed a leisurely toilet. A nap before midday meal. Then midday meal taken in his bedroom, a sunny room. Mrs. Wilson practically gave him his meal, and either read to him, or some visiting friend read to him about matters of information. After midday meal, a nap. At three o'clock he saw those whom he wished to see. At four, a drive. He had mapped out the vicinity of Washington into certain specified drives. One through Arlington, over into Virginia, sometimes across the Maryland border, and the Sunday drive was always through the Soldiers' Home and around 'the Hill' as the Capitol is sometimes called. As an invalid in driving, he was entertaining in his remarks and stories, in admiring the scenery, and in speaking of things which pleased him. When passing the flag he was accustomed to remove his hat, and, placing the hand holding the hat over his heart, to say that he wished the men of the country could feel as he did in honoring the flag.

"At times he would occupy the front seat of his car, where he was punctilious in showing courtesy to those who accompanied him. As in other things, he was punctiliously careful in observing the courtesy of the road. He was frequently recognized while driving and was especially pleased when children saluted him, which he invariably promptly returned.

"After the drive he rested, then came to the library where, in an armchair beneath a high electric lamp, he had his supper. Mrs. Wilson often read a summary of the evening paper, or some friend with him would read to him something else. Then he played solitaire, Mrs. Wilson keeping his score, and at ten o'clock was ready to rest for the night.

"Saturday evenings his diversion was going to Keith's theater. This came to be a Washington event for the populace. There was a side entrance to the rear of the theater by which he gained immediate access to seats on the last row. These were reserved for him. The managers were always present, plain-clothes men kept him from annoyance, and the people gathered in the street and in the theater to see him. They greeted him warmly, which he much appreciated. On leaving the theater the crowd was even greater, and his welcome and goodbye on theater nights, in spite of the weather, were always cordial and delightful.

"As an invalid he was uncomplaining and patient,

doing cheerfully whatever he thought could be of use. From time to time he desired to know what he could expect in the way of convalescing, and whether he was doing his share. He had great faith in the recuperative powers of nature, and placed confidence in his physicians.

"January 5 was an anniversary in his wife's family. It was Saturday, and to honor the occasion, he drove in the afternoon, although the weather was cold. A friend remarked to him: 'It is cold for you to be out.' Says he: 'You know I am not a quitter.' To do full honor to the occasion the usual visit to Keith's was carried out. Next day, Sunday, being cold, he did not drive, but on Sunday evening at supper some one read to him the splendid poem of Francis Thompson's 'The Hound of Heaven,' which illustrates the overwhelming presence of God and the futility of human escape from the Divine Presence. He greatly enjoyed and appreciated this splendid poem.

"One of the most striking things concerning his passing from human life was his extraordinary appearance after death. Near the window in his bedroom in which the sunlight fell softly and freely, upon a couch lay Woodrow Wilson, in appearance thirty-five or forty years of age. His hair was prematurely gray for his features. The lines of care, of anxiety, and of weakness had disappeared. The outlines of the face were smooth and beautiful. It was as if a distant sunrise had touched the features."

This intimate picture, by one of the oldest and most intimate friends, of the daily regimen of the life of the invalid President sums up much of the thirty-five months after he left the White House.

The days were made cheerful when old friends

would call, and they all went away with a sense of the triumph of the mind over bodily ailments. It cannot be said that he took excursions into new lines of thought, but his interest in the policies and principles which had interested him before his illness was unabated. Indeed, the hope and faith that they would prevail upheld and sustained him.

In recent months he kept in touch with the outside world in a way, his radio set being a source of real enjoyment. He was glad to take advantage of the suggestion, that he broadcast a message to the people on Armistice Day. Quietly seated in his study, he addressed millions in audiences invisible to him. He spent hours in preparing the message—(did he know it was his last?)—and delivered it with unwonted emphasis. The Armistice Day address was in these words:

"The anniversary of Armistice Day should stir us to great exaltation of spirit because of the proud recollection that it was our day, a day above those early days of that never-to-be-forgotten November which lifted the world to the high levels of vision and achievement upon which the great war for democracy and right was fought and won.

"Although the stimulating memories of that happy time of triumph are forever marred and embittered for us by the shameful fact that when the victory was won—won, be it remembered, chiefly by the indomitable spirit and valiant sacrifices of our own unconquerable soldiers—we turned our backs upon our associates and refused to bear any responsible part in the administration of peace, or the firm and permanent establishment of the results of the war—won at so terrible a cost of life and treasure—and withdrew into a sullen and selfish isolation which is deeply ignoble because manifestly cowardly and dishonorable.

"This must always be a source of deep mortification to us, and we shall inevitably be forced by the moral obligations of freedom and honor to retrieve that fatal error and assume once more the rôle of courage, self-respect and helpfulness which every true American must wish and believe to be our true part in the affairs of the world.

"That we should thus have done a great wrong to civilization, and at one of the most critical turning points in the history of mankind, is the more deplored because every anxious year that has followed has made the exceeding need for such services as we might have rendered more and more manifest and more pressing, as demoralizing circumstances which we might have controlled have gone from bad to worse, until now—as if to furnish a sort of sinister climax—France and Italy between them have made waste paper of the Treaty of Versailles, and the whole field of international relationships is in perilous confusion.

"The affairs of the world can be set straight only by the firmest and most determined exhibition of the will to lead and to make the right prevail.

"Happily, the present situation of affairs in the world affords us an opportunity to retrieve the past and render to mankind the incomparable service of proving that there is at least one great and powerful Nation which can put aside programs of self-interest and devote itself to practicing and establishing the highest ideals of disinterested service and the constant maintenance of exalted standards of conscience and of right.

"The only way in which we can show our true

appreciation of the significance of Armistice Day is by resolving to put self-interest away and once more formulate and act upon the highest ideals and purposes of international policy.

"Thus, and only thus, can we return to the true traditions of America."

From the front steps of his house, on Armistice Day, he addressed the waiting thousands in a brief impromptu talk concluding with these sentences:

"I am proud to remember that I had the honor of being the Commander-in-Chief of the most ideal army that was ever thrown together—pardon my emotion—though the real fighting Commander-in-Chief was my honored friend Pershing, whom I gladly hand the laurels of victory. Just one word more. I cannot refrain from saying it:

"I am not one of those that have the least anxiety about the triumph of the principles I have stood for. I have seen fools resist Providence before and I have seen their destruction, as will come upon these again—utter destruction and contempt. That we shall prevail is as sure as that God reigns. Thank you."

From time to time friends and admirers would write asking his opinion about men and measures. Rarely after his retirement did he volunteer advice or counsel as to legislation or politics, but when his counsel was sought he wrote frankly, with a candor and directness that was characteristic. If he was asked about a candidate, who in the crucial fight for the Covenant had not given that Magna Charta of Peace his support, Mr. Wilson advised that he be not re-elected. People said these letters showed he was bitter in his illness. Not so. They showed he was so devoted to a cause he could not forgive those he felt had failed to advance it. Now and then he wrote a letter to some organization and summarized doctrines and called for consistency and devotion to ideals. He craved for his party a return to power, not as a partisan, but because he wished it to be the agency for carrying the Republic into the League of Nations. His brief letters were all in that spirit. And they all breathed confidence that the people of America would yet be found co-operating with other nations to end war. He died with that faith undimmed.

Only once did Mr. Wilson in his retirement respond to the request that he write for the magazines. In the *Atlantic Monthly* of August, 1923, the following article from his pen appeared. (It is published here by permission of the Atlantic Monthly Press, Inc.)

## THE ROAD AWAY FROM REVOLUTION

By Woodrow Wilson

In these doubtful and anxious days, when all the world is at unrest and, look which way you will, the road ahead seems darkened by shadows which portend dangers of many kinds, it is only common prudence that we should look about us and attempt to assess the causes of distress and the most likely means of removing them.

There must be some real ground for the universal unrest and perturbation. It is not to be found in superficial politics or in mere economic blunders. It probably lies deep at the sources of the spiritual life of our times. It leads to revolution; and perhaps if we take the case of the Russian Revolution, the outstanding event of its kind in our age, we may find a good deal of instruction for our judgment of present critical situations and circumstances.

What gave rise to the Russian Revolution? The answer can only be that it was the product of a whole social system. It was not in fact a sudden thing. It had been gathering head for several generations. It was due to the systematic denial to the great body of Russians of the rights and privileges which all normal men desire and must have if they are to be contented and within reach of happiness. The lives of the great mass of the Russian people contained no opportunities, but were hemmed in by barriers against which they were constantly flinging their spirits, only to fall back bruised and dispirited. Only the powerful were suffered to secure their rights or even to gain access to the means of material success.

It is to be noted as a leading fact of our time that it was against "capitalism" that the Russian leaders directed their attack. It was capitalism that made them see red; and it is against capitalism under one name or another that the discontented classes everywhere draw their indictment.

There are thoughtful and well-informed men all over the world who believe, with much apparently sound reason, that the abstract thing, the system, which we call capitalism, is indispensable to the industrial support, and development of modern civilization. And yet everyone who has an intelligent knowledge of social forces must know that great and widespread reactions like that which is now unquestionably manifesting itself against capitalism do not occur without cause or provocation; and before we commit ourselves irreconcilably to an attitude of hostility to this movement of the time, we ought frankly to put to ourselves the question, Is the capitalistic system unimpeachable? which is another way of asking, Have capitalists generally used their power for the benefit of the countries in which their capital is employed and for the benefit of their fellow men?

Is it not, on the contrary, too true that capitalists have often seemed to regard the men whom they used as mere instruments of profit, whose physical and mental powers it was legitimate to exploit with as slight cost to themselves as possible, either of money or of sympathy? Have not many fine men who were actuated by the highest principles in every other relationship of life seemed to hold that generosity and humane feeling were not among the imperative mandates of conscience in the conduct of a banking business, or in the development of an industrial or commercial enterprise?

And, if these offenses against high morality and true citizenship have been frequently observable, are we to say that the blame for the present discontent and turbulence is wholly on the side of those who are in revolt against them? Ought we not, rather, to seek a way to remove such offenses and make life itself clean for those who will share honorably and cleanly in it?

The world has been made safe for democracy. There need now be no fear that any such mad design as that entertained by the insolent and ignorant Hohenzollerns and their counselors may prevail against it. But democracy has not yet made the world safe against irrational revolution. That supreme task, which is nothing less than the salvation of civilization, now faces democracy, insistent, imperative. There is no escaping it, unless everything we have built up is presently to fall in ruin about us; and the United States, as the greatest of democracies, must undertake it.

The road that leads away from revolution is clearly marked, for it is defined by the nature of men and of organized society. It therefore behooves us to study very carefully and very candidly the exact nature of the task and the means of its accomplishment.

The nature of men and of organized society dictates the maintenance in every field of action of the highest and purest standards of justice and of right dealing; and it is essential to efficacious thinking in this critical matter that we should not entertain a narrow or technical conception of justice. By justice the lawyer generally means the prompt, fair, and open application of impartial rules; but we call ours a Christian civilization, and a Christian conception of justice must be much higher. It must include sympathy and helpfulness and a willingness to forgo self-interest in order to promote the welfare, happiness, and contentment of others and of the community as a whole. This is what our age is blindly feeling after in its reaction against what it deems the too great selfishness of the capitalistic system.

The sum of the whole matter is this, that our civilization cannot survive materially unless it be saved only by becoming permeated with the Spirit of Christ and being made free and happy by the practice which springs out of that spirit. Only thus can discontent be driven out and all the shadows lifted from the road ahead.

Here is the final challenge to our churches, to our political organizations, and to our capitalists—to everyone who fears God or loves his country. Shall we not all earnestly co-operate to bring in the new day?

On every Armistice Day (to him it was a holy day, for it was the end of the war) and on his birthday gatherings of friends and admirers would assemble at his home on S Street to do him honor. These visits were grateful to him, with a hint, however, of sadness that he could not greet them as before he was stricken.

On the day the body of the Unknown Soldier—the brave lad Wilson had called to battle—was carried with fitting ceremony down Pennsylvania Avenue from the nation's Capitol to Arlington, the sincerest man to uncover in his honor was Woodrow Wilson, the Known Soldier and Executive.

"It is a fearful thing to lead this great peaceful people into war," he said on that memorable April evening. "It was his regret," said his life-long friend, Dr. Davis, "that he could not personally enter the army." He was comrade to every man who wore the country's uniform in the great war. Therefore he followed the Unknown Soldier as one who in perfect comradeship of spirit had shared his hardships, slept with him in the mud, and charged through the deadly barrage.

The great concourse, seeing the feebleness of the former Commander-in-Chief as he rode toward Arlington, paid their tribute first to the Unknown Soldier, and then to the broken body of ex-President Wilson. Perhaps no American has received a tribute so spontaneous, mingled with the feeling of the people that Wilson, too, was a war casualty, and not many days hence would be borne to rest with the boys he had called to fight the battle of world freedom.

The ceremony over, the steps of thousands turned to S Street in pilgrimage to Wilson's home. The dead hero could not hear their tribute. The living hero heard and saw, his eyes blurred with tears.

When President Harding died, his predecessor joined

the ranks of mourners, and gave evidence of his respect for the dead and tender sympathy for the living.

The last reception given by Woodrow Wilson was at his home on January 16, 1924, to the members of the Democratic National Executive Committee. They had met in Washington to fix the time and place for the next Convention, and their first act was to send greetings to the leader, who had twice borne their banner to victory. They called in a body, and he welcomed them, not as the militant champion they had loved to follow in 1912 and 1916, but as the leader broken in body at the end. But his spirit was as dauntless, even as he received them sitting in his great armchair in the library and shook hands with them. He gave personal greeting to those he knew well, and welcome to all. These party associates, who had hoped against hope that he might recover and again lead the hosts to victory, left the home saddened. "He plainly showed the effects of his long illness," said one. "He has aged perceptibly; his hair has grown whiter, and his face was stamped with marks of pain. His left arm, limp at his side, rested against the cushions of the chair. His right hand was raised with an effort to clasp the hands of his callers. It was with difficulty the women kept back their tears."

He talked of the League of Nations with friends not long before the end, and said, "I am not sorry I broke down." They were surprised and told him what a great personal triumph it would have been for him to have led it to universal acceptance. "But," said Mr. Wilson, "as it is coming now, the American people are thinking their way through, and reaching their own decision, and that is the better way for it to come."

Faith to the end.

## Chapter XXXIV

# THE END OF THE ROAD

"THE OLD MACHINE HAS BROKEN DOWN"—"YOU'VE DONE YOUR BEST FOR ME"—"BUT IT IS BETTER THAT I SHOULD DIE THAN LIVE ON, A HELPLESS INVALID"—"TELL MRS. WILSON I WANT HER"—"I AM READY"

*"There is a Providence to which I am perfectly willing to submit."*—WILSON

IT was on January 31 that the loving and trained eye of Mrs. Wilson observed that her husband was not as well as usual. Alarmed, she called in Dr. Sterling Ruffin, who had been one of his physicians since his first illness in 1919. Dr. Cary Grayson had gone for a brief hunting trip. He was summoned and hastily returned to Washington. After a consultation, Mr. Wilson was ordered to bed. He did not recover from the digestive disorder. He grew weaker and realized his condition. He looked death in the face unafraid, not with the spirit of a stoic, but with the fortitude of the Christian. His mind was clear. No pain benumbed his brain. Waiting for the end, his thought, as always, was first for his beloved wife. He watched for the moment (there were few such moments) when she was not in the room. His thin hand was stretched out under the covering. He drew Dr. Grayson close to him.

"The old machine has broken down," he said calmly and with difficulty. "You've done your best for me, but it is better that I should die than live on, a helpless invalid. Tell Mrs. Wilson I want her. I am ready."

The loving physician pressed the hand of the friend he was to lose so soon, not trusting himself to speak

He called Mrs. Wilson, who was near at hand. Quietly and alone these two lovers and partners exchanged the last words before his passing. He made known his wishes, but there was little he had not told her in the talks and drives of the months of close companionship. She understood. He understood.

That was Friday, February 1. Connected speech was never possible again. Beyond a whispered "yes" or "no" in response to inquiries about his comfort, he could not speak. After Saturday there was no recognition of those about him. The end came as of going to sleep. Loved ones watched and waited. They knew the loosing of the cords was near at hand. The inanimate things he had used—his cherished books, his cane (he called it "my third limb"), the golf sticks long unused—all had a new value to those who loved him.

The hush of the Sabbath came. The nation shared the suspense and anxiety of the watchers. Sympathetic friends wended their way to his home to inquire how went the last battle with "the lame lion of S Street." His brother Joseph, his daughter Margaret, and other loved ones shared the vigils of the loving wife. The faithful colored man who had served and loved him stood near. The minutes passed as his wife held his hand in hers until the pulse ceased. As the church bells summoned the nation to prayer the soul of Woodrow Wilson took its flight.

The War President was dead.

## Chapter XXXV

# SPIRITUAL SATISFACTION

TO THE CHRISTIAN MAN "OLD AGE BRINGS HIGHER HOPE AND SERENE MATURITY"—THE QUEST OF LIFE IS "SATISFACTION"—FOUND IN SPIRITUAL AIR—"RATHER HE WAS RULING ELDER THAN PRESIDENT," SAID HIS FATHER

*"Our civilization cannot survive materially unless it be redeemed spiritually."*—Wilson

"I DO not understand how any man can approach the discharge of the duties of life without faith in The Lord Jesus Christ."

That public confession of faith was made by Woodrow Wilson in a very unusual place. On a visit to Raleigh, N. C., in February, 1919, he had been invited to make the address presenting a portrait of Stonewall Jackson to the Capital Club. The beauty and chivalry of the city were gathered for the annual ball. Preceding the dance, Mr. Wilson spoke briefly on Stonewall Jackson. He dwelt little upon his military achievements, which he said were too well known to need his commendation. It was of Jackson, the Christian, whose faith in God was the dominant force in his life. Then he added his own confession. Solemn pause and impressiveness fell on that company. There was no thought of gayety until Mr. Wilson and party withdrew. The incident lingers still in the memory of those privileged to have heard a statement of that character in so unusual a place.

Mr. Wilson's reticence in speaking of the things that

he held dearest was an inheritance from his father. He once related this incident to some friends: "One time my father was attending a religious meeting when other ministers were relating their religious experience. My father did not join. A minister, turning to him, said: 'Have you no religious experiences, Dr. Wilson?' 'None to speak of,' was the reply."

The President quoted that remark to friends with approval, showing his belief that feelings which were deep and sacred were not to be freely discussed.

One day Mr. Wilson's father dropped in to see his friend, Dr. James Sprunt, in Wilmington, N. C. He was very happy and told Dr. Sprunt the cause. "My son, Woodrow, has been made Ruling Elder in the Presbyterian Church. I would rather he held that position than be President of the United States."

On his table by his bedside lay his well-worn Bible from which the minister read at his funeral. He knew its contents and walked in its precepts. His addresses and papers show his familiarity with the Scriptures and his belief in their authority. In February, 1913, a few days before he became President, in an address at Trenton, he said:

"The opinion of the Bible bred in me, not only by the teaching of my home when I was a boy, but also every turn and experience of my life and every step of study, is that it is the one supreme source of revelation, the revelation of the meaning of life, the nature of God and the spiritual nature and need of men. It is the only guide of life which really leads the spirit in the way of peace and salvation. If men could but be made to know it intimately, and for what it really is, we should have secured both individual and social regeneration."

No one can read Wilson's history without feeling, as he himself said once, that Lee had profoundly influenced his life. Probably Wilson never expressed his own feeling about death better than when he told his doctor that it would be better for him to die than remain an invalid; as Lee had expressed his feeling in 1869 in a letter to a friend upon the death of General Dodge: "But those who are gone are happier than those who remain. They are spared what we have to see and meet; but my trust in the mercy of God is so great and my faith in the good sense and probity of the American people is so strong that I know that all things will in the end come right."

In "When a Man Comes to Himself" Mr. Wilson reveals himself perhaps better than in all his other books. It is a small book of only forty pages, but in it is compressed the philosophy that guided his thought and life. He concludes it by saying, "what every man seeks is satisfaction." How shall it be attained? Here is his answer: "He deceives himself as long as he imagines it to lie in self-indulgence—so long as he deems himself the center and object of effort. His mind is spent in vain upon itself. Not in action itself, not in 'pleasure' shall it find its desires satisfied, but in consciousness of right, of powers greatly and nobly spent. It comes to know itself in the motives which satisfy it, in the zest and power of rectitude."

Then comes the climax of ripe wisdom:

"Christianity has liberated the world, not as a system of ethics, not as a philosophy of altruism, but by its revelation of the power of pure and unselfish love. Its vital principle is not its code, but its motive. Love, clear-sighted, loyal, personal, is its breath and immortality. Christ came, not to save himself assuredly, but to save the world. His motive, His example is every man's key to his own gifts and happiness. The ethical code he taught may no doubt be matched, here a piece, there a piece, out of other religions, other teachings or philosophies. Every thoughtful man born with a conscience must know the code of right and of pity to which he ought to conform, but without the motive of Christianity, without love, he may be the purest altruist and yet be as sad and unsatisfied as Marcus Aurelius.

"Christianity gave us, in the fullness of the perfect image of right living, the secret of social and individual well-being; for the two are not separable, and the man who receives and verifies the secret in his own living has discovered not only the best way to serve the world, but also the one happy way to satisfy himself. Henceforth he knows what his powers mean, what spiritual air they breathe, what ardors of service clear them of lethargy, relieve them of all sense of effort, put them at their best. After that fretfulness passes away, experience mellows and strengthens and makes more fit, and old age brings, not senility, not satiety, not regret, but higher hope and serene maturity. Perfect love casteth out fear."

He found spiritual satisfaction.

## Chapter XXXVI

## "THE WAY OF PEACE"

IMPRESSIVE AND TOUCHING SIMPLICITY MARK THE FUNERAL SERVICES AT THE HOME AND AT THE CATHEDRAL—COMRADES OF THE WORLD WAR BORE HIS BODY—THE VACANT CHAIR BEFORE THE FIREPLACE—PRAYER THAT THE HIGH VISION OF A WORLD AT PEACE MIGHT BE REALIZED

"A BUGLE calling softly in the fading day told that Woodrow Wilson had passed today down 'The Way of Peace' to his earned and honored rest.

"It sang the same soldier requiem that once before, at the lips of the same loyal comrade, it sang to lull America's Unknown to his sleep in glory."

With these words the Associated Press commenced its account of the simple but impressive funeral of Woodrow Wilson, the remainder of the article being as follows:

And as the bugle called, out over the hills that look down on the city, a stricken woman turned away from the entrance of the stone crypt down in the dim chapel, leaving her dead to the mercy of God.

At the end, there still stood beside the vault one staunch friend of the dead President, a friend who had battled death for him to the bitter end, who had shared in the great days of triumph, the bitter days of disappointment, even as now he stood to render the last loyal service. Not until the great slab of stone had been swung back to close the vault did Dr. Grayson end the vigil he has kept with Woodrow Wilson for more than a half score of years.

To-night the somber casket of black steel lies in the western niche of the great vault below Bethlehem Chapel. Above, towering from the hillside, looms the gray mass of the cathedral. Below the lights of the city that has turned back from its day of sorrow to the crowding cares of life twinkle through the dark of an overcast night.

And on that casket, where the great dead lies alone at last for his endless rest, beside the plate that sets forth only his name and the days of his birth and death, there still lies the handful of soft-hued blossoms that were the last touching gift of the grief-worn widow.

Distant rumbling of saluting guns in the cloud-darkened dawn ushered in the day when the nation would pay to Woodrow Wilson the simple tribute that he had claimed of it. The busy life of the Capital surged on for a few hours before its course was checked in the last moments of silent respect for the dead. But to the door of the stricken home and into the dim chapel where the last rites would be paid poured an endless stream of flowers that banked and overflowed every space with tender beauty. The names of kings and the great of the earth were on these tributes, and the names of loyal, humble friends and comrades.

As the hour of the double services drew on, thousands took their places along the way from house to chapel to stand long in the chill air, unmindful of the flurries of snow and rain that beat about them. The wide avenue over which the dead War President would make his last journey was banked with people and kept clear of traffic until he should have passed.

Before the house, across the street, a solid rank of people had gathered before the first of those who would join with the family in the home service had arrived. They stood oblivious of cold, waiting to bare their heads a moment. Opposite them the guard of honor came to stand in ranks before the house—soldiers, sailors, and marines.

Singly and in groups the little company that could be admitted to the house came and passed within. Thus came President and Mrs. Coolidge, the honor guard saluting as their Commander-in-Chief passed to stand beside the bier of a dead colleague. Thus came others who had stood shoulder to shoulder with Woodrow Wilson in his days of greatness and came also those few humble ones who could not be forgotten at such a moment, the faithful friends of the old days.

Within, on the second floor of the house, flowers were everywhere. They covered the walls and sent their soft fragrance down from every niche and corner. There are three rooms and a short hallway on this floor, the living rooms of the house. Wide doors had been opened to make them one room, that all who should be present at this intimate service in the home privacy the dead man loved might at least hear what was said.

In the study, where a great vacant chair before the fireplace stood untouched since last he had sat there to ponder in the warm glow, the casket had been set. On the walls about clustered the old, trusty friends of many years, books ranking row on row from floor to ceiling save in the spaces where old pictures made sacred by ties of memory looked down. At one side stood the piano brought from the quiet, scholarly home at Princeton of those other years before greatness had found

Woodrow Wilson out and called him forth to battle and to death.

It was among these surroundings of a quiet, home-loving thinker, the precious memory-laden things of home, that old friends were now gathering to pay him last honors. For a little while before the service began the casket was opened that a few who knew and loved him best might gaze a moment at the still, pain-worn face into which death had brought at last something almost of the placid look of the years long past. Not all of those who crowded the rooms had this opportunity. It was reserved only for intimates, of whatever station in life, who mingled in this silent company.

There was dim light in the rooms. The shades were drawn and only the soft glow of wall lights filled the chambers as those came who gently placed the steel covering above the tired face, and men had known their last sight of Woodrow Wilson. All of the rooms were filled and even the doorways blocked with those standing silently about.

Out in the hallway by the stairs stands a great clock, which ticked solemnly in the hush. As the President and the old friends and companions of the trying days at the White House grouped about the casket, the members of the family came down stairs, leaving only Mrs. Wilson and the two daughters of the dead President in the refuge of the landing above. The three clergymen took their places at the head of the bier.

The mellow chime of the great hall clock beat three solemn strokes through the stillness. As the last tone dwindled and died, Dr. Taylor, the pastor in Washington under whom Woodrow Wilson sat in all his years of Presidential greatness, raised his voice:

"The Lord is my Shepherd," he read,—the old, comforting words of the Twenty-third Psalm carrying out through all the rooms and up the stairs to the tearful women waiting there in deepest black. As he read, faint sobbing came from the landing where Mrs. Wilson's courage faltered for a moment in the long strain she had known.

As Dr. Taylor said the last word of the psalm there was a murmured "Amen" and he gave place to his colleague from Princeton, Dr. Beach, Mr. Wilson's pastor in those far-off quieter days. With raised hands, the minister bade the company to prayer, pouring out his earnest plea that Divine aid be given in the realization of the high vision of a world at peace the dead President had glimpsed. "Especially we call to remembrance Thy lovingkindness and Thy tender mercies to this Thy servant," the minister prayed. "For the wondrous vision Thou didst give him of universal peace and good will, for his zeal in behalf of the Parliament of Man, in which the mighty nations should be restrained and the rights of the weak maintained, for his unswerving devotion to duty, for his courage in the right as God gave him to see the right, for his unflinching integrity, for the fervor of his patriotism which ever flamed upon the altar of his heart, we give Thee thanks." There was sobbing again as he besought God's compassion on the grief-bowed family.

The prayer over, Dr. Beach gave place to Bishop Freeman, whose deep voice sounded the Scriptural quotations dearest to the dead leader. They had been copied from the little book of devotional exercises it had been his wont to read at night and stirred again the bitter grief of the widow and daughters.

"Now unto Him that is able to keep you from falling, and present you faultless before the presence of His Glory with exceeding joy;

"To the only wise God, our Saviour, be glory and majesty, dominion and power, both now and evermore, Amen."

As the solemn words were spoken, the clock chimed the quarter hour and the simple home service of Woodrow Wilson, plain American, had been said as he wished it said.

Into the room came eight men from the honor guard, their sun-tanned youthful faces set in solemn recognition of the dignity and honor of the place that had been given them. They stood soldierly and erect a moment beside the black casket upon which now lay the cluster of orchids, Mrs. Wilson's favorite flowers, the flowers her dead husband often had sent her in the glad other days. Then the soldier, sailor, and marine comrades stooped and raised the fallen chieftain to bear him out for his last journey.

Outside, the other men of the guard had double-lined the short way across the sidewalk to the waiting hearse. As the house door swung back and the three clergymen stepped out to take their places beside the hearse door, up and down the steep, narrow street the multitude which had waited long for this brief glimpse uncovered in the chill air. The men of the guard stood at stiff salute as their comrades bore the casket down through the double rank and lifted it gently into the hearse.

Behind the casket came Mrs. Wilson in deepest black, with a thick veil guarding her sadness from curious eyes. She leaned on her brother's arm, and was helped into a waiting car that moved off at once down the hill behind the hearse. The honor guard was formed in rank on each side.

Next from the house came William G. McAdoo. The daughters of the dead President were supported on his arms as he helped them to the car awaiting them. Behind these came the other members of the family, the brother and nephew and those less closely kin to the dead. There was but one vacancy in the immediate family circle left by the place Mrs. Sayre, the third daughter, and her husband would have filled had time permitted their arrival.

Behind the family came President and Mrs. Coolidge, heading the group of distinguished men and old comrades who made up the funeral party. They were taken in the slow moving row of waiting cars and gradually the funeral train reached down to Massachusetts Avenue and swung around to the right for its slow journey up to the cathedral.

There are few houses along the broad street in its two-mile tree-lined length to the cathedral close. Police and soldiers and marines were strung along the way to keep back the crowding thousands who stood in deep ranks on either side all along the way. The military guardians were without arms, but they and the police, as the cortège passed, silent but for the noise of its own motion, each rendered his stiff salute to the dead. Behind them in the ranks of citizenry that had waited so long, standing five and ten deep at every vantage point, heads were bared and there was weeping among the women.

It had taken long to get the funeral train in motion and still longer for its slow progress up the hill to wind in through the cathedral grounds to the chapel entrance past other thousands. Already the company that would take part in the last public ceremony was gathered in the narrow compass of the chapel. For an hour the organ had sounded from the building in mournful cadence, and as the funeral train wound in through the cathedral gate, the great chimes rang out in slow tones, sending the old, consoling melody of "Nearer My God to Thee," ringing through the chill air to catch the ear of many thousands in near-by streets.

Within the chapel, banked with flowers, the Cabinet members and the diplomatic corps were already seated, and with them the delegation from Senate and House and those from societies of veterans. The only vacant chairs were those that awaited the funeral party. Scores stood for hours in the open space behind.

Led by the cross, the choir moved into the aisle leading to the altar, which was banked on either side with the flowers that filled every nook and corner and flowed over into the outer corridor, lining both sides of the approach to the chapel entrance. Thus between walls of bright blossoms the honor guard was lifting the casket down to bear it into its place at the rail.

It is over this outer door of the chapel, cut deep in the stonework, that the inscription, "The Way to Peace," is set. And through that portal of peace Woodrow Wilson was tenderly carried, with the clergymen walking ahead and the saddened widow following after.

As the casket was carried through the inner door and into the aisle, the choir moved slowly toward the altar in hushed silence. Then, from his place as he walked, Dr. Taylor raised his voice:

"I am the Resurrection and the Life, saith the

Lord," he read, and on down through the Scriptural passages until the choir had filed on to its place beside the altar. The clergymen took up their stations, standing before the altar, the two Presbyterian ministers in their black gowns, the bishop and his colleague of the Episcopal cathedral in white vestments.

Just before them the body bearers set down their burden again and withdrew to join their comrades in the standing group at the back of the room. The black-gowned widow, the two daughters and the other members of the family moved to their places on the left, while President Coolidge and the honorary pallbearers and old friends turned to vacant seats to the right, where the Cabinet members already stood.

Then Bishop Freeman began the reading of the Thirty-ninth Psalm. "Lord, let me know mine end," the murmur of the response filling the dim chamber. He read through the lesson: "Now is Christ risen from the dead, and become the firstfruits of them that slept," and at the close, the choir sang softly, and without organ accompaniment, the dead President's favorite among the old hymns. Only the men's voices of the choir shared in the tender melody. The boys were silent.

"Day is dying in the West;
"Heaven is touching earth with rest."

The blending voices, led by a clear, pure tenor, gave the old hymn an infinitely sweet appeal and it seemed that Mrs. Wilson's head was bowed in tears behind her heavy veil.

"Gather us who seek Thy face,
"To the fold of Thy embrace,
"For Thou art nigh."

The last tones rang softly in the deep cut vaulting of the chapel roof, followed by the solemn chords of an "Amen" and then the Bishop led in the Apostles' Creed.

At the close, as he called the company to prayer, those who were seated sank to their knees with bowed heads until, with raised hand, he pronounced the solemn blessing that ended the service. The organ sounded again softly and the choir moved slowly out again into the aisle, around the sombre bulk of the casket with its single cluster of color. The chanting tones of the recessional hymn sounded: "The strife is o'er, the battle done." Following the choir went the clergymen, down the aisles and off to the right through the doorway, the chanting voices growing softer and softer in the distance and fading at last to a faint whisper as the door was closed:

"That we may live and sing to thee, Alleluia," came the last line, then the faint far-away chords of the last "Amen."

As the organ took up again its softly chanted note of sorrow, Mrs. Wilson was led by her brother out into the chapel robing room on the right and behind her went the members of the family to seek seclusion there until the chapel should be cleared for the private entombment. They did not need to pass through the thronged room again, a door close to the altar letting them escape that trial.

As they left, President Coolidge rose and moved out of the chapel, to be whirled away at once to the White House. Behind him the gathering slowly made its way out to the waiting cars, leaving the honor guard and those who would lift the great slab from the vault entrance alone in the dim room.

None but the eyes of the dear ones and closest friends and of the religious comforters and the loyal comrades of the sister services saw this last moment. The vault entrance lies in the very center of the chapel floor and below it is the place of utter rest many feet down. It was not until the great stone had been put to one side and the honor guard men stood ready to lower the casket gently into the hands of the comrades waiting below to lift it to its secluded niche in the western end, that the family came back for that last farewell. The clergymen stood at the head of the entrance, while Mrs. Wilson took her place at the foot, facing the chapel altar.

At the last the Presbyterian ministers whom the dead man had worshipped with in life joined in saying over him the form of burial service his church knows. Bishop Freeman concluded the service, repeating verses from Tennyson's "Crossing the Bar," with its message of resignation and faith in God's goodness. Then the casket sank slowly into the stone work and from outside, beyond the double walls and where the gray end of a gray day was coming swiftly, the bugle rang out in "taps," the soldier farewell to a fallen comrade. There were only a few remaining about the chapel entrance as that last, clear message was sounded. They stood bareheaded and the soldier and marine guards at salute until the last note died.

Behind them in the chapel, Mrs. Wilson was sobbing as she turned from the vault with the members of the family to go back to the vacant, still house on S Street, where the great chair stood vacant beside the fireplace, and the books waited for the friend to come no more. She took heart, a little, to greet the handful of close friends who had waited without to offer her comfort in her sadness, but it was a grief-bowed woman who went back down the long hill into the city.

And at the vault still stood the friend and physician who had been with Woodrow Wilson through the years of greatness and world-wide acclaim and the years of pain endured with stoic fortitude that followed; the friend who had pledged his word to another woman in the White House years before, ere she came to her death, that he would watch over his chief to the end.

Not until the great stone had sunk again into its place did this friend turn away, his pledge redeemed to the uttermost.

The honorary pallbearers were: Cleveland H. Dodge of New York, Cyrus H. McCormick of Chicago, Dr. Edward P. Davis of Philadelphia, and Dr. Hiram Woods of Baltimore, all members of his Princeton class; Frank L. Polk, former under secretary and at one time acting Secretary of State; David F. Houston, former Secretary of the Treasury; Newton D. Baker, former Secretary of War; Josephus Daniels, former Secretary of the Navy; Albert S. Burleson, former Postmaster General; John Barton Payne, former Secretary of the Interior; Thomas W. Gregory, former Attorney General; William C. Redfield, former Secretary of Commerce; William B. Wilson, former Secretary of Labor, and Edwin T. Meredith, former Secretary of Agriculture. Vance C. McCormick of Harrisburg, Pa.; Bernard M. Baruch of New York; Norman E. Davis of New York; Jesse E. Jones of Houston, Texas; Dr. F. X. Dercum of Philadelphia and Winthrop M. Daniels of Princeton, N. J., all personal friends.

Senators Glass and Swanson of Virginia and Representatives Garrett and Hull of Tennessee. Charles S. Hamlin, former governor of the Federal Reserve Board; Robert Bridges, a classmate; and Rear Admiral Cary T. Grayson.

Major General Tasker H. Bliss, formerly Army Chief of Staff and a fellow member of the Peace Commission; Chief Justice William Howard Taft; Justice Louis D. Brandeis; John Sharp Williams; and Charles R. Crane.

The active pallbearers were: Sergeant Raymond M. Daugherty, Lincoln, Neb., who won the Distinguished Service Cross; Joseph Dloughy, San Francisco, Technical Sergeant; David Friesel, New York City, Staff Sergeant; William E. Wheaton, East St. Louis, Ill., Staff Sergeant; Sergeant James G. Bryant, Seattle; Corporal Harold L. Mitchell, Jarratt, Va.; James Chadwick, Roxbury, Mass., private, first class; Louis M. Kell, Baltimore, private, first class.

The Navy guard of honor and body bearers were drawn from the U. S. S. *Mayflower*. They were: Claud Alexander Ezell, Coxswain, Ware Shoals, S. C.; William Lafayette Cole, Radioman, Naples, Tex.; Oscar Herbert, Sailmaker's Mate, first class, Brooklyn, N. Y.; Arthur Francis Picard, Motor Machinist's Mate, first class, Windsor, Vt.; John Trellis Sharp, Coxswain, Morristown, N. J.; Roy Lester Sherman, Yeoman, third class, Dayton, O.; Louis Silbereisen, Quartermaster, first class, Elkridge, Md.; John Edward White, Seaman, first class, Oklahoma City, Okla.

The Marines were: Ellwyn C. Rowe, Gunnery Sergeant, Sidney, N. Y., who wears the Croix de Guerre with Bronze Star; Willard C. Clopton, Gunnery Sergeant, Smithland, Ky.; John J. Agnew, Staff Sergeant, Baltimore, Md.; John Dunn, Sergeant, Paterson, N. J.; Richard S. Perkins, Sergeant, Montgomery, Ala.; Jesse W. Coleman, Corporal, Lanett, Ala.; Paul O. Moyle, Sergeant, Elm City, N. C.; Frank J. Moran, Corporal, Syracuse, N. Y.

## L'Envoi

The last words of the service were significant of a faith common to great spirits like Tennyson and Wilson. The poem repeated by Bishop Freeman was produced only a few months before Tennyson's death, and by his orders printed as a farewell at the end of every authorized edition of his poems. It is a fitting *vale* to a career of a great American whose idealism visioned a happier day for all mankind. Well does it express the sense of work accomplished and the simple faith in the Pilot to a brighter life:

Sunset and evening star,
  And one clear call for me!
And may there be no moaning of the bar,
  When I put out to sea,
But such a tide as moving seems asleep,
  Too full for sound and foam,
When that which drew from out the boundless deep
  Turns again home.

Twilight and evening bell,
  And after that the dark!
And may there be no sadness of farewell
  When I embark;
For though from out our bourne of Time and Place
  The flood may bear me far,
I hope to see my Pilot face to face
  When I have crossed the bar.

# INDEX


ABC Conference, 184
Abney, Benjamin L., 55
Adams, Anne, 28
Adams, Herbert B., 60
Advisers to the President, 302
Agricultural distress in 1920, 163
Alaskan railroad, 201
Alderman, Dr. Edwin A., 59
Aldrich, Senator Nelson W., 166, 170
Alexander, Joshua W., 139
American Academy of Arts and Letters, 84
Ancestry, 27 *et seq.*
Anderson, of South Carolina, 41
"An Old Master," 61, 90
Arlington Cemetery, speech at, 313
Armistice, 295
Armistice Day, Address by radio, 348, 349
  Message on steps of home, 350
Army program, Garrison's and Wilson's, 144
Article Ten of League Covenant, 329
Athletic interests, 48, 69
Augusta, at school in, 39
  First Presbyterian Church at, 33
Author, Wilson as, 84 *et seq.*
Authors, favorite, 49
Atlanta, Wilson a lawyer in, 59
*Atlantic Monthly*, Wilson's last article in, 351
Axson, Ellen Louise, 61
  Rev. S. Edward, 62
  Dr. Stockton, 231

Bagehot, 49
Baker, Newton D., 111, 137
Baker, Ray Stannard, 302
Ballingerism, 116
Baltimore Convention, 105 *et seq.*
Bankers and the Federal Reserve, 169
Barnwell, Charles Heyward, 40
Baruch, Bernard, 205
Baseball, 42, 48
Beecher, Henry Ward, 39
Bellamy, John D., 45
Belmont, August, 107
Bermuda, Wilson's trip to, 135
Bible, Wilson's appraisement of, 359
Big Four, The, 306
"Bitter-Enders," 318
Blaine, James G., 161
Blake, of South Carolina, 41
Bolling, John Randolph, 345
  W. H., 336
Bones, Jessie Woodrow, 38
  Helen Woodrow, 63
  Mrs. James, 38
Boston, Reception at, 318
Boyhood days, 36 *et seq.*
Brandeis, Louis D., 138, 205
Brest, Wilson lands at, 298
Bridges, Robert, 49
Brougham, 49
Bruce, William Cabell, 55
Bryan, William Jennings, 83, 105 *et seq.*
  appointed Secretary of State, 136
  on currency reform, 168
  peace treaties, 314
  resignation, 141
  resolution at Baltimore, 107
Bryant, David, 236
Bryn Mawr, Wilson at, 62, 66
Buckingham Palace, the President at, 303
Burke, Edmund, 49
  John, 205
Burleson, Albert S., 138, 205

"Cabinet Government in the United States," 131
Cabinet making and breaking, 135 *et seq.*
Cabinet meetings, procedure at, 140
Caldwell, M. H., 56
Campaign of 1912, 115 *et seq.*
Carlisle, Wilson's visit to, 34, 304
Carnegie, Andrew, 70, 241
Carranza, Wilson's recognition of, 185
Catt, Carrie Chapman, 203
Chaumont, Wilson at, 302
China and Shantung, 311
Christianity, Wilson's appraisement of, 360
"Christmas present for the American People," 173
Circus episode, 56
Clark, Champ, 108, 121
Clark, Prof. John B., 123
Clarke, of Arkansas, Senator, 145
Clemenceau characterized, 306
Cleveland, President, 132, 155
Coffin, Howard E., 208
Colby, Bainbridge, 139
Colleges, Democracy in, 81, 83
College days at Davidson, 41
  Princeton, 46 *et seq.*
  Virginia, 54 *et seq.*
College Voters, League of, 118
Columbus, Wilson's speech at, 327

Congress of Vienna, 316
"Congressional Government," 59, 84, 131
"Constitutional Government in the United States," 88
Coolidge, President, 188, 322
Country Club, Princeton as a, 76
Covenanter heritage, 27
Covenant of the League of Nations, 318 *et seq.*
Croker, Richard, 100
Crowell, Benedict, 208
Currency System, 165 *et seq.*

Daniels, Josephus, 138, 182, 205
Danish West Indies, 192
Davidson College, 41
Davis, "Boss" Bob, 97
Davis, Dr. E. P., 50, 341
  intimate picture of Wilson by, 344 *et seq.*
Davis, Jefferson, 37
Dawes, General Charles G., 322
Day, David T., 61
Death of Woodrow Wilson, 357
Debates, Wilson in, 50, 55, 157
Deeds, Edward A., 208
Degree of Ph.D., 61
Democratic National Convention, 105 *et seq.*
  and the Philippines, 191
Democratic National Executive Committee, 355
  organization in New Jersey, Wilson and the, 98
  platform, tariff plank, 157
Dercum, Dr. Francis X., 339
Derry, John T., 39
De Schweinitz, Dr. George, 339
Dewey, Admiral George, 189
  Davis R., 61
Disability of the President, 153, 340
"Division and Reunion, 1829-89," 85
"Dollar Diplomacy," 193
*Dolphin*, U. S. S., 180
Duane, William, 29, 30
Dubois, Ex-Senator, 113

Eight-hour day, 197
Election to Presidency, 125
Elkus, Abram, 205
Ely, Richard T., 60
England, Wilson arrives in, 303
Eumenean Literary Society, 41
Europe, the President in, 298 *et seq.*
Europe, Wilson's second visit to, 309

Father of Woodrow Wilson, 31, 39, 92
Federal Farm Loan Act, 174
  Reserve System, 165 *et seq.*
  Trade Commission, 60, 124
Fiume, Italy's claims to, 310, 320
Fletcher, Admiral, 183
Foch, General, 296
Food restrictions, 37
Forces in the world, the greatest, 90
Fordney Emergency Tariff, 163
Foster, John W., 146
Fourteen Points of Peace, 291
France, Wilson's reception in, 298
Funeral of Woodrow Wilson, 362 *et seq.*

Galt, Mrs. Edith Bolling, 335 *et seq.*
Garfield, Harry A., 208
Garrison, Lindley M., 137, 143 *et seq.*
Gauss, Professor Christian, 53
*George Washington*, Wilson sends for the, 310
German propaganda in Mexico, 187
Glass, Carter, 139, 168, 171
Glass-Owen Currency measure, 170
Glee Club, 48, 58, 60
Glenn, Governor R. B., 42
Gompers, Samuel, 118
Goodwin, "Pete," 47
Gould, E. R. L., 61
Governor of New Jersey, 95 *et seq.*
Graduate School at Princeton, 79 *et seq.*
Grandfather of President Wilson, 29
Grant, President, 140
Grayson, Dr. Cary T., 64, 338, 341
  appraisement of Wilson, 342
  Wilson's last words to, 356
Gregory, Thomas W., 139
Guildhall, the President at the, 304

Hadley, Herbert S., 121
Haiti, 194
Harding, President, 164
  Wilson at funeral of, 354
Harmon, Judson, 108 *et seq.*
Harrison, Francis Burton, Governor of Philippines, 192
Hawaii, 193
Hearst, William Randolph, 121
Hernia, operation for, 344
Hindenburg's disapproval of peace plan, 296
Historical Fellowship, 60
"History of the American People," 86
Hitchcock, Senator, 325
Hoar, Senator, 190
Hoover, Herbert, 208
Horner, J. M., 55
House, Colonel, 138, 314
Houston, David F., 138, 205

Howe, Dr. George, 33
Howe, Mrs., 341
Hubbard, Governor of Texas, 57
Huerta, General Victoriano, 176
Hughes, Charles Evans, 267
Hunt, Dr. Theodore Whitefield, 52

"I am ready," 356
Illness of Wilson, 335 *et seq.*
Imperialism, Wilson on, 136
Inaugural Ball, why there was no, 63
Inauguration of Wilson, 127 *et seq.*
Indianapolis speech, 176, 315, 329 *et seq.*
Ingle, Edward T., 61
Inherited traits, 27 *et seq.*
International Control, Commission on, 301
  justice, 317
*International Review*, 48, 131
Interstate Commerce Commission, 173
Invalid President, the, 344 *et seq.*
Ireland, freedom of, 320
Irish ancestry, 28
Island territories, 189 *et seq.*
Italian delegation withdraws from conference, 310
Italy, the President in, 305
  and Fiume, 310, 320

Jackson, Andrew, 85
Jackson, "Stonewall," 358
Jackson Day Dinner, 136
Japan's claim to Shantung, 311
Jefferson College, 31
Jenkins, W. O., 150
Johns Hopkins University, 60 *et seq.*
Johnson, Dr. Alexander, 70
Johnson, Hiram, 122
Joline, Adrian, 82
Jones Act, 192
Jugo-Slavia and Fiume, 310, 320

Kant's "Critique," 47
Kennedy, Ross, 33
"Kept Us Out of War," 273
Kern, Senator, 111, 119
Keswick, England, 63
King and Queen of England, 303
King and Queen of Italy, 305

Labor Legislation, International, 301
La Follette, Senator, 125
Lamar, Judge Joseph R., 39, 184
Lane, Franklin K., 137
Lansing, Robert, 146
  resigns, 153
  statement on Haiti, 194
    Wilson, 225
Latimer, of Virginia, 41
Latin-American States, Wilson's policy on, 184
Lawrence textile strike, 123
Lawyer, Wilson as, 59
League of College Voters, 118
League of Nations, 294 *et seq.*
  result of Senate disapproval of, 295
  tied to treaty, 309
League to Enforce Peace, 314
Lecky, William, 42
Lee, Robert E., 37
Lehman, Frederick W., 184
Levermore, Charles B., 60
"Lightfoot Club," 38
Limerick, a Wilson, 99
Lincoln, President, 37, 139, 140
Lind, Ex-Governor, 177
Lloyd George and the khaki election, 300
  characterized, 306
Lobbies at Washington, 158
Lodge, Senator, 323
Los Angeles, Wilson at, 328
Low, A. Maurice, 132
Ludendorff's memoirs, 296
*Lusitania*, 252

McAdoo, Mrs. William G., 62
  William G., 117, 136
McCombs, W. F., 110, 117
McKinley, President, 155
McReynolds, J. C., 137, 205
Madero, Francisco, 176
Magna Charta of Peace, the, 350
Manchester, the President at, 304
Manson, N. C., Jr., 56
Marriage, first, 62
  second, 335
Marryat's novels, 40
Marshall, Thomas R., 114, 119
Martin, Colonel William, 41
Martine, James E., 100
Mebane, Dr. David, 43
Medary, Samuel, 30
Memorial Day, 1916, speech, 315
"Men and Manner in Parliament," 47
Meredith, Edwin T., 139
"Mere Literature," 91
Message to Congress, first, 158
Mexico, relations with, 150, 175 *et seq.*
Minneapolis, Wilson at, 124
Minor, John B., 54
Mobile, Wilson at, 184, 193
Money, glorification of, 80
Money-bags campaign blundering, 120
Monroe Doctrine, 194, 316, 321
"Monsieur Mouton," 42
Morgan, J. Pierpont, 107

Morgenthau, Henry, 205
Morris, Prof. Charles S., 61
Mount Vernon, speech at, 317

National Defense, Council of, 118
National Guard, 145
Naval Oil Reserves, 133
Navy, fondness for the, 44
"New Freedom," 89
New York, "greatest Italian city in the world," 306
Nickname, 42
Nobel Prize award, 25
Nomination ballots, 112, 114
Novels by Wilson in days of youth, 40

Obregon, President of Mexico, 188
Oil Reserves, Naval, 128, 133
Old Guard Republicans, 122
Omaha, speech at, 326
"Omit No Word or Act," 253
Orlando of Italy characterized, 307

Page, Roswell, 58
Palmer, A. Mitchell, 139
    Dr. Benjamin M., 39
Panama Canal Tolls, 195
Pan-American Conference, 194
Paris, Peace Conference at, 301 *et seq.*
Paris, why Wilson went to, 317
Parker, Judge, 95, 106
Patton, Francis Landey, 73
Payne, John Barton, 139
Payne-Aldrich Tariff act, 116, 161
Peace, a vision of world, 313 *et seq.*
    Conference, opening of, 301, 306
    outlined in fourteen points, 291
Peaceful penetration, 290 *et seq.*
Penfield, Frederic C., 205
Percy, Leroy, 56
Perry, Bliss, 91
Pershing, General, 238, 302
Phi Kappa Psi, 55
Philippine Islands, 145, 189 *et seq.*
Phillips, Dr. Charles, 41
Pittsburgh papers, 30
Pope, Wilson's interview with the, 305
Porto Rico, 193
Potts, Rev. George C., 29
Precedent breaking, 77, 220 *et seq.*
Presbyterian elder, Woodrow Wilson as, 359
President and the Presidency, 127 *et seq.*
Press censorship, 29
Princeton, matriculation at, 46
    president of, 77 *et seq.*
    professor at, 70
    the Wilson home at, 62
*Princetonian, The*, 48
Procter, William C., 79
Progressive party, 122
Protection, 157
Pueblo, last speech at, 334

"Quad" system at Princeton, 78

Radio, Wilson's message by, 348
Railroad strike, 197
Raleigh, Wilson at, 358
Ramage, B. J., 61
Redfield, W. C., 138
Reed, Thomas B., 155
Reforming the Currency, 165 *et seq.*
Religion of Woodrow Wilson, 358 *et seq.*
Renick, Edward Ireland, 59
Renick & Wilson, 59
Reparation Commission, 301
Reservations to treaty, 324
Restoration program, Wilson's pre-war, 129
Richardson, of Mississippi, 41
"Road Away from Revolution," 351
Rome, Wilson at, 305
Roosevelt, Theodore, 120 *et seq.*
    and League of Peace, 25
    and tariff revision, 156
Rosenwald, Julius, 208
"Round Robin" of Senators, 133, 320
Ruffin, Dr. Sterling, 339, 356
Russell, Mrs. Joseph R., 43
Russian revolution, 351
Ryan, Thomas F., 107

St. Louis, speech at, 332
"Sand Hills," 38
Sayre, Mrs. Francis B., 62
"Scholar in Politics," 96
Schwab, Charles, 208
Scotch and Irish strains, 28
Sea, Wilson's love for the, 44
    Wilson's stories of the, 40
Seattle, Wilson at, 338
Sea Girt, Wilson at, 110, 117
Seward, William H., 140
Shantung, 311
Shaw, Albert, 61
Sherman, James S., 121
Silver plank, Wilson's attitude toward, 136
Smith, Adam, 61
Smith, Rev. Herbert S., 336
    James, Ex-Senator, 96
Sonnino, of Italy, President Wilson's reply to, 306
South, Cabinet members from the, 205

Southern Presbyterian Theological Seminary, 39
Speaking tour, President begins his, 322
Sprunt, Dr. James, 94, 359
"State: Elements of Historical and Practical Politics," the, 85
Stettinius, E. R., 208
Stitt, Rear Admiral E. R., 339
Stonewall Jackson, Wilson speaks on, 358
Stovall, Pleasant A., 38
Strike, Lawrence textile, 123
    railroad, 197
Suarez, Vice-President of Mexico, 176
"Swing around the circle," the, 328

Taft, Ex-President, 115, 176, 190, 319
Talcott, Charles A., 66
Tariff reform, 155 *et seq.*
    measure signed, 161
Taussig, Professor, 162
Taylor, Rev. James H., 336
Teapot Dome, 120, 128, 133
Thilly, Prof. Frank, 236
"Thinking Machine," Wilson as a, 27
Thornwell, Dr. James H., 34, 39
Toast that failed, the, 104
"Too proud to fight," 81
Treaty of Versailles, 312, 321, 323
Trenton, address at, 359
Tumulty, Joseph P., 148 *et seq.*, 205
Turin, Wilson at, 306

Underwood, Oscar, 108 *et seq.*
University and the State, 73
Unknown Soldier, Wilson at burial of, 354

Vanderlip, Frank A., 171, 208
Vaudeville, Wilson's interest in, 346
Vera Cruz seized, 183
    service in honor of dead at, 188
Vest, Senator, 161
Veto by Wilson of high tariff on farm products, 163
Victory Loan and the Federal Reserve system, 171
Vienna, Congress of, 316
Villa, Francisco, 185
Virginia, the "Mother of Presidents," 36
Virginia, University of, 54
Virgin Islands, 192

War, 281 *et seq.*
    aims, 290, 316
    between the States, 33
Warren, Charles B., 208
    F. M., 61
Washington and "Alliances," 328
    Wilson's life of, 36, 61, 86
"Watchful waiting," 179, 184
Wesleyan University, 62, 69
Western Theological Seminary, 31
West Point, address at, 315
"When a Man Comes to Himself," 360
Wichita, Wilson stricken at, 327
"Wilful men," 263
Wilmington, recuperating at, 43
Wilson, Ambassador Henry Lane, 177
    Annie Josephine, 33
    Eleanor, 62
    James, 28
    Jessie Woodrow, 62
    Joseph Ruggles, 31 *et seq.*
    Joseph Ruggles, Jr., 33
    Margaret, 62
    Marion, 33
    P. W., 146, 154
    William B., 138
Wilson-Gorman Tariff Act, 156, 161
Winder, M. B., 58
Witherspoon tradition, 47, 71
Wood, General Leonard, 286
Woodrow, Janet, 32
    Rev. Dr. Thomas, 304
Woman suffrage, 134, 203
"World made safe for democracy," 297
World peace, 313 *et seq.*
World War, 281 *et seq.*
Wytheville, Virginia, 336

Yager, Arthur, 61